Call
of the
Litany Bird

To Those Who Were There And Survived
And To Those Who Didn't

Call

of the

Litany Bird

Surviving the Zimbabwe Bush War

Susan Gibbs

Cover Illustration: © Loose Chippings Books

Published by Loose Chippings Books
The Paddocks, Chipping Campden, Gloucestershire, GL55 6AU
www.loosechippings.org

Printed and bound in Great Britain by CPI MacKays, Chatham, ME5 8TD

Hardback ISBN 978-1-907991-00-4
Ebook ISBN 978-1-907991-03-5

Foreword

Over these last unhappy years we have read a great deal of the problems, privations and miseries of the Zimbabwean people Black and White.

In this book, Susan Gibbs gives a vivid account of what it was like in Matabeleland before and after Independence. In the pre Mugabe days her love of the country and its fauna and flora captivate her and she becomes part of a family and friends who were pioneers for over a hundred years in the development of Rhodesia. Later on after Independence and the hostility Mugabe showed to Nkomo and the Matabele the life of those who lived on their farms and ranches changed dramatically for the worse. Security fences were put up; arms were provided for protection, terrorists roamed the countryside.

The farmers were resolute in their determination to stay, protect their livelihood and hope for a return to what had been one of the most prosperous countries of Africa. It was not to be and the seizure of white farmers' land and the intimidation of the population Black and White grew worse. Understandably, the Gibbs decided that for them there was no future in that sad country and this book reminds us of the courage which they and so many of their friends and neighbours showed and the catastrophe which has engulfed the people of Zimbabwe under Mugabe's regime.

Lord Carrington
Foreign Secretary 1979 - 1982

Author's Note

In writing this book I have drawn on my own memories – still vivid after so long – journals, diaries, press cuttings, photographs, and notes sporadically tapped out at the time on an old typewriter as some of the events unfolded, together with the recollections of others who were there.

This account of our lives on the farm during the Rhodesian Bush War, the transition to Zimbabwe, the experiences of escalating security problems due to both dissident activity and the actions of Mugabe's Fifth Brigade was originally written for the family to record the experiences of their childhood, but others felt it might also be of wider interest.

Times have changed and whereas today some may regard certain things I have written as politically incorrect I have portrayed life as it was lived and accepted then and not as some might see it today. Words and phrases – most obviously the name of the country – are as would have been used at the time.

I have, however, changed a few names in order to protect the identities of those I have been unable to contact and who may still be there.

I have avoided writing too much about my husband, Tim, in this account for his intention has been to write his own story one day.

Despite the generous suggestions, help and contributions from others, these are my own recollections and any mistakes or omissions are entirely mine.

Susan Gibbs

Introduction

This book is a gem. The early years of Zimbabwe's independence were a tense, difficult and dangerous time in Matabeleland in the south west of the country. While peace returned to the rest of Zimbabwe after years of civil war, in Matabeleland tension and danger increased, fuelled by the historical suspicion of the majority Shona people for their Ndebele neighbours, who a hundred years previously had held them in subjugation. While a British military training team helped to amalgamate the rival armies of the Smith government, Joshua Nkomo and Robert Mugabe, into four brigades of the new Zimbabwe army, a fifth, all Shona, brigade was trained by North Korea on different lines, and parts of Nkomo's Ndebele army, ZIPRA, either held aloof or were excluded and took to the bush in Matabeleland, with dire consequences for all.

Sue Gibbs tells the story of the harrowing times that followed. Her tale is all the more compelling and effective for the restraint with which she writes. She avoids the wider political canvas and confines herself to a vivid account of day to day events, some of which were ghastly, in a hauntingly beautiful landscape. Her father-in-law, Sir Humphrey, was the governor who refused to accept Ian Smith's illegal declaration of independence and remained loyal to his sovereign, in splendid isolation in Government House; he was also a man of very great charm.

Towards the end of my tour of duty as British High Commissioner, my wife and I went to say farewell to the Gibbs. On the Saturday Molly Gibbs and my wife Jilly, who shared a love of painting, went off into the bush to sketch. They were not long gone when Agric-Alert announced an attack on a nearby farm. Humphrey and I dived into the Land Rover and drove out to scoop them up. Tension was still high the next morning when Tim drove us to the airport with rifles under our feet. I remember hoping that, in case of ambush, he would prove to be a better shot than was I.

I have enjoyed every page of this charming book and I am sure that all who read it will do so too.

Robin Byatt CMG
British High Commissioner to Zimbabwe 1980 - 1983

ECCLESIASTES 9: 12

Moreover, no man knows when his hour will come:
As fish are caught in a cruel net,
Or birds taken in a snare,
So men are trapped by evil times
That fall unexpectedly upon them.

1

Duncan's approaching death, unlike so many others at the time, was brought about by natural causes. It was October 1977, the hottest, driest month of the year in what was then Rhodesia, and a month after his thirty-sixth birthday.

Standing in the hospital room that day, already grieving and longing somehow to snatch him back, to slam shut the door of death before he went through, I was dimly aware that some deep place within me also held a sense of gratitude – gratitude for thirteen years of a never-dull marriage, for two wonderful children, for the fun he'd brought to life, and gratitude too that his was not a violent death.

We'd woken early that morning, just as the sky was lightening, and I got out of bed and opened the curtains so we could watch the dawn; but as I turned back to speak to him and saw the blood trickling from his mouth I knew. I called Paul Fehrsen, our GP, from the phone in the study. Within ten minutes he arrived at the house, quickly followed by Eric Cohen, the consultant, a friend of ours who, on his way to the hospital, happened to pass Paul on the road.

One glance at Duncan told them there was no time to call an ambulance and after gently carrying him to Eric's car we sped off to the Medical Complex. He joked about Eric's driving on the way. "You crazed already?" he said, playing with Eric's Jewishness, "After all, only last week a stray hippo was shot wandering down here, this Cecil Avenue? Run into its wife, who's probably out looking for him by now, and we'll all end up on the ward."

The Private Ward of the Bulawayo Central Hospital was 'my' ward, the one I worked on part-time at night, and I knew Sister Matheson, the ward sister, well. She gave us two large private rooms next door to each other which opened out on to a wide verandah, and in one of them, during the long hours as Duncan drifted in and out of consciousness, Duncan's brother John, his wife Fam and other close friends set up a quiet vigil. Some stayed the whole day, popping in from the verandah to check on us from time to time, taking care not to intrude.

As the day wore on the early morning chill gave way to stifling heat.

"It's obvious why they call it suicide month" Sister Matheson said, just for something to say, as she topped up jugs of iced water. "Nothing we can do about it here, and the fans are quite inadequate."

The morning wore on and from time to time, as word spread quickly round Bulawayo, more friends arrived to offer their support and then, seeing there was nothing they could do, left again.

Late in the afternoon, after a long, hot day, Duncan quietly and naturally slipped away.

At home again a few hours later as friends and relations milled around the verandah talking to each other, I sat there looking at them, numbed, trying to take in what had happened. Scents of jasmine and roses filled the cooling evening air and S'iponono brought a drinks tray out and set it down beside me.

"Nkosikasi[1]," she said, "Don't say anything to the children. Not yet. Not tonight. Later, after they are asleep, go to their room and gently shake them until they are nearly awake. Not fully awake. Nearly awake. Then tell them what has happened to the Boss."

"David is only three and Sarah just a few weeks old. They are so young, especially Sarah. They will not understand."

"You must tell them, Madam. Do this in the night. Then, somewhere inside, they will already know when you talk in the morning. Then they won't be so sad. Because inside, in their spirits, they will already know. Even Sarah."

I wasn't the only young widow in Matabeleland; several of my friends had been widowed before me – almost entirely due to the violence of the bush war – and I had seen the vulnerability of other widows left behind with young children, the sense of responsibility the community felt towards them, and before too

---

1 Nkosikasi: literally the head-woman of a tribe but is used as roughly equivalent to Madam.

long I would need to give thought to our future, where it would be, and when.

As I went to bed that night I caught sight of Duncan's certificate on his desk proclaiming him a member of the Pioneer and Early Settlers Association, and lying there alone I reflected on his life and how he happened to be born in Rhodesia.

His grandfather had arrived as a pioneer in 1896, the year before the first railway line arrived in Bulawayo, and two generations further on that same pioneering spirit, with all its sense of adventure and courage, had continued to live on in Duncan.

In the 1940s Duncan's parents, MG and GG Fleming, had bought two hundred acres of virgin bush six miles south of Bulawayo which they named Mzinzini Estate. On top of the highest hill they built a large, colonial house complete with verandahs and balconies with views over-looking the Matshemhlope River, as it descended down the valley and disappeared into the picturesque Hillside Dam in the distance. In between the rocky outcrops of the kopje[2] GG created imaginative gardens and planted sweeping lawns from the house to the lip of the hill. It was an idyllic place in which to bring up their three children, a place where they could range in freedom and safety. They fished, swam in their pool, hunted for small animals, felled birds with well-aimed catapults, hit balls around a packed-mud tennis court and played on the crashed light aircraft which had somehow been manoeuvred on to the property for the boys' enjoyment.

Bulawayo lacked a boys' prep school and the Flemings, having two young sons, felt the need and decided to build one on the edge of the estate which they named Whitestone School. John, Duncan's elder brother, was the very first pupil, followed three years later by Duncan. The majority of the boys came from farming families and so, later, no one was particularly surprised when, as young man, Duncan chose farming as his career.

MG and GG bought a 33,000 acre cattle ranch north of Bulawayo which was extensive enough for both John and Duncan to farm

---

2   A kopje: a rocky outcrop.

separate sections, John taking charge of the cattle and Duncan, who by then had graduated from Gwebi Agricultural College in Mashonaland, took on the arable areas and grew tobacco.

Duncan's house was a small cottage not far from the main house where John, his wife Fam, and their four children were already established and Duncan, living alone, was ready for a wife of his own. Early in 1963, I'd met Duncan in Australia where I'd recently completed a nursing training and when his mother wrote inviting me to call in to Rhodesia on my way to England I accepted. It was intended to be a short visit but he overcame my plans for travel and adventure by proposing. We'd not been married long when he first became ill with lymphosarcoma at the age of twenty-five and his parents, with great consideration and forethought, had seven acres of land surveyed on the river further up the valley and transferred it into my name.

"Shouldn't it be joint names?" I asked, amazed by their generosity.

But they simply said, "A woman always needs the security of a roof over her head."

A grader came and fashioned a winding dirt road, through the valley and at the end, nestling into some kopjes, we built what to us was a perfect home which we named Hoopoe Hollow. It had large airy rooms and red quarry tiled floors under a deep thatched roof and we designed particularly low windows so we could sit up in bed in the early mornings watching the dawn lighten the colours and bring out the garden scents as we talked over plans for the day. And, during times of illness, Duncan could lie in the stillness watching game – mainly kudu – come down past the windows to drink in the river.

After a few years, as Duncan's parents became older, they sold their family home with a portion of the estate and built themselves a cottage tucked out of sight on land marching with ours. They were especially vigilant and helpful with the children following Duncan's death and later, when I was asked to take over the Matabeleland Red Cross, with the particular task of training a black African to take over in anticipation of Majority Rule, with their encouragement, I accepted. What I didn't know was that the board had not informed the director of thirty-three years that they were easing her out and that I was taking her place, which made for a challenging situation. Of necessity this was a temporary position. Sometime later when my brother Campbell Rankine offered, as both an accountant and solicitor, to deal with all the financial and legal aspects of moving us to Australia (reassuringly adding: "You can't afford me, so don't even think about that side of it") I began to seriously consider cutting my loses, taking the children and the memories, and leaving before becoming a burden to those who had their own lives to lead. But when I eventually began making plans and told friends there were hearty protests.

"We are small enough in number as it is, and shrinking", one remonstrated.

"Where else would you be able to give David and Sarah such quality of life, living with nature, surrounded by all of us!" another said.

Yet another insisted, "You can't go and abandon S'iponono".

But the most original protest of all came from Tim Gibbs who said: "Stay here and marry me instead."

I'd known Tim, but not very well, for many years. The Fleming's cattle ranch lay beyond the Gibbs' dairy farm in the same district of Nyamandhlovu and we met from time to time at the Farmers' Club and occasionally at Bulawayo dinner parties. For ten years I'd tried to find a wife for Tim, and each time a new girl, especially if she were an English Rose, turned up in Bulawayo, I gave yet another dinner party and invited him. But he never saw the potential in any of them and he displayed no interest.

During the days following Duncan's death MG and GG watched over us with loving concern and I pretended not to know that my servants reported daily to their servants who, in turn, passed on reports to MG and GG, giving them the details of those things I neglected to tell them: if I was eating properly, getting enough rest, and how I was coping generally.

As time went on they began to observe the to-ing and fro-ing of Tim's car driving down the track to my cottage but no one said anything until one day, as I was giving lunch to the children, S'iponono handed me a note brought down by their cook. These 'Chatty Chittys' as we called them were a regular part of daily life, but this one was different. It read more like a command than an invitation.

"Darling Sue, Please come for a drink at 6pm. There is something we wish to discuss with you."

I was fairly sure I knew why I was being summoned and was a little apprehensive. That evening as we sat in their drawing room with our whiskies enjoying the view over the veldt and the valley sweeping down to the dam they broached the subject immediately.

"It is obvious to us," GG began, "that this man is courting you. MG and I have discussed this and we wanted to say to you that we think you should make a decision as soon as possible, he's no longer young and so don't keep him hanging around."

"What we really want to say," MG interjected, picking up on the one-sided conversation "is that when you feel ready to make a decision, we are right behind you regardless of what that decision is, and will give you our full support. However," he went on, "if you do decide to marry Tim, there are two things we hope you will consider. Firstly, as your own father is no longer alive, I, as your father-in-law, would like to give you away in a service in the Cathedral."

"And secondly?" I asked stunned by the extent of their support.

"Secondly, we would like to give the wedding reception here in our garden. We would wish Bulawayo to know that you had our blessing."

The announcement of our engagement delighted friends and lifted spirits in a community under strain with some good news. Pre-wedding invitations to lunches, dinners and drink parties began arriving and unexpected presents were delivered. One in particular took us by surprise: a large silver salver inscribed:

"Susan and Timothy
From
Jairos Jiri MBE"

And with it a covering letter explaining that Jairos Jiri had read in the *Bulawayo Chronicle* that we were to be married and had presumed he was not invited. However, this letter was to advise us that he would be coming anyway.

I'd not met Jairos but had long admired all he had done for the poor and disabled amongst his own people. His large modern shop in Bulawayo sold goods of excellent workmanship – table mats, baskets, beaded work, wood carvings, salad bowls and servers, woven hats and numerous other articles all produced in the workshops he had set up in the townships to train and produce an income for the needy. I'd seen his photograph on the walls of the shop – a prosperous looking man with a prosperous looking girth and we were delighted that he wanted to join us.

One Saturday afternoon, shortly after the announcement of our engagement, we gave a party in the compound for the farm workers. The rains had not yet begun and I regretted not taking a hat with me as we stood under the punishing sun, watching writhing ebony bodies glistening with sweat in uninhibited dancing and singing. Old women in assorted finery, abandoned themselves to the beating of the drums and I marvelled, hypnotized by the rhythm, at their stamina. Dust kicked up into our eyes and it was a moment before we noticed that from time to time one or other of the women shuffled forward on her knees, hands extended as in supplication, bearing gifts. There was a small grass basket, hand woven in reds and blues, six eggs nestling in a small box of thatching grass, a yellow-beaded jug cover, an earthenware pot and a brace of scrawny chickens bound together at the legs. Treasures put together with care. I was reminded of the Widow's Mite, and in the receiving felt I was holding something precious beyond measure.

The children and I needed to return to Bulawayo before the curfew caused by the worsening security situation, and so we left the party knowing the celebrations would continue late into the night, and we went for a cursory look around the Little Bonisa cottage to plan which pieces of furniture I would bring out from town.

Despite Tim's mother's offer to swap houses, I felt it would be right to begin our married life in Little Bonisa. Since Humphrey and Molly's return from Government House to Big Bonisa in 1969,

Tim had moved back into Little Bonisa and, apart from a certain sentimentality about it, I was also aware that, as Tim had not married until he was forty, I needed to be conscious of wider family feelings. And so, disappointing as this was for Molly, I opted to begin our married life living in the tiny thatched cottage the other side of the kitchen garden[3].

I loved Little Bonisa. The luxuriant garden had ample water from a bore hole and the cottage, U-shaped like Big Bonisa, looked as if it had sprung, self-seeded, out of the lawn. Couch grass was ideal in these conditions and, although spiky and coarse, it remained hardy, green and springy all year round. A prolific bougainvillea swarmed up the trunk of a tall camel thorn tree and splashed deep-pink blossoms to the ground. Around the garden Pride-of-India in several shades of pink and mauve; yellow, white and pink frangipani trees; Yesterday-Today-and-Tomorrow, and oleander, along with other shrubs vied with each other in displays of colour during the day and, as darkness fell, Queen-of-the-Night revealed herself in her full glory and the long, creamy trumpets of the moonflower unfurled, releasing sweet perfume to fill the night air.

The bedroom and living wings of the cottage were joined by a verandah, with a green cement floor under a low thatched roof. On the east were two large bedrooms, separated by a bathroom, the smaller of which would be adequate for David and Sarah, who were still young enough to share. In the western section a large, beautifully proportioned drawing room stretched out into the garden and a small dining room behind it led into an even smaller kitchen, no bigger than a narrow passage, which looked like a somewhat begrudging after-thought tacked on the back. It was clearly a bachelor's cottage. No one had seen any reason to make provision for hot water, work space, or storage beyond a couple of wobbly, makeshift shelves.

Initially my views regarding the need to 'do something about this' were not well received. Sensing resistance beginning to take

3   Tim's parents, Sir Humphrey Gibbs and his wife Dame Molly owned Bonisa farm in the Nyamandhlovu area north west of Bulawayo. It comprised three houses Big Bonisa, Little Bonisa and New Farm. Sir Humphrey was Governor of Rhodesia.

hold I realised that fussing about it would not help – we probably disagreed too profoundly to dispute – and so, with a studiously neutral expression on my face I went away and wrote two lists: one of 'essential' and one of 'desirable' improvements. Unless the essentials were met I would refuse to move out to Nyamandhlovu with the children.

Topping the list of non-negotiables were: a security fence, hot water in the kitchen and decent accommodation for S'iponono, our T'stwana[4] maid who had been with me for many years and had asked to come out with us from Bulawayo.

Within a week and without further reference or discussion a forty-four-gallon drum was rigged up on a stand outside the kitchen, a fire built underneath it and a woodpile stacked nearby. This hot water supply, although haphazard as the fire flared up and died down, was better than nothing and many of the farmers survived using what was known as a 'Rhodesian Boiler'.

The security fence was another matter and a very much more expensive proposition. I stood firm. The children must have the utmost protection and I personally was neither hero nor martyr. Big and Little Bonisa homesteads were separated by less than an acre of kitchen garden and, with the security situation deteriorating, there seemed little sense in securing only the cottage, leaving Tim's parents exposed in Big Bonisa. And so a high, diamond-mesh fence of pig-wire topped with rolls of barbed wire went up, encompassing the two houses and gardens. Although a constant and ugly reminder of what lay in the bush beyond, we were able, because of the topography, to erect much of it on the northern side more or less out of sight below the escarpment, and it did eliminate the need for sand bags in front of the windows. I was glad of the fence. Later, when Mugabe sent his Fifth Brigade down to Matabeleland, when the tribes began warring and the security situation grew worse in Nyamandhlovu,

---

4 T'stwana: a tribal people of Botswana and other parts of eastern and southern Africa.

drawing in the white farmers, it became necessary to alarm the entire circumference.

The peace of mind this gave far outweighed the irritation of false alarms during the night, usually set off by an owl or night ape. A couple of years later, after we had moved into Big Bonisa and the situation deteriorated even further, two armed guards were employed to patrol inside the fence at night. Although reassuring, when the area became 'hot', spot checks became necessary to ensure the guards had not curled up under a tree and gone to sleep.

2

Tim and I were married at 6pm on 9th December 1978 in St John's Anglican Cathedral by The Rev. Jonathan Siyachitema, Dean of Bulawayo – a large, black-bear of a man – for whom it was also a special ceremony. This was the first time he had officiated at the wedding of a white couple, and he diligently took us through several pre-nuptial preparation talks about 'leaving and cleaving', commitment and sex!

My mother came over from Australia for the wedding and we took a few days to go shopping in South Africa for a dress. In one of the boutiques my mother found what she declared to be the most perfect and exotic Italian silk confection in the palest mushroom pink. I was tall and slim and I hesitated, wondering if the thin silk ribbons cascading down the skirt made me look like a Maypole. My mother stood determined, and dismissing my uncertainties talked me into it for which, later, I was very grateful.

On the other hand Tim went in for improvisation – when his belt got left behind, he had managed to hold his trousers up all evening with someone else's borrowed brown shoelaces tied together with added bits of string.

The stickiness of the hot, sultry day continued into the evening but, ignoring the discomfort, the Dean conducted the service dressed in heavy celebration robes of gold, blue and red brocade, bearing up under them with dignified delight.

After the many grievous services in the same cathedral in recent times, this was an uplifting and reassuring occasion, a counter balance, a reminder of the good things in life.

Duncan's mother had planned well. Her garden, always well tended, now looked spectacular. In the glow of sundown long scarves of pink and orange streaks filled the sky above; flowering trees, climbers and shrubs of roses, frangipani and moonflower, scenting the air. We walked down an avenue of roses to the marquee where the interior was filled with perfume from homegrown flowers picked from gardens around

Bulawayo. Arranged by friends, they spread down the centre of each table and spilled riotously down from the ceiling.

Paul Fehrsen made an excellent speech and although dinner and dancing continued until midnight (when it was whispered that it was time for us to leave) the evening finished all too quickly. As we began to walk out I glanced over at the three formidable women in my life talking together. Each one a rugged individual, each living out their own legends; leaving their marks: Duncan's mother, Tim's mother and my own. I had hoped they would like each other but I was suddenly aware that some sort of invisible powerhouse of matriarchal opinion was being forged between them and was not sure if this was a good thing or not.

Tim didn't feel that he could spare much time away from the farm and arranged for us to fly, the next morning, for a three-day honeymoon in the noble, old-colonial hotel at Victoria Falls. Built as a railway hotel in 1904 it overlooked the Zambezi River where it hurtled into the gorge, creating a rain forest and the Falls themselves. White spray cannoned upwards from the gorge; 'Mosiatunya', The Smoke That Thunders, as the African's called it, before David Livingstone discovered and renamed it in 1855.

At the centre of the hotel a courtyard dripped with various colours of bougainvillea and hibiscus. Inside, palm trees and marble floors with overhead fans and pillars reflected days of departed grandeur, enhanced by black staff wearing red fezzes and sashes over white, stiffly-starched uniforms padding silently on bare feet through the cavernous rooms.

On the first morning I began to feel unwell and ran a temperature, but we went down to breakfast which was taken on the terrace under the shade of a gigantic Msasa tree, home to a family of monkeys which swooped down to snatch food from the unwary. I'd been there often and it was my favourite place on earth. As the day went on I felt more and more wretched, my temperature soared and I was confined to bed with malaria for the remainder of the honeymoon, while Tim sat patiently writing endlessly cheerful postcards to what seemed to me to be everyone he'd ever known.

Following our return to the farm I set about making Little Bonisa our home. S'iponono settled in and got on well with the other staff. I employed Manka – the daughter of Molly & Humphrey's cook Lavu – to take over the washing, ironing and polishing of floors and silver while S'iponono and I shared the care of the children, the cooking and dusting. Tim, having not married until he was forty, had a very good collection of paintings – mainly water colours – but he had always expected to marry at some stage and didn't waste time on decorating his cottage, expecting instead that his future wife would have her own ideas on furnishings and fabrics. In a way it was gratifying that the rags on each individual window were neither matching nor of the same length. They smelled like dust from an old tomb stuck with mummified beetles which gave me every justification and a free hand to replace them all.

Knowing we would eventually be moving into the Big Bonisa homestead I had inexpensive curtains made of heavy, coarse cotton in natural tones, traditionally known as 'Kaffir Sheeting' but recently renamed, 'Heavy Sheeting' for political reasons. Thick and weighty, they let surprisingly little light through, and at night we drew them before turning the lights on, secure in the knowledge that we could not be easily picked out as targets from beyond the fence or garden. Many people used this fabric and, aside from the fact that I thought it attractive, the heavy drapes would help dampen the effects of any explosion should there be an attack.

Tim's dog, Ticky, a large Alsatian, quickly accepted Koki and Snoopy as part of his new family which both pleased and surprised me as he was accustomed to having Tim to himself, and two more large dogs invading his territory could have caused problems.

A few days after moving in to the cottage Tim was appalled to discover that I had noticed, and dealt with, the profusion of spider webs swathed around the two wagon wheels suspended from the rafters in the drawing room which, topped with hollowed out ostrich eggs served as light fittings.

"You can't remove those," he insisted. "In the morning I will show you something."

As dawn broke we crept quietly across the verandah to the stable door and peeped over into the drawing room. There, clinging to a wagon wheel, was the most beautiful bird trailing an exceptionally long, rufous-coloured tail, its greenish head, iridescent in the morning light as it pecked ravenously at insects caught in the webs.

"It's the Paradise Flycatcher," Tim whispered. "He comes to feed every morning and he also raids the silk of the web and uses it to bind his nest together and form a neat little cup to attract a mate."

Having seen this beauty of nature at work I dropped my standards to levels which, before now, would have been thought improbable and quickly learned to adapt more fully to living with nature. I even agreed to use the little crocheted doilies weighed down with coloured beads – gifts presented to us by the women in the compound during the pre wedding party – to cover bedside glasses of water. Drowning rose-beetles, hawk-moths and other insects I could live with, but swallowing them during the night was a step too far.

Although there were relatively few scorpions on Bonisa, they still filled me with panic having one night, years ago, been stung on the neck by one which had dropped out of the thatch, and I'd woken with rapid swelling and excruciating pain radiating out from the puncture wound. It had become routine to shake out our shoes first thing in the mornings but now we also stood each bed leg in a jar of paraffin to prevent any crawly thing from scaling up and joining us in bed.

We slipped into a daily routine which began with 6am Roll-Call on the Agric-Alert system set up in the bedroom – a system that was an assured link with the outside world. It was not completely dependant on an electricity supply which could be vulnerable to lightning strikes or being cut off by hand. It was our life-line providing a method for farm to farm contact, and we relied on it heavily. Early systems were cobbled together from disused telephone handsets and spare parts and powered by old car batteries lashed together with string and bits of wire; but now they were marginally more professionally made to provide communications with all the other homesteads and with the Police Camp, where a large board hung on the back wall.

Down one side ran a list of individual call-signs each with its own tiny light which lit up when an Agric-Alert caller made contact. An alarm from a remote Agric-Alert also set off the lights and over-rode the volume controls both in the Camp and in each homestead. There had been increased terrorist activity recently and now the Roll-Calls had increased to three times each day – 6am, 12midday and 6pm – providing a reassuring awareness of being part of a community that worked together and looked out for each other.

I'd seen much less of old friends since moving out from town and I missed the companionable, tight-knit friendships. But the days were full and, although we kept in touch, telephone conversations were short because of the possibility of an urgent security call on the party-line. Occasionally friends came out to the farm for a night, but because of the dawn-to-dusk curfew, lunch parties were the only alternative for getting together.

A few weeks after we'd settled in to the cottage we gave a Sunday lunch party to thank the many friends who had so generously helped prepare for our wedding and reception. Molly and Humphrey were getting older and beginning to find the heat trying. Knowing beyond doubt that the day would be blazing hot but still not wanting to exclude them completely, we suggested they join us for a drink beforehand, which seemed to please them. However, as the first convoy of cars drew up outside the security gate the private telephone linking the two houses suddenly rang.

"I've filled the zinc bath with water and tick muti[5] but the animals are too strong for me," Molly said. "Would Tim please come over now and wash the dogs?"

To be fair, we were amused that during the years since leaving Government House Molly had come to rely on Tim as, in his words, her replacement "Lady in Waiting".

Soon after the last car drove in through the security gates Tim returned from Big Bonisa, eagerly followed by wet dogs smelling of chemicals who nuzzled and pawed everyone they could, before

---

5   Medicine

one made off with half a ham from a table under the trees. I was furious.

"This wouldn't have happened if you'd let me put out the food in the dining room," I muttered fiercely to Tim in passing. "At least we could have closed the door on it."

"It's only for a season," he replied, astonished that I could have been heartlessly more concerned about the ham than for the peace of the Spotted Eagle Owl and her five chicks living in the dining room chimney.

Tim's godmother, Mary Buxton, had been a regular visitor to Rhodesia over the years, staying with various friends in-between her times on Bonisa. We'd met her frequently at Paddy and Paul Fehrsen's and although life had been a disappointment for her and she was not very robust, I liked and admired her honesty and courage. She'd not married and had children of her own and she'd immersed herself in Tim's life and well-being. It must have been hard for her to have someone else come first in Tim's life, but she accepted me with warmth and generosity and so, when her letter arrived announcing she planned to visit us, I was delighted and we agreed she would come in May and so avoid the hotter months.

By April I was beginning to feel unwell again. At first I suspected a recurrence of the malaria, or perhaps one of the other African bugs that afflicted us from time to time but no temperature developed. Nausea, thirst and fatigue came and went and, drawing on my nursing background, I decided I probably had diabetes. It was possible if not probable; after all my mother, grandmother and brother all had it. Eventually I made an appointment to see Paul Fehrsen who had become more than a doctor to us, guiding and supporting us through the ten years of Duncan's illness and then becoming David's godfather. After explaining the symptoms to him, he asked for a specimen, which his nurse bore off to check immediately, while Paul and I sat in his room and reminisced about safaris we had done together in Botswana, in the days when it was safe and we were free to roam, before the days of rules and regulations and strict border checks. We were steeped in nostalgic memories when the nurse called him.

I waited feeling mildly apprehensive, hoping it wasn't bad news. When he returned he looked at me gravely for a moment. "Well, you don't have diabetes," he said and paused. "I'm afraid that what you do have is a slight attack of pregnancy." He laughed, delighted, as I just sat there speechless. He did some rapid calculations. "The date to look forward to is some time in October."

Driving back along the Falls Road I wondered what the reaction of David and Sarah would be. The potential for dissensions and rivalries as they grew up could be considerable, and I determined to work at building a united family and would plan well ahead to prepare and involve them. I also wondered what my reaction would be. Would anything change?

David was excited that there would be another baby in the family and although Sarah didn't quite understand, not to be left out, she beamed with delight and each evening, as I lay in the bath, they both perched on stools chatting and watching as I grew larger. And then one evening, the baby kicked sending a leg shape pistoning out from my abdominal wall. David pointed and laughed.

"How did the baby get in there?" he asked.

I nonchalantly reminded him of the times he'd observed nature at work amongst the animals.

"What? You did that?" he exclaimed indignantly and after a moment's pause: "Well, why didn't you wait for me to watch?"

"You were busy," I said, clutching at straws, "out fishing with Ben."

"Oh," he said and wandered off.

It was clear that, with a baby on the way, more space would soon be needed and the exchange of houses with Tim's parents would be necessary sooner than I'd hoped. It was also obvious that the cottage would be too small for Molly and Humphrey's long term needs. We decided to stay in Little Bonisa until after the baby was born, using the time to enlarge the accommodation and spare them the mess and disruption of builders.

Both Hum and Molly were pleased with the plans for the cottage and, with no requirements for planning permission, we paced out a good sized area and brought in a few farm workers to dig foundations, joining together the two wings of the cottage at the back. They were delighted with the completed building which included a large study for Humphrey and a studio for Molly where she could paint her pictures without interruptions.

The security situation deteriorated. Nkomo's ZIPRA[6] forces had been quiet lately but rumours of 'sightings' in the area began to circulate, making us alert and hyper vigilant again; and I became concerned about Mary's impending visit. But Mary herself was not to be put off. She insisted that not only would she still come, she had decided to bring her trip forward to the beginning of March, and I began to wonder if, in her drab, lonely London life, she looked forward to the stimulation of the unpredictable hazards of Africa. By the time she flew in we were once more resorting to Roll-Call three times a day and taking extra precautions. It was clear that, for Mary, it was a treat to be a part of something, to feel a belonging which we didn't completely share. She arrived laden with gifts for us all and, as international sanctions bit deeper, petrol rationing was becoming more of a challenge, so we were particularly grateful for the 'Tourist Petrol Coupons' she claimed on our behalf.

The morning sickness, which lasted all day, continued for months, but I couldn't have been more content. Although the political situation was tense, security problems in the Nyamandhlovu District had abated and each day, following the children's afternoon rest, we put on shoes and hats and I took them for a walk – to the dairy to watch the cows being milked or down the path to the dam, tracking spoor in the dust and hoping for a glimpse of their favourite vervet monkeys.

A few years before Duncan died we'd lived on a remote cattle ranch in the low veldt, just north of the Limpopo. The area was sparsely populated: the nearest neighbours lived several miles distant, and we rarely saw them. We spent the days dipping cattle, fishing in the Lundi River or hunting for the pot, both ours and for the workers'.

---

6   Joshua Nkomo's Zimbabwe Peoples' Revolutionary Army.

Our tracker from the local tribe had never been out of the area, never seen a town or city, but his knowledge and love for the bush and game verged on reverence. Duncan also had excellent bush knowledge, an instinct which saw him through some challenging times, and each time we went out Mkava taught us more about tracking: how to recognise tracks, blood spoor on low vegetation, the time since the game had passed that way, and its urgency. But there are some things which can't be taught, they can only be 'known', and as I watched him I tried to assimilate as much as possible. What Mkava had taught me about tracking in those days I now taught the children on our daily excursions. Sometimes Mary came with us but she was not strong and, finding the heat trying, she usually turned back to the homestead after a short distance to sit reading on the verandah until the relative coolness of the evenings.

At the end of each day we gathered on the verandah with our sundowners listening to the six o'clock news. At the beginning of February DC Rosenfels had been murdered on his farm in Marula and now, with Mary there, came the bulletin "Security Forces regrets to announce the death today of Mr Charlie Rosenfels in the Kezi..."

I glanced over at Mary. To my relief she was completely calm, interested, but untouched by the news, despite having met Charlie a few weeks earlier. They were part of a dynastic farming family which owned vast tracts of land and we'd known them through the farming community. Charlie died as a result of a land-mine, leaving behind a wife and three children.

Neither Marula nor Kezi areas are in the Nyamandhlovu district; nevertheless they are in our region of Matabeleland and we wondered how long it would be before Nyamandhlovu also had another attack.

3

The government issued all the farmers, and their wives, with G3's – automatic weapons which looked cumbersome but once mastered proved effective and deadly. Joint Operations Command (JOC) in Nyamandhlovu provided a medical course in basic war-specific injuries and when I, along with several other wives, joined the paramilitary Police Reserve we were offered weapons training with a roving army instructor.

The high-veldt winter morning was cold when six of us gathered at the camp, wearing battle fatigues, pistols belted on our hips and carrying our G3s with spare magazines. In our own vehicles we followed the lead Land Rover in convoy from the JOC Camp down a mile of so of deeply corrugated track of heavy sand, through dry mopani scrub for another two miles or so. Eventually the vegetation opened into a clearing about 150 yards long. At one end of the man-made vlei stood eight larger than life mock-ups of men in camouflage uniforms charging towards us, assault rifles clasped across their chests.

It was obvious from the start that Sergeant Barry Viljoen of the Rhodesia/Zimbabwe Army was hostile. A short, stocky Afrikaner, with a thin, black moustache slicing across his face, he paced around, scowling, impatiently slapping his thigh, as if to emphasise his irritation at having to train women who, after all, had husbands to protect them. He gave a cursory nod in reply to our greetings.

"Get into line, three paces apart," he ordered.

We glanced at each other in resignation and lined up at the opposite end from the targets.

The air was crystal clear, and behind the targets a low, glacial sun shone in the palest of blue skies. Maggie Goldman lifted her hand to shield her eyes against the glare.

"Put your hand down," Sgt Viljoen bawled. "In an attack, you can't position the bloody enemy to suit yourself."

Angie Summers, her natural vivaciousness subdued, stood on my left at the beginning of the line. From under her cap strands of blonde hair escaped and whipped around her face in the bitter winter wind. Carol Wagner looked over from my right and cast her eyes heavenwards while the three beyond her waited in silent scorn.

"Right," our instructor went on, "the procedure is this: You will learn to strip and re-assemble the weapons in thirty seconds. When you are perfect, and only then, you will run up to the mark... here." He dragged a foot to make a line across the sand. "You will throw yourselves on the ground, take aim at your targets and fire until you are ninety percent accurate. We will begin with assault rifles." He paused, raking his gaze across us before continuing.

"Weapons must be protected from dust, so take off your jackets and put them on the ground – to your right." Six jackets were removed and obediently laid out on the sand. No one dared complain of the cold.

"Place sidearms and automatic weapons on the jackets."

Step by step Sgt Viljoen took us through the stripping process. The G3s were heavy, the metal cold and the smell of gun oil hung in the air. With few repetitions we moved rapidly on to the re-assembling procedure. We were good – far better than he expected – and we surreptitiously exchanged satisfied glances.

"OK", he said curtly and strode away to his line in the sand. "At my signal, this is your mark." He paused.

"Go!"

We ran. I lowered myself down carefully and I took aim.

"Hold Fire!" he bellowed. "You. I told you to throw yourself down."

"I can't," I retorted, "I'm six months pregnant." Surely he could see that.

"Then dig a bloody hole and throw yourself into that!"

Ignoring his protests Angie darted over to help me and we dug together with our hands until we had made a reasonable ditch.

Sgt Viljoen was tapping his leg again. "Start over."

Once more we ran from the base line to the firing positions and hit the ground, skinning our elbows. Choking, blinding dust rose, and when it cleared the targets looked intimidating. It was hard not think of them as real men; hard to aim for their hearts.

It was slightly warmer now and the wind had died down as the sound of automatic fire splattered through the air. We were surprisingly accurate, and we sensed this was not as he'd expected as he gruffly announced that we would now follow the same procedure with the side-arms. As these were not army-issue but our own personal pistols, they varied. We had bought them privately when the troubles first began a few years before and most of us had used them – mainly for snakes – they were old friends, familiar, and dependable. We knew how to clean and look after them, and moving easily through the drills we advanced rapidly to target practice.

Angie missed every shot.

"Stop!" Viljoen ordered. "Place your weapons on the ground." Striding over to Angie, he picked up her pistol and turned to face us.

"You will never hit the target by jerking up like that. I have told you, you must hold the pistol absolutely still then very gently squeeze the trigger. Watch ." With exaggerated deliberation he clasped Angie's pistol in his right hand, clamped his left hand under the butt and, fully extending both arms, he slowly and almost imperceptibly squeezed the trigger.

A shot rang out. The world froze.

Carol dropped to the ground beside me. We watched in horror as, through the dark green of her camo-kit a darker patch began to spread.

I sprang over to her and clamped my hands around the warm wetness flowing from the top of her thigh. She lay there staring up at me, mute, unbelieving. Angie stripped, frantically popping buttons off her shirt, and held out her bra. As we struggled to wind it around Carol's thigh a shriek pierced the air.

Spinning around, we watched, in disbelief as Sgt Johannes Viljoen, weapons instructor to the Rhodesian/Zimbabwe Army, slowly lifted Angie's pistol to his head and held it against his temple. His career was finished he wailed. He was finished.

30

Jo and Viv lunged like wild cats knocking him to the ground sending the pistol flying out of his hand. Debbie threw herself astride his chest, winding him. Viv sat on his knees immobilizing his legs, and Jo pulled his arms flat on the ground above his head and stood on his hands. Pulsing with anger she repositioned her feet with little twisting movements.

We turned back to Carol. Blood squirted into our faces from her wound as, with slippery hands, we got the tourniquet in place. Twisting a stick in the fabric, we tightened it until the flow stopped. It looked like a flesh wound but she had lost a lot of blood and we wondered if a major vessel had been hit. Shock set in as we loaded her into the back of Angie's estate and I covered her with a collection of camouflage jackets and dog blankets. Beyond sips of water and reassurance there was little else that could be done. Angie drove carefully over the corrugations on the track back to the Nyamandhlovu Road. Leaning over to the mobile Agric-Alert, she pressed the 'speak' button.

"Control, this is One Nine, do you read?"

"Come in One Nine."

"Roger, Urgent casevac requested at Firing Range. Copied?"

"Affirmative, One Nine, on our way."

Angie turned and grinned at us before pressing the speak button again.

"Control,... One Nine"

"One Nine... Control... Go. "

"Special bandages required for serious ego wounds. Over."

I laughed.

"Watch the road," Carol muttered as she grinned back.

31

4

On Sundays, when petrol rationing permitted, we made an early start with the children and drove the thirty miles to St. John's Cathedral in Bulawayo in time for the 7.30am service. Gilded sunrises drenched the veldt with promises of the day ahead and anointed the bush with a particular glory, whilst game, frisky in the cool morning, gave an sense of hope and expectancy. It was also a time we were less likely to run into an ambush – the usual time being early evenings just before the cover of darkness obliterated tracks and thwarted follow-up attempts until morning light.

Because of the security uncertainties I moved in to a rented flat in Bulawayo with David and Sarah two weeks before the baby was due. Tim came in for a few hours from time to time but returned to the farm before curfew to safeguard his parents and supervise the work. The days dragged on. September became October and, as the temperatures soared to new heights, the air felt thin and I felt bovine, lethargic and very large. (I held on to the memory that I used to be slim and that when I first met Molly she'd asked if I was anorexic. Perhaps one day I would return to what I regarded as my natural state.)

"It must be a boy," Tim noted. "Bull calves are always late." Eventually, on the 13th October, on one of the hottest days of the year, James arrived, three weeks late via caesarian section. Long, thin and rangy, he was born, as one of the nurses said, "With that Gibbs look on his face." So pronounced was it that Duncan's mother was moved to whisper, "I'm very pleased to see you haven't strayed, Sue".

Return to the farm was delayed for another three weeks when I developed septicaemia. I knew I was seriously ill and asked the surly nurse, who had been drafted in from the townships, to call the doctor. She refused, slightly defiantly, saying it was his day off and, as my condition deteriorated over the next few hours, I began to panic. Several times I asked, then pleaded and then, angrily informed her I was qualified staff and knew what I was talking about; but she remained unmoved and through a semi-conscious haze I wondered if she had actually been properly trained.

Eventually I told her to send for my solicitor. I thought I was dying and wanted to up-date my will, not done since our marriage. Perhaps she began to suspect I was not doing well because she went off and rang him. He came quickly and together we drafted a new will which he took away to be typed up and made ready for signing.

Some time later, despite it being his day off, Paul Fehrsen popped his head around the door unannounced, and I suspected the solicitor had 'phoned him. He entered the room, took one startled look at me, said nothing, turned around and disappeared. A few minutes later he returned with another friend, Eric Cohen, a cardiac consultant and physician. I was dying! They took James away from me and the next few days passed in a hideous blur of dreams, sweats and pain. A nurse stationed constantly at my bedside monitored vital signs frequently, injected antibiotics into muscle and stuck needles into my arm to set up a transfusion pumping cold, too cold, blood into unwilling veins. At one moment I opened my eyes and caught her watching me. I told her I had a curious feeling I might be dying. "Nonsense," she said. "You're fine, and anyway the whole hospital has been praying for you." *Why?* floated through my mind as I drifted off again.

A few days later, Paul asked if I would like to share my very large room with Severine Barry, a good friend, still in the delivery room having just given birth to a daughter named Helga. As my health improved it was good to have Sev's company, but after another week I became restless and longed to return to Bonisa, to the other children, to Koki and Snoopy, to the bush and the coolness of the thatched roof. I'd been off the farm for many weeks and had had enough of town. I wanted to hear again the crowing of cockerels in the distant compound just before dawn and the drums beating on Saturday nights and to see if the gecko which lived on the bedroom wall had grown another tail, and just to sit in the garden, now full of colour, where the solitude had a spiritual, almost narcotic quality.

At last, two weeks later, James and I returned to Little Bonisa and began slipping into family life again. The mornings were busy with the children and domestic concerns but in the heat of the afternoons all I felt like doing was sitting under the camel thorn tree, James alongside me under a mosquito net in a pram, while I wrote letters and dozed, listening to the incessant chatter of the colony of masked weavers noisily making their city of nests in the acacia tree.

Through eyes half closed I watched yellow flashes darting around, weaving grass into roughly spherical chambers. To each fully-formed chamber the male added an entrance tunnel, directed downwards, making access more difficult for predators. I watched in awe as, when the little homes were ready, the birds stripped leaves off the branches, leaving them naked so that they would expose approaching predators, mainly snakes, intent on raiding their eggs and babies.

When a nest is completed Mrs Weaver is called to inspect it. House-proud and fussy, if the quality fails to please she rips it apart casting frequent disdainful glances towards her hapless husband perched forlornly on a nearby branch. I may have imagined it, but it seemed to me the unsuccessful builder sighed before resigning himself to beginning the work all over again. Perfectionist females sometimes made their mate rebuild several times before accepting his offering but then, when satisfied, she set about lining the interior herself, decorating it with leaves and grass tops. The weaver's domestic life fascinated and absorbed me for many afternoons and I looked forward eventually to watching chicks emerging from the tunnels.

Most days were spent out-doors. Tim, out and about on the farm, came in for tea and meals and to catch up with book-work in the office. The farm office, a cavernous room which he shared with his father, formed the corner of the bedroom wing of Big Bonisa. It had been a sleeping porch for the five sons and instead of windows two sides were covered with mosquito gauzing to allow through-drafts. Despite a good roof overhang, driving rain sometimes splattered in through the gauze, forcing the desks to positions in the centre of the room.

One day when Tim was working there alone a shadow fell through the open doorway. He looked up and squinted to make out the figure against the bright sunlight behind. The silhouette was tall, straight and dignified and he recognised it as Egalandi. Egalandi had been named for England and no one was quite sure how old he was, not even Egalandi himself, but everyone was agreed that, whatever his age, he was tough and timeless.

"Yes, come in," Tim said.

Huge black feet padded softly across the polished concrete floor and stopped in front of the desk.

"Please Boss, I want a day off."

Tim put down his pen, astonished.

"How long have you worked here Egalandi?" he asked.

"Forty-five years Boss."

"And have you ever before asked for a day off?"

"No, Boss." He had never wanted one.

"Why now?" Tim was intrigued.

"I want to see the amanzi... the water," was the reply.

Little by little the story emerged. It seemed that at 5.30am, every morning for forty-five years, Egalandi had left the compound and walked the mile or so to Red Bank Siding to meet the train from Bulawayo as it passed through on its way to Victoria Falls. After collecting the newspapers and exchanging a few words with the guardsman he then faithfully walked back to the homestead in time for the newspapers to be placed on the Master's dining room table. Each morning he had stood on the platform and watched the trains pull out and puff away into the northern distance. He had watched and wondered. Now the mystery he had been pondering for years had become too much for him. He wanted to go and see for himself where the trains went.

He knew with certainty that a railway engine could not turn on the single tracks, so how could it always be at the front? Of course he had asked the guards who had told him about a turntable at Victoria Falls and how, after the carriages were unhitched, the engine drove onto the table which then turned. In this way the engine would once again be at the front of the train for the return journey. The improbability of such a thing filled Egalandi with considerable doubts. He had heard that there was a mighty river called the Zambezi, full-full of water which fell over rocks and became 'Mosiatunya'... The Smoke that Thunders. He could imagine and believe this, but he could not discount the possibility of his own theory – that the train engines themselves were discarded each time they reached the mighty river and a new engine produced for the return journey south.

He wanted to see for himself.

"Egalandi," Tim leaned back in his chair, "take as many days off as you need to find your answer and don't come back until you are satisfied."

The old man padded out of the office to make his plans. Alternative arrangements would be made for the newspapers.

We did not see him go, but a few days later the bush telegraph was buzzing with the excitement of having seen Egalandi, dressed in a spotless white shirt and his best trousers, walking resolutely down the dusty track to Red Bank Siding at an odd time of day. And not returning. Perhaps his ancient mother knew the reason, for he was not a married man, but when asked she simply smiled to herself and said nothing.

After several days Egalandi appeared as usual for fencing duty. Offering no explanations to the rest of the bursting work force, he carried on, quietly stretching and cutting wire. Tim drew him to one side.

"Well Egalandi?" he enquired. "What did you find?"

Egalandi stood erect, his weathered, mahogany face set firm, not inviting further questions.

He turned to gaze out towards the horizon.

"Well?"

"Maningi Amanzi," was all he said. "Plenty-plenty water."

5

The extension to Little Bonisa, now nearly completed, formed an oblong courtyard between the bedroom and living sections of the cottage which I planted up with sweet smelling shrubs and flower tubs. James spent much of the day there, protected from the elements, asleep in his 1930s pram from Tim's childhood, being gently rocked by David or Sarah as they passed through. They were so fiercely proud of him, they even dragged travelling fertilizer salesmen over to admire him.

Although life was often unpredictable, we attempted to establish some sort of routine. Missing the social contact with old friends, Tim suggested I took Thursday off each week to go to town. S'iponono helped load the car with vegetables from the kitchen garden, fresh cream from the dairy and game meat for friends in Bulawayo, and some treats for her friends in Mpopoma township.

Our first call was on Boo Mavros in one of the wide avenues in Suburbs. Spreading jacarandas joined overhead, cooling the air underneath and in season dusting the ground with delicate, sweet-smelling mauve blossoms. Boo's husband Mav, Medical Superintendent of Mpilo African Hospital was rarely there during the day and we sat drinking coffee in the garden of their large old colonial home, catching up with news and reminiscing about the fun we used to have, about the parties, and the achievements and the wonderful weddings of their children. We were almost as proud as they were of their son, Patrick Mavros, and others who we knew were Selous Scouts. The Scouts were held in awe, the elite, not talked about for security reasons or, if they were, it was in whispers. They were ones for which we knew we had a lot to thank, and it was generally recognized that they must have had the toughest experiences of the bush war. And so, when, at the wedding reception for Patrick's sister Danaë and George Lambert-Porter, about a dozen Selous Scouts gathered in the garden, the atmosphere changed. Leaning into a circle, lusty young men, arms resting on each others' shoulders, rhythmically chanting and singing blood stirring songs known only to them, white and black, they shared a bond we could not enter into.

Patrick and his wife, Catja Halsted, went to live in Mashonaland where Patrick set up a workshop of outstanding ivory and silver sculptures, sometimes resting on ebony plinths, and became an international success.

Boo loved babies and as her own children all left to make their own lives she more than welcomed mine and generously looked after James on our trips to town, leaving me free to tackle the shopping lists with David and Sarah in tow. Having James was "an absolute pleasure," she claimed, "No trouble at all," but when I collected him later in the day it was clear he'd not been changed. "Oh I couldn't possibly do that," she said cheerfully, "he looks so much like Humphrey it would be indecent to undress him."

After leaving James with Boo we drove to Advance Wholesalers, a large warehouse shed in the hot, dusty industrial sites, where farmers and retailers obtained stock for their stores.

We didn't run a store for the workers, as many farmers did, but we were given a permit to buy such goods as were available: Rhodesian grown tea; sugar; flour; disgusting, sticky, black coffee essence; loo paper; cartons of Madison or Kingsgate cigarettes in packets of 20, 30 and 50; matches; masses of candles and wooden crates of Fanta Orange, Crème Soda and Coca Cola in glass bottles, which I rationed, one per child, on a Sunday. There were large plastic bags of sticky sweets coated in dust which, kept in the car, were given out to picannins for opening farm gates or running small errands. Advance also stocked tinned hams from Colcom (who made the best pork products in the whole world) and GibCan tinned fruit and vegetables, which were canned in Mashonaland in a factory begun by the family. We bought quantities of waxy, green soap in eighteen-inch bars to be taken home, grated and put on the roof to dry in the sun for a week before being used in the dairy, for the washing of clothes and for producing permanently smeary drinking glasses.

Shopping trips could not be hurried. David and Sarah wanted to explore, stop and examine everything. I never locked the car and often left shopping bags on the seat with the roof down on my Caravelle and nothing disappeared. However, going into the larger stores we were searched for security reasons and one day I cringed as a guard plunged his hand into my bag, and pulled out a wet cake of soap and an old chop bone. David and Sarah stood wide-eyed. It was nothing to do with either of them, they said. Nothing. They were very, very sure of that.

There were a few shops all selling much the same range of locally produced clothes, which often tended towards the gaudy and badly made, and I looked instead for fabric. Small Greek, Jewish and Indian stores stocked excellent materials and a wide range of prints mainly woven from cotton grown in Mashonaland, from which I made nearly all the children's clothes and many of my own.

By late morning, hot and thirsty, we drove to Christian Vigne's. Vigne's had been started as a Book Shop, Coffee Shop, and Library by Duncan's parents a few years before for the purpose of providing employment for a friend who found herself suddenly and tragically widowed with two young children and no means of support.

The Flemings still owned the business and, although new books were in frustratingly short supply and difficult to obtain because of sanctions, the staff there did a remarkable job of ferreting out secret suppliers. They hid under the counter books they thought we'd enjoy before offering them to the public and, while Enoch loaded the car with the morning's shopping, which had already been delivered to the back door, we sat at a low coffee table browsing through the selection, making our choices and sipping ice-cold mango and pineapple juices.

Bulawayo (the name means a 'place of slaughter') stands west of the Great Dyke at an altitude of 4,500ft and Baden Powell, when investigating it 1896, wrote that he found 'A red earth flat laid out by ditches, in blocks and streets, over two miles long and half a mile wide.' The original planners stipulated that the streets had to be wide enough to turn a wagon drawn by sixteen in-spanned oxen.

The streets, now tree lined with flamboyants, jacarandas, frangipani and spathodea (the African Tulip tree), were reputed to be the first streets in the world to be lit by electricity at the time when London was still lit by gas lamps.

I much preferred the small, out-of-the-way supermarkets and Solomon's, in particular, could sometimes be persuaded to produce tins of fish and other exotic luxuries (presumably smuggled into the country) from under the counter at inflated prices. The shortages included honey which could rarely be found anywhere and I resolved that, when we moved into Big Bonisa, I would take up beekeeping and sell the produce to these small stores. We already supplied Meikles and the other large supermarkets in departmental stores such as Haddon and Sly with fish and citrus.

The children especially enjoyed visiting the Indian leather workers of Jacob's shoes, away from the smart part of town towards the townships, before Lobengula Street. Their store, festooned with hides, belts, sandals, watch covers, bags and repaired shoes, smelled strongly of new leather, hot glue and sweat. It seemed the Indians could make anything anyone could possibly want. Their workmanship was professional, their prices reasonable and nothing was too much trouble. They suggested the best style of sandal for farm children and then, with the children, solemnly discussed their preferred style of catapults.

The morning passed quickly and eventually we drove to Suburbs for lunch with Paddy Fehrsen. David took charge of putting our perishable shopping in her fridge and placing the car keys on top, so we couldn't leave without them, and then stayed in the kitchen with Sarah where Aaron, the cook, plied them both with treats I thought guaranteed to spoil their lunch and rot their teeth, but I pretended not to notice.

Paddy and Paul's home was neat, compact and stunningly beautiful. To one side of the verandah she'd put in a black-painted swimming pool, with a fountain splashing shivers of light through the ripples and, while the children swam, we sat under streamers of Lady Slipper draping yellow trumpets down from the latticed roof and watched the young as we talked. I loved having time away from the farm for a day. It was refreshing being in the company of other women who although understanding of the daily difficulties of life in the bush were uninvolved with it. They had other horizons; other conversations; other problems to discuss.

Ineke Williams and her daughter, Sasha, often joined us, coming in from their Turk Mine ranch east of Bulawayo. Neat, vivacious and chic – not what was usually expected in a farmer's wife, Ineke came from Holland where, it was said, she had been briefly married to the watchmaker Tissot, but no one knew what brought her to Rhodesia. I still had a slight pang of conscience about Ineke. Each time we met I remembered the day, a year before, when the phone had rung just as I was leaving the house and I'd ignored it.

"Just say I've gone out and take a message S'iponono," I'd said.

"It's Mrs Fehrsen," she called after me, but I was running late.

"Tell Madam to come now, come quickly," Paddy said to S'iponono. But I'd already gone. I thought we could catch up later when we were all having dinner together later that evening to celebrate the return of Huntsman, Ineke's husband, from the forest area up beyond Lupane, where he'd been on call-up. Paddy, Ineke and I loved any excuse for a celebration.

It was two hours before I got the message. Huntsman would not be coming back from call-up. There would be no celebration dinner. The rocket that hit his vehicle had ripped his arm off at the shoulder. There were no medical supplies in his area. He quickly bled to death.

I got back in the car and drove straight to Suburbs. All we could do was sit with her, in the agony of it all. Paul Fehrsen was Ineke's doctor as well as ours and he sedated her. I never did confess the ignored phone call, it weighed heavily on me. I would have if I'd thought it might have helped Ineke in any way – but it wouldn't and it took a long time to forgive myself.

Huntsman's funeral took place on their farm. We could hardly bear it as, in the heat and the dust and the flies, we stood around the grave with other friends. His old father, Benjie, looking stony faced and numb, and Ineke, sobbing, threw herself on his coffin and had to be removed before it was lowered into the sun-baked, red earth.

But now, a year later, there were signs that Ineke was beginning to make a new life and although we knew there was a long way to go, she said these times together, reminiscing about Hunty and shared memories, helped and the Thursday lunches became important for the three of us.

We called David, Sarah and Sasha out of the pool before Aaron sounded the gong calling us in for lunch. He affected surprise when the children weren't interested in lunch despite him having fed them with cake and biscuits earlier in the kitchen and he would hear no criticism of them when all they wanted was ice-cream.

When it was time to leave Paddy and return to the farm before curfew the children were tired but we always made a small detour to the Eskimo Hut on Burnside Road for a final indulgence. Enormous ice-creams with names like Green Mama, Bee Hive, Wimbledon Wonder and Chocolate Mountain Rock kept them quiet as, sitting on tree stumps at the hut, we raced to lick the instantly melting goo dripping down the cones.

"Like the sweat on our faces," David said.

On the road home I watched the way ahead, alert for signs of abnormal activity, while the three children slept peacefully in the back. Everything was quiet when, after leaving the Nyamandhlovu Road, we reached the tarmac strips on the home stretch and I noticed a log lying across the road ahead. There weren't any trees around and, in the dry arid area, I wondered if it was a trap. I quickly scanned either side of the track. Apart from tufts of brown grass and an occasional dry bush there was nothing to be seen. Puzzled, I turned back to the road just in time to see the 'log' rise up and lunge towards us. Too late to swerve, we ran over it. I glanced in the rear view mirror, it had gone. Terrified that it may have curled around the axle I put my foot down and raced for home. Outside the security gates we sat in the car blasting the horn until Tim came out. He was sceptical.

"It stretched from side to side of the strips?" he replied, "They don't come that big here." But he checked under the car before letting us out and then returned with me to the spot where I'd thought it had been. There was no sign of anything untoward and I was beginning to wonder if I'd imagined it when a movement, just off the road, caught the eye of each of us at the same time. In the dry grass, still writhing but badly injured, a ten foot Black Mamba was in its death throes. I am cautious, but not afraid, of any snake except the Mambas, black or green. They're aggressive, fast, deadly and they terrify me.

But Tim hates all snakes. He swore at it, drew his pistol and with one, probably never to be repeated, lucky shot, blew its head apart.

6

By the middle of 1979 Tim was spending more time in Salisbury, trying to develop an export business, and he felt the time had come to employ a farm manager. When John Zurnamer applied for the position Tim invited him for an interview. A no-nonsense young bachelor in his early twenties, he had a quick sense of humour and an endearing stutter, which was strangely absent in his spontaneous wit. It was also apparent that he had an excellent grasp of all aspects of farming in Matabeleland. I knew instantly John was the right person and, almost more importantly, it was obvious at first meeting that Samson, the 'boss boy', and Mkava, my right hand man, immediately respected him.

A month later John arrived loaded up with a few items of furniture, some basics groceries, a plentiful supply of Madison cigarettes and Zonda, his energetic young Weimaraner. Several miles down the track leading to the Mpopoma River on a section of Bonisa known as New Farm was an empty cottage, completely isolated apart from a small building of feeding pens for calves, and John said he would be happy to live there alone. I was apprehensive for him but we were also glad to have the far end of the farm occupied. Occasionally, when Tim was away overnight John volunteered to come up and sleep in the drawing room in Little Bonisa as protection for the children and me and I was grateful to have the added security.

Monica Barrington also regarded John as an asset. Living, as she did, opposite the entrance to Bonisa, just off the strips close to Red Bank Siding, she looked upon anything to do with Bonisa as also to do with her. Her a tiny cottage with its typically functional corrugated iron roof was surrounded by a security fence which she reluctantly agreed to have when it was explained that it was not fair to expect the neighbours to protect her if she didn't take some basic measures herself. Its whitewashed walls were splattered with red-brown mud from last seasons torrential rains, which should have been hosed down but never were. A volunteer crop of something that looked like mealies heroically fought to grow through the impoverished soil and a few hardy plants: Bizzie Lizzies, Christ Thorn and Bethlehem Star interspersed with prickly pears survived, untended, in the one bed. It was not her fault that she wasn't really interested in gardening; her bore hole, although only fifty yards from the Khami River, yielded a mere one hundred gallons of water a day which was enough to knock gardening aspirations out of anyone.

Monica held lightly the things of this world, keeping her mind focussed on a higher plane, a way of life re-enforced during the years she, with her husband Albert, had run St Thomas' Mission since founding it in 1950 just outside Nyamandhlovu. Content in her cottage she rarely ventured out since that dreadful day, five years earlier, when Nyamandhlovu police arrived with the news that Albert had been killed in his Morris 1100 on the Gwaai Bridge. It was an accident they said; it was late afternoon, the sun was in his eyes, he didn't see the two African buses careering towards him side by side from the opposite direction. He didn't stand a chance and had, mercifully, died instantly.

Monica, now alone in the world, became more and more reclusive. Many of us tried to draw her out but she made it plain that she did not want to be drawn out; did not want to be included or loved, only to give love; to devote herself, as she had always done, in the service of The Lord, in whatever way she felt called. There was an added assumption that we, and John, (although we may not have known it) had also been called to help her. It was mostly the local children who interested her and sometimes, as we passed through Red Bank Siding, she could be seen dancing with them outside her cottage, singing in fluent Ndebele, her long, grey hair flapping around her like a flag in the wind.

Following Albert's death, Monica lived her life in the constant expectation that 'The Lord would provide.' She was certain of the natural flow of this provision – The Lord, who always looked after his own, would nudge her neighbours and those she regarded as 'better off' to enquire of her needs and then meet them. Since her cottage clung to the bottom of our farm track and we lived in a large house, we fell into the categories of both 'neighbour' and 'better off'.

If natural providers ignored supernatural nudgings, or were slow off the mark, Monica stepped in to do a little nudging of her own until another farmer, a large, blunt Africaaner had had enough and burst out, "Ja, Monica, Hell, man, in Nyama you're 'The White Man's Burden' – all by yessself".

We saw less of Monica, however, than we did of Mpofu. Mpofu had been a young student from a nearby kraal in the early days of the mission who fastened on to Monica and Albert, taking advantage of their good natures and later, when they retired, he offered himself as their house boy, garden boy, messenger, and guard.

We didn't trust Mpofu. John Zurnamer loathed him and claimed that the years Mpofu had been with Monica were entirely on his own terms and for his own benefit.

"He's a skellem[7]," John told her, "He manipulates you." But Monica steadfastly clamped her lips into crows feet and refused to discuss Mpofu.

"He's ripping you off Monica, he's lazy and he needs a good wash," John persevered but Monica simply feigned deafness. She took the view that Divine Providence had sent him to her and that, regardless of whatever we may think less than perfect in him, it was not for her to sit in judgement.

Mpofu often appeared at Little Bonisa bearing notes from his mistress. S'iponono refused to let Mpofu beyond the kitchen door, and brought the notes to us herself, her back rigid, her face set in disapproval.

"The bore hole has packed up, could you come and fix it?" the notes frequently read, or, "Mpofu is not well, he would like some vegetables from your kitchen garden to make him better," or "Could you take Mpofu to the clinic in town and pick up some things for me on your way back…?" usually adding that she would pay us later. But then forgot.

---

7   Skellem: an untrustworthy rogue.

It was with some surprise that, after not hearing from Monica for a while, I received a note from Mpofu bidding me to come and see her, alone. She didn't often invite visitors and, curious, I called Mpofu and set off in the Land Rover for Red Bank Siding. In the far corner of the small property, next to Mpofu's two roomed kia[8] I could see his own thriving patch of well-watered mealies provided a little shade for an assortment of chickens, three legged pots and the embers of last night's cooking fire.

I climbed the steps to Monica's cottage. Inside was dark, unkept, and, apart from a picture of Douglas Bader in a spitfire, an old rug and four utilitarian chairs, there had been no attempt to decorate it. Mpofu was supposed to keep the place clean, but he quite clearly didn't and a faint, stale smell of neglect permeated the air trapped inside the closed windows. Monica apparently didn't notice, or, if she did, chose to ignore it.

She called out from the bedroom where she was lying face down on the bed: "Maggots in my bum." I immediately understood why. It was a one of the hazards during the rainy season. Damp washing on outside clothes lines risked having Putzi Fly eggs laid in the fabric. On contact with human skin the eggs hatch, the larvae buries itself under the skin and develops into itchy, painful boils containing maggots. Diligent ironing prevents this but Mpofu apparently didn't think it his place to iron Monica's knickers and, for once, I privately agreed with him. Eventually fully grown maggots eat their way out and emerge of their own accord. Picking up a pair of tweezers on the bedside table I began gently pulling out the fat, white, wriggling maggots one by one. It was a slow job and I took the opportunity to ask Monica how she came be so fluent in Ndebele.

"My parents were missionaries in Swaziland," she said, "and I grew up speaking Zulu – Real Zulu, not your chilapalapa mumbo-jumbo stuff. But no one bothers to learn it properly these days," she scoffed. "Ndebele derives from Zulu, so I had a good foundation."

---

8   Kia: a small hut.

As the discomfort eased she became more expansive. "My parents were very popular; in fact one of their old friends wrote last month and asked if I needed anything."

"And?" I encouraged.

"I told them I needed a new car."

That's a bit excessive, I thought.

"And? they are giving you one?"

"Ah, yes! God is good to me," she sighed.

7

Humphrey approached his 80th birthday in good health, if a little stooped and very deaf. A shock of thick, white hair crowned his handsome, almost gaunt, and permanently tanned face. We suspected his deafness was selective as, apparently, did a member of the Portland Cement board who claimed:

"Humphrey is an excellent Chairman. He has a brilliant method for keeping order and getting what he wants – He simply pretends not to hear unwanted comments or interruptions and talks over them with his own agenda."

Although still a crack shot, an unerring billiard player and retaining his sharp wit, the initial in Governor's Lodge and later incarceration in Government House had taken its toll and left both Humphrey and Molly with a tiredness from which, we felt, they never fully recovered. Since being given leave, by the Queen, to stand down in 1969, they had lived quiet lives on the farm[9].

Harold Wilson offered Humphrey a peerage which he turned down saying: "The British Labour Government sacrificed Rhodesia on the altar of expediency. I'll not accept anything from them." He had already received the KCMG from the British Government in 1959, followed later by the KCVO and the GCVO, which were in the Queen's gift, but refused to accept an honour from the Harold Wilson Government. When pressed further he stood firm saying no, what he had been given was enough, but implied that something for his wife might be suitable. After all, Molly had borne much of the

---

9   On 11 November 1965 Ian Smith, the Prime Minister of Southern Rhodesia, had broadcast a Unilateral Declaration of Independence (UDI) in the name of "the safeguarding of justice, civilisation and christianity." Humphrey had disagreed and refused to stand down. With substantial national support he had remained incarcerated in Governor's Lodge, and later Government House, until 1969 when Ian Smith declared a republic. With ties with Britain cut, the Queen gave permission for Humphrey to stand down.

brunt during the difficult beleaguered years, and so she was created a Dame of the British Empire. Along with refusing the honour, he also refused to accept his salary or to pay to the Rhodesian Government the monthly bill for £250, being 'rent for Government House.' Over the four years from UDI to 1969, other large expenses mounted up, which Humphrey paid from his own pocket and from the Governor's Fund which had been set up by sympathetic Rhodesians, refusing reimbursement. Eventually an agreement was reached for these funds to be deposited in a Trust Fund in Molly's name in the Bahamas, not for himself, but for eventual distribution to his five sons some of whose lives (especially Tim's and Nigel's) had also been so disrupted by the politics of the times.

It was over one of our weekly bridge games (during which Humphrey was a partner with perfect hearing) that I pressed the issue of his birthday.

"We can't let eighty years pass without marking it. Your friends will want to beat the drum and cheer you into the future," I said. But they were not, as a couple, given to noticing birthdays and, tired of the endless formal entertaining of the government house days, they dismissed my suggestion of a celebration. At least Molly did – Humphrey was suffering deafness.

"I'd love to give a lunch party for you at Little Bonisa," I persisted, which was not entirely true. For, although the spirit was willing, unrelenting heat and constant vigilance left the flesh feeling weak. However, as it became clear that I intended doing all the preparations without calling on them for help, Molly reluctantly agreed and we drew up a list of names from the dwindling number of friends in both Bulawayo and the Nyamandhlovu District. About forty replies came in – all sounding delighted – galvanizing my own enthusiasm and we set about arranging an armed convoy to bring the guests from town out to the farm.

During the oppressive October heat I'd drawn copious amounts of water from the bore hole and by 22nd November the garden looked luxuriant – a green oasis in an otherwise pale, withered veldt. On the lawn under spreading shade trees, tables covered with white cloths were set out, and down the middle of each I arranged masses of garden flowers and foliage.

Unable to spare any chickens I made coronation guinea fowl which was passable, if not as good as the original, and ordered one of the York hams from the Bulawayo Club, for which they were renowned. A number of prominent Bulawayo Jews had been black-balled from membership of the Club and they no longer allowed their names to be put forward. Although I never discovered whether or not this was policy, it was embarrassing. Bulawayo had a significant Jewish population and as a number of our guests would be Jews – some orthodox – we also killed a lamb to offer as an alternative to the ham.

For once I hoped and prayed that it would not rain and, as the day arrived and the temperatures soared, there was not a cloud in the sky.

From the front lawn we could see dust rising from the direction of the turn off and a few minutes later, just as the convoy drove up, S'iponono came to me in a panic.

"Nkosikasi, the coleslaw, she is boiling, she is smelling, now she is like silage."

I probably should have known not to prepare the coleslaw too far ahead at that time of the year and certainly not in a plastic bucket.

"Quickly, get help," I told her. "Find the garden boy, the tractor driver, (a terrorist, anyone). Bring more cabbages and carrots from the kitchen garden and do what you saw me doing to them." And, hoping for the best, I went to greet the arrivals, leaving her to it.

Molly and Humphrey walked over from Big Bonisa, through the kitchen garden, as they heard the cars draw up. Molly, elegant in a flowing green silk dress which she had made herself, changed her shoes and went to greet their friends. I'd not expected Humphrey to dress up and I was right. Even on the hottest days he wore his battered old tweed jacket, one side dragged down by the weight of the pistol in his pocket. He refused to wear a holster and, beyond abiding by the curfew and trying to remember to pocket his firearm, he took little interest in safety or security. Even the alarms left him unmoved, and Molly nervy and jumpy.

MG and GG Fleming came in first bearing a large painting – a striking picture in muted blues and greens of African trees, birds and animals surrounding a black St Francis of Assisi wearing nothing but a loin cloth and impressive pectoral cross. Humphrey recognized it and received it with great pleasure. It was an appropriate present, the work of Richard Rashid of Cyrene Mission near Plumtree. He'd been trained by Rev Canon Ned Patterson, an old friend of Humphrey and Molly and an accomplished artist himself. It had been a great pleasure to everyone when Ned's daughter, Barbara, had married Humphrey and Molly's second son, Nigel.

At the last minute Monica agreed to join us and proudly drove herself the mile or so from Red Bank Cottage in her newly 'donated' car and immediately began seeking out John Zurnamer. He avoided her. She in turn avoided the Jewish guests, probably not because they were Jewish but because she was uncomfortable with their glamour and sophistication. She looked tidy with her grey hair scraped back into a bun and had added white beads to a dark blue dress I'd not seen before. It suited her and after admiring it I introduced her to Paddy Fehrsen who was a particular friend of several missionaries including Garfield Todd. Although Gar was under house arrest at the time and not able to join us, Paul, as Gar's doctor, had permission to visit him on his farm and had the latest news of them. I thought that they, at least, would have something in common to talk about.

I would have loved to have asked Peter Baker what he made of Monica but couldn't bring myself to be quite so obvious. Peter, the psychiatrist in charge of Ingutsheni, the mental hospital in Bulawayo unwittingly intimidated some people who uncomfortably wondered if he could see into their souls, but I enjoyed him and invariably found myself put next to him at dinner parties. His wife Jill was a dear friend and I still missed the afternoons in Bulawayo when I stood-in as a substitute in the regular bridge four she had with Paddy. I'd not wanted to be tied down to a regular group and being a floating substitute for several sets suited my unpredictable life style.

Most people knew each other and, clutching drinks, milled around under the shade trees catching up with the gossip and the latest on 'the situation'. I watched silently for a moment and recognised again how much I missed these occasions.

Paddy cast imploring looks in my direction. Monica had apparently been enjoying quantities of something that looked like water – but wasn't – and it was making her chatty and not entirely easy to understand. I turned around and indicated to GG Fleming that it was her turn with Monica. GG was astute with little sympathy for the less robust but her manners would never let her down. Although she didn't suffer fools gladly, Monica was not a fool – just different. GG summed up the situation in a flash, her strong sense of duty rose to the fore, as I knew it would, and after a few words of conversation she tactfully drew Monica off into a circle of general conversation.

Time passed quickly. S'iponono produced a credible substitute coleslaw, the gin held out and helped smooth over known prickly subjects. It was good seeing Humphrey and Molly enjoying what was, despite their initial resistance, a very happy day. For the rest of us, who were aware that we were a small and haemorrhaging community, it provided another addition to the bond of shared experiences.

8

The rest of November remained dry. Listless cattle wandered down to the dam or lay down under trees. Sporadic bush-fires flared up in the murderous heat and dust-devils spiralled off dry lands. In the afternoons black clouds rolled up from the direction of the Congo bringing hope, only to dissipate by evening. The mood was strained and fractious and conversations largely centred on dying crops and the need for rain. Then, on the last night of the month, it broke.

Deafening, window-shaking thunder exploded somewhere near and rolled closer. Dazzling blazes of lightning fractured the black skies, putting out the lights. We didn't complain. Our spirits soared when, initially, as if unsure, a few large drops of rain fell, and then rapidly gained momentum, swelling into great artilleries, then torrents, hammering on the thatch, gouging canals in the earth below.

Thunder rumbled continuously all night, sometimes accompanied by sheet lightning which briefly lit up the land, like a flare. The children clambered into bed with us and I told them what GG always said: "It is only God moving his furniture around up there," which partially reassured them while Koki and Snoopy cowed, terrified, underneath. The relief was tangible, as if some tightly stretched unseen force had snapped, releasing pent-up tension, and I knew other farmers would feel the same. Maybe flash floods would follow, maybe cupboards would smell as shoes and belts grew mould – what did it matter? For a while the lands might be too heavy to plough and red mud would stick to everything; but in a few days the veldt would turn green bringing the heady, evocative smells peculiar to Africa – smells of wet dust, of musty wet thatch and pungent Matabele ants – and the rains would signal that new life was about to begin, the way it should.

We could also be fairly sure that no one would be attacked on a night like this.

The precariousness of life was never far from our minds. Despite the improved security situation no one was seduced into complacency.

We avoided sticking to routines, especially for travelling, and were amazed that the milk tractor, on its daily trip to and from Bulawayo, never came under threat. However, we did decide to ignore the 'confidential letter' sent to all farmers by the Matabeleland Farmer's Co-op announcing that they had been 'appointed the distributors for a Government-tested, and approved, internal window safety bullet protecting box' which, they claimed, would 'protect against standard rifle fire but not against armour piercing rounds.' A sketchy diagram came with the letter. Made on legs, adjusted according to window height, and filled not with sand but with small, well-tamped granite chips, they sounded awful and would not, in any case, provide sufficient protection against the sort of attack which we anticipated – which might include tracer bullets into the thatch. Security fencing, Agric-Alert and other standard precautions seemed more appropriate for our needs, especially as the homesteads were built on top of a steep plateau making direct rifle fire unlikely to be effective and tracers difficult to project on to the roof due to the angle.

And so we continued to wear sidearms, keeping them within arms length when in bed or in the bath and there were other small precautions – the men wore snap-on, thick, leather wrist-watch covers – to prevent sunlight glinting off the metal and revealing their position and, on call-up, soap was abandoned, its lingering smell a powerful give-away in the bush.

Previous experience had shown that the quiet times could be the most dangerous, with the safest periods in the immediate aftermath of an attack when the area swarmed with security forces and the terrorists went to ground.

Monica Barrington refused to have Agric-Alert.

"God will protect me," she said – although she was at a loss to explain the recent Elim Mission massacres in the Eastern Districts. "One day it will be over, one day the lion will lie down with the lamb."

"Really?" John said "the lamb won't get much sleep. Well the least you can do is lock your security gate at curfew. You are a perfect soft target and then we will have to respond." John remonstrated with her and instructed Mpofu to "stop being so idle and see to it."

Snatches of information regarding Red Bank Cottage were whispered by the bush telegraph and by John's loyal workforce, headed by Arras Ndhlovu, but from time to time we also had news from Monica herself. Eschewing her own party-line, she drove up the track to use our direct-line to Bulawayo which had been installed on Humphrey's return from Government House.

"It's so much cheaper," she explained and of course we recognised the economic sense of not having to pay your own telephone bills.

Monica lit up in the company of picannins but was surprisingly indifferent to white children, including our children, and I excused this by rationalising that, although we had little money and our children had few toys, they could not be regarded as disadvantaged in the same way as the little black ones in the compound. Her attitude didn't impinge on the children's lives at all but it annoyed John, who thought her rude. And said so.

Despite having little contact with other young, the children had full, interesting lives. Tim and John took them around the farm in the open-backed Land Rover and David, in particular, revelled in the bush – in the birds and the game which he could identify accurately, and in rescuing injured or abandoned animals which he brought back to the cottage and helped nurture. Various young antelope on bottle feeds, a tortoise, a pygmy hedgehog, and a young monkey all joined the menagerie over time.

But David's constant companion and best friend was a short-haired German Pointer, named Snoopy. Snoopy had been wished on us by the widow of a friend who'd committed suicide and, when she begged us to take the dog, I'd felt it was the least we could do.

Looking after Snoopy was David's priority. He insisted on grooming and feeding him and, with an eye for detail regarding his creature comforts, he kept Snoopy's droopy ears out of the feeding bowl by stapling them together above his head.

Although being, as he was, a useless gun dog David was besotted and they were inseparable until the day Snoopy chewed one door handle too many and, with swift retribution, was shot dead. David wept beyond comfort.

"But I didn't even say goodbye," he sobbed.

In desperation I rang Stephen Mills, a distant farmer and explained that although David didn't know Snoopy was dead, only that he'd gone, his grief was devastating and that I didn't know what to do.

"Put him on the phone," Stephen said.

"David, hello. I'm Stephen, Snoopy's new owner. I'm very sorry you are missing him but I want you to know that he is happy. He has lots of friends – other pointers – to keep him company. They play and hunt together on my ranch up at Gwaii River. He sends his love to you – would you like to hear him bark? I'll call him."

Every night, only slightly comforted, David knelt by the bed and prayed for Snoopy.

Over the next few weeks I searched for distractions. I read him stories and taught him things I'd learned about the bush.

"How come you know so much about everything?" he asked me one day. "I've lived a long time and that's what mothers are for," I told him, "They learn things and then teach their children about life." The next morning he ran into the bedroom before breakfast.

"Mum, I'm going fishing with Ben in a minute but before he comes could you just quickly teach me about life?"

Ben, the son of Enoch, the garden boy, took him fishing and game tracking and taught him to make animals and toy bicycles out of fencing wire which they raced against each other across the top lawn. They were about the same age, were both approaching the time of beginning formal education.

For Africans it was the only hope of advancement to a better life, an increased earning capacity later on, and the parents instilled an eagerness to learn in the children from an early age. Farm schools – usually little more than a thatched room with one teacher – made some form of education available in most, even remote, areas. Officially, for those who knew their birth dates, lessons began in the January following a child's fifth birthday but the test for picannins of uncertain age, was to tell them to extend their right hand over their head and touch the left ear – an impossible feat before the age of six.

From the age of three, David had attended the Hebrew English Nursery School in Bulawayo but, since we'd moved out to the farm, this had been reduced to twice a week on random days in accordance with security advice. However, David had turned five and schooling needed to become serious and orderly. Petrol rationing and the security risk of routinely using the same road at the same time meant Day School was out of the question. Too young to board, the only other option was for me to teach him at home myself with the help of Correspondence School which, based in Salisbury, had been set up specifically for farm children, and for that we needed a dedicated schoolroom.

The cottage extensions we'd undertaken for Molly and Humphrey were completed and the builders had moved out and the time to move was closing in.

But we decided, before leaving Little Bonisa, to have a holiday, probably the last one we'd be able to have outside the designated school holidays for years ahead. MG had given us several sheets of mint stamps commemorating the ascension of Edward VIII which were now quite valuable and we sold some to pay for a trip for the five of us to Kenya with a week on Lamu Island. We flew from Malindi in a privately owned, six seater aircraft to Manda Island and boarded a dhow to cross to the Peponi about three miles north east of Lamu Town. Free from responsibilities and security concerns, it felt like paradise on earth. Our rooms opened onto an almost deserted Shela Beach – clean white sands for as far as we could see. And was exactly what we needed.

There were no cars on Lamu, the only way to go from place to place was on foot, or by donkey or dhow. Behind Peponi was a small village which we didn't intrude into until one night the locals generously invited us to a feast following Ramadan as a way of thanking me for treating one of their top people who had stepped on a stone-fish. He was in great pain and I'd expected him to die but, although my nursing training didn't include stone-fish poisoning I must have done something right because he fully recovered.

At first it felt both odd and liberating to be without firearms and I briefly recognized how unnatural our daily lives had become in

Rhodesia and, when the time came to fly home and re-enter that world, I wished things could have been different.

Little Bonisa had grown cosy and friendly with a family in it and although I regarded it as 'our' home and had anticipated several more years there, it was clear that the moment of exchanging houses with the parents had arrived. Molly, especially, was delighted. But it was much sooner than I'd hoped and I approached the inevitable with sadness.

Through a wet and steamy early December we packed our things until, one morning, on its return from the milk run to Bulawayo, the tractor and trailer turned up at the cottage. Farm hands hauled David and Sarah up to ride on the flat bed with each load as it trundled off through 200 yards of sticky red mud, in between downpours of rain, to our new home in Big Bonisa.

The children were jubilant, but as the last loads went off and Little Bonisa stood empty again, a small place within me died.

9

Big Bonisa homestead sprawled across the lip of a plateau overlooking miles of scrubby bush veldt, interspersed with acacia thorn trees, mimosa, wachambickie with their hooked, 'wait-a bit' thorns, and tall, solid camel thorns away to the north.

Humphrey had bought 6,000 acres of virgin bush in 1927, not a large spread compared with cattle ranches in the area, but having good arable land and underground water there was the potential for creating a viable farm growing crops and breeding cows for a dairy.

The Khami River meandered around the western and part of the northern boundaries but, despite being fed by the Mpopoma River from further up the watershed, it often became little more than a sandy bed during the dry season and when Agrictex told him there was no suitable place on the farm to build a dam, Humphrey simply diverted the river and built his (very successful) dam. He also sank two bore holes into the aquifer which produced good water over future years.

As if by telepathy, twelve Africans appeared to look for work. In a clearing at the bottom of the escarpment they built themselves a compound and moved in with their families, their scrawny chickens and equally scrawny dogs. As word spread that work was available and that this boss was 'a good one', several others joined them, bringing the total labour force to twenty-eight.

They worked hard in all seasons: fencing, grading roads, drilling further bore holes, cultivating the lands with an ox-drawn plough, and constructing cattle pens and a dairy. Soon after his marriage to Molly Peel Nelson in 1935, Humphrey built the basic Bonisa Homestead about 200 yards from the site of the dairy and, although in some ways inconvenient, it was a spacious home, erected of homemade mud bricks under a low-slung thatched roof around a courtyard of flower beds, low shrubs and a fish pond with a fountain which gave an illusion of coolness. As the years went by and sons arrived – five in all – other rooms were added to form an east wing.

A huge billiard room had also been added behind the kitchen and some of the bedrooms in the wing had been converted to other uses – a sewing room, a gun room and a farm office.

Despite my reluctance to leave Little Bonisa I welcomed the extra space and the children loved it. Preferring to stay together they shared the capacious night nursery which overlooked the courtyard and, being an internal room and only separated from our bedroom by the family bathroom, it was practical from a security point of view.

Security advice recommended installing an additional water tank above the bathroom which, when shot into through the ceiling, created a small wet-room for a degree of protection in the event of a tracer bullet finding its way from beyond the fence and setting fire to the thatch. Elisa Godfrey, a family friend who'd married a farmer in Esigodini told me she'd followed that advice. As automatic fire tore into their house she crouched on the bathroom floor, hugging her two children to her. "Isn't this fun?" she said, "Like cowboys and Indians," and jiggling them up and down on her knees pretended they were the goodies escaping on their horses from the baddies.

We'd not long been settled in the homestead when it became obvious that S'iponono was restless and unhappy. She had firmly-held views which I'd tried to accommodate over the years, such as her refusal to accept her wages after the sun had gone down.

"Why?" I'd asked.

"My mother told me it was wrong to accept money from a man after dark." I didn't know if she realised the significance of that but she stuck to it to honour her mother.

But now nothing seemed to cheer her up.

"What's wrong S'iponono?" I asked.

"Aziku Nkosikasi, Nothing." But she continued to be preoccupied and clumsy.

"S'iponono, what is it?" I asked again after she'd fallen down a step.

"Sore eyes Madam," she said, turning her head away.

After a few days, when the basic medicines from my clinic failed to help, I took her to Mpilo Hospital on the outskirts of Bulawayo townships. A concerned and compassionate doctor out from England on work experience took us in to a room and examined her carefully.

"I'm afraid nothing can be done," he said, explaining that some sort of worm had burrowed into her eyes. She was in the early stages of irreversible blindness. It was not uncommon, he said.

"Stay here with us and we will look after you," I assured her, but she remained uncertain and edgy. We'd known for sometime that her husband in Botswana had taken a number-two wife, one who was jealous of S'iponono and spoke spitefully against her but when news came that she was also being unkind to S'iponono's only child, a five year old son, she decided she had to return to her kraal to protect him and take care of him herself.

Saying goodbye broke our hearts. After all these years she was part of the family and she'd loved each child since birth as if it were her own. But now, as far as she was concerned, there was no alternative and, very depressed, she boarded the Bulawayo bus for Botswana. We didn't hear from S'iponono again and my letters to her were all answered promptly by her husband. He didn't give any news of her, he asked for money and then more money. Eventually the correspondence stopped. We were sure she would not receive money sent via her husband.

Manka, the daughter of Humphrey and Molly's cook, Lavu, took S'iponono's place. Having been our laundry maid, she and the children knew each other well. It was not the same, but she was patient and kind with them and, although illiterate, she would often spend hours pouring over pictures books with them, making up stories which were at variance from the ones the authors intended, but often more colourful and interesting.

I had privately wondered if perhaps Manka may have been a little too timid until one day, shortly after she arrived up from the compound, she presented me with Teresa who, she said, would now take over the washing and ironing. It was evident from the start that Manka had no doubt about her superiority, disdainfully rejecting any ironing she considered unsatisfactory and doing so with a frequency that made me wonder if Teresa would stay. Teresa, however, understood the natural order of things and gave in to Manka's demands.

A few weeks later a tall, dignified and very black Malawian came to the gates looking for work.

"I am Peter. Already I am very good cook," he said, but when asked was unable to produce any references.

"There was a fire in my kraal. Every thing gone," he claimed. Although this might, or might not, have been true I liked the look of him. I took to his gentle, thoughtful manner which I later discovered could stiffen into stubborn opposition if he disapproved of something, and the one thing he disapproved of was the one thing I believed in – discipline of the children. Scowling and tut-tutting under his breath followed my reprimands or my withholding of treats from them when they needed to learn that certain behaviours result in certain consequences and neither he nor I altered our views over the following years.

Peter's presence brought out a competitiveness between the two women. Manka, no longer in the first bloom of youth, became positively girlish and displayed an obsessive interest in the children's food which kept her in the kitchen longer than necessary. Teresa, who was young and pretty, turned coquettish and sly. But Peter understood hierarchy and dealt tactfully with both.

He took pride in his responsibility for the kitchen, dining room, hall, drawing room and verandah and although both his cooking and reading skills were negligible, he was a fast learner. Recipes had to rely on memory and repetition was the key. Week after week Monday's lessons were repeated until Peter could cook unaided and with confidence, but at that point it became impossible to try and vary the methods or ingredients in anyway.

We'd not been married long before visitors began arriving. One of the first, Nick Mangnall, a Green Jacket, had come out to Rhodesia as part of the Commonwealth Monitoring Force which, under the British Command of Major General Acland, kept an eye on the process of the elections in preparation to handing over from the white government to Majority Rule. Nick's team of six, drawn from other Commonwealth Nations, covered an area which stretched from Bulawayo north to Victoria Falls, south to Beit Bridge and east to Gwelo, soon to be renamed Gweru. Although Nick had been given our names to contact before he left the UK, and we'd been given his, neither of us had done anything about it until we met at a dinner in Bulawayo. We instantly liked him and over the following months he came out to Bonisa whenever he could manage a break. An easy guest, he would pick up a gun and disappear, returning a couple of hours later usually with guinea fowl, francolin or a duck from the dam, for the pot. Humphrey had given Tim No.1 of his pair of Holland and Hollands which I helpfully described to Nick and then discovered that his middle name was Holland. I also told him that when the day arrived and he decided to marry he must bring his bride out to Bonisa as part of their honeymoon and, sometime later, he did.

Although visiting men often went off and occupied themselves one way or another, the women, with the domestic side of life already taken care of, tended to sit on the verandah writing letters, reading or doing tapestry. Except for Aunt Helen. Aunt Helen, the strong-minded matriarch of six children and Clifton Hampden Manor[10], gathered up her binoculars and *Roberts' Birds of Southern Africa* and took herself down to the dam and beyond, enthusiastically watching and identifying large numbers of species. She'd heard of Albert Barrington's death which occurred at much the same time as her own husband, one of Humphrey's brothers, had died and she asked to meet Monica. Unsure about how compatible they might be but, hoping for the best, I despatched Mkava to Red Bank Cottage with a note, inviting Monica to tea the following day. She accepted which was unusual, arrived on time and, after making a call from our telephone, she joined us on the verandah. It was comparatively cool under the thatch and we sat admiring the healthy looking

---

10 Humphrey's brother's house in England.

crops below the escarpment while Aunt Helen entertained us with stories of her bird-watching on the dam until Peter brought out a tea tray.

"In just a few days I've spotted ninety-nine different varieties including pelicans and a pair of flamingos; quite young ones, I think," Aunt Helen said.

But Monica wasn't interested in bird life and countered with her own stories of the picannins and of The Lord's provision before launching into the discomfort she'd experienced with maggot flies and announcing, with an air of martyrdom, "I am making sure it will never happen again because I don't use underwear any more."

A mortal quiet fell over the verandah.

Aunt Helen rose briskly from her chair and strode off.

Returning a few minutes later, she paused and thrust a cheque into Monica's hand. It was for £100.

"Go and buy yourself some decent underwear," she instructed, "and iron them yourself if you have to. You can not go around without pants on!"

As Monica looked at the cheque I braced myself for an argument but, looking up, she beamed an angelic smile on Aunt Helen.

"Thank you," she said. The Lord had done it again!

10

I enrolled David with the correspondence school in Salisbury/Harare beginning in January. After two years of home schooling he would have to go to Whitestone's – the prep school for boys in Bulawayo – where he would be a weekly boarder and I would have to begin again, teaching Sarah. Teaching had never been an ambition of mine and it was obviously going to be a long haul.

With the help of Morden, (the headmaster and only teacher of a small, thatched, one-roomed school provided for local picannins on Kirby's farm beyond the Khami) we worked on gutting the end room of the L-shaped east wing and converting it into a dedicated schoolroom. In an excellent elevated position, far enough away from the main house and telephone, but within range of Agric-Alert broadcasts it provided panoramic views stretching for miles over the northern veldt.

Morden's other skills included woodwork. More than a carpenter, he was also a gifted, if basic, cabinet maker. With limited opportunities for using his expertise, he took care and pride in his work. He was also delighted for the chance to augment his meagre income. Working in Mukwa, a local hard wood of an attractive, warm, mahogany colour wrapped around a blonde heart wood, he erected shelves and store cupboards and added a bench 'In case it might be useful.' Back at his own school he secretly made easels from the off-cuts which he presented to the children when we moved into the completed room.

"Painting," he said, setting them up with poster-paints and paper under shade trees in the garden, "is a very important part of education."

Every second Friday, a chrome-yellow, zip-up bag arrived from the Correspondence School containing the lessons for the following two weeks and a constant reminder for mothers to make the lessons 'fun' for their children. Fun wasn't something I'd associated with teaching. I wasn't proud of my attitude and realised this would have to change if David were to make progress. Steeling myself to setting aside all thoughts of homicide I, eventually, more or less got the hang of it and began to enjoy David's enthusiasm and aptitude for learning.

An old dining table served as a desk under the large window, and in idle moments we paused to watch the daily steam trains puffing coal smoke as they wound their way down from Victoria Falls and, in season, the tractor rhythmically ploughing up and down the front lands trailing billows of dust. We traced the course of the Khami River as it meandered across the dry baked plains towards the Gwaai, a bigger river, which in turn flowed into the Zambezi. We noted the behaviour of birds in the wide skies as we watched for signs of rain, and we stopped, drawn to the haunting, strangely reassuring cry of the fish eagle, as he took off from his perch in the spreading jacaranda on the edge of the garden to hunt on the dam. Distractions were everywhere and it took discipline to return to work.

Mrs Patterson of Pioneer Pharmacy in Bulawayo thought all insects and snakes should be left well alone but reluctantly obliged when I begged large jars and quantities of formaldehyde for pickling specimens of snakes, scorpions, spiders, insects and small animals. But the curator of the Bulawayo Museum was more enthusiastic. Looking earnestly at me through thick glasses, he assured me we could work well together; by which I discovered he meant that he would appropriate the best specimens and those of unusual interest for the museum and in return he would help me identify and label my own collection.

We didn't have to look far for snakes and they often found us. The nineteen stable doors of the homestead were made of unseasoned Mukwa which, during the rains, warped leaving gaps through which snakes slithered into the house – twenty-three of them in one season, mainly spitting Egyptian Cobras. Cats helped to keep them down but occasionally even they were not quick enough and caught the deadly accurate squirts of poison in their eyes which, unless immediately washed out with milk, resulted in blindness.

Although prudent I am not afraid of snakes and when word spread around neighbouring farms that I was the one to call when the shotgun missed, it was not what I'd have chosen. However this did mean that over time we had an enviable collection on the schoolroom's nature table and the museum happily gained a few interesting items.

I woke early one morning to shouting from the direction of the hall. Dragging on a dressing gown I raced across the courtyard.

"Madam! Madam! Madam!" Peter was standing on a chair in a state of panic. "Nyoka, Nyoka." Tim ran in the other door but Peter yelled at him, "No! Not you!" raising his voice, "Madam, Madam." Beneath the chair a small, harmless grass snake, having been flung from one of the brushes when Peter turned on the electric polisher, writhed frantically trying to get a purchase on the shiny floor. I was sure it looked as alarmed as Peter and Tim and for just a moment I was tempted to go off and leave the men to cope but I rescued them all.

A mission station in the Chimanimani Mountains of Manicaland produced soft and extremely thick sisal matting, and I sent off for large quantities to cover the cement floors of the bedrooms and study. It arrived several weeks later in great rolls made of twelve-inch squares sewn together and adjusted for the size of our rooms. The pale cream colour allowed us to see, before stepping on, any creepy-crawlies that found their way inside – a great advantage as we mainly lived in either bare feet or open thonged sandals and, with no call for them, the children did not possess proper shoes.

In the days before UDI we'd been determined to do all we could to try and turn the political tide, and we put a great deal of energy and resources into fighting the 1974 election. Only whites had the vote and Ian Smith had a stranglehold on the country. He played on white fears with posters showing white children's legs going off to school alongside young black legs and won the election in a landslide victory. Through the media he slated us as 'sell-outs' and threatened to imprison Tim as an 'enemy of the state.'

The United Nations introduced international sanctions which began to bite hard. They specifically covered petrol and diesel which had the potential to cripple the country and bring it rapidly to a grinding halt. Being a landlocked country, and since Moçambique turned it's face away, we had only South Africa on which to depend and rescue us with shipments from their ports. The British knew that, of course, and sent po-faced observers to take up positions on the South Africa-Zimbabwe border at Beit Bridge, where sanction-busting bowsers crossed the Limpopo. International oil companies co-operated by erasing their logos, painting all their oil tankers the same colour. With large signs at the front of the vehicles proclaiming: 'Cold Tea', 'Tia Maria', or 'Sea Water', they trundled across the bridge trailing an unmistakable smell of fuel.

Luxuries quickly disappeared, soon followed by more and more shortages of basic goods – from time to time matches, sugar, light bulbs and, worst of all, loo paper became unavailable. But this also brought out the innovative spirit in human nature. Rhodesians could always 'Make a plan.' Creative new businesses sprang up producing goods largely manufactured from natural resources and often based on agricultural endeavours.

I particularly minded doing without honey and decided to start a cottage industry on the farm, producing honey for ourselves and selling the surplus to small Indian and Jewish stores in town. Tim's own small farm marched with Bonisa (which belonged to his parents) and from that I appropriated the name and had labels printed:

Deeside Honey, Fit for a Queen.

"Why a queen?" asked David.

"Because hives are made up of workers and a single Queen – no Kings," I replied, upsetting his five-year-old male view of the natural order of things.

A Bee House already existed, hidden deep inside the gum plantation opposite Red Bank Siding and a few hundred yards from Monica's cottage. From a security point of view the site was a double edged sword. Although invisible from both the road and the line of rail, the narrow, winding track running to it through the trees provided good cover for ambush, and escape, if not impossible, would certainly be difficult in an emergency.

Inside the rectangular, timber-framed building, Mkava and I placed ten new hives, and aligned the bee's landing pads with narrow slits to the outside. The padlocked, steel door fitted tightly and it was a mystery to me how the snakes which we frequently encountered got in.

Because of the extreme ferocity of the African bee, cropping needed be done after dark when the bees were inside, replete and hopefully exhausted. Besides, after sunset temperatures dropped and the work became more bearable as the infernal heat leached out of the bee house.

I asked Mkava what he thought about informing security forces of our intentions. After all, by going to the bee house after dark we would be acting if not illegally then certainly dangerously.

"No Madam," he said.

Part of me agreed with him. We were uncertain where the loyalties of certain individuals in the squad lay, and decided it might be safer to take a chance with breaking the curfew and hope to escape being noticed, reported, or shot at.

The following week ten queens arrived in the post bag, each one tucked alive and well inside a hair curler and ready to begin the new colonies. By early September, the dry, shrivelled veldt began to green and the garden coloured with sweet-smelling blossoms. The bees emerged from their sluggish wintering, presumably glad to get away from sugar feeds, and forage for themselves, and Mkava and I slipped into a routine.

After night fell I drove slowly out of the security fence with Mkava riding on the bonnet of the Land Rover, clutching an automatic rifle across his knees. I drove down the sandy track without lights, taking care not to rev the engine, towards the railway line where we paused, listening for trains (which also travelled without lights) before bumping on down to the gum trees. We'd cleared a turning point in front of the bee house and overlaid it with branches to prevent wheel spin in case there was a need for a hasty retreat. After doing a cursory check of the area and went inside sweeping torches around, over rafters and under hives. Mkava had what was probably the better attitude towards snakes: fear, and it fell to me to deal with them. Shooting in an enclosed area was not an option – they had to be caught and popped into a sack for either the museum or schoolroom which, by torch light, couldn't be hurried.

Working quickly, and quietly, Mkava lit smokers of dried cow dung and puffed white smoke into the hives while I removed the lids and lifted off the supers with their heavy frames of waxy, capped cells dripping with honey. Outside, the usual bush noises, the call of a Nightjar, or Litany Bird as it was known, an owl, or the bark of a jackal reassured us – silence would have been ominous and unnerving – and we emerged to load the supers in the Land Rover before carefully returning to the homestead.

Back in the kitchen, using a hot knife Mkava cut the caps off the honey-comb, while I slotted the frames inside a centrifugal extractor before taking turns to wind the handle, and watch golden streams of honey run down the inside walls of the drum.

Mkava talked hesitantly about his life and his family. It had not been easy for him.

"My father and mother and three sisters all burnt. The soldiers came. They made them go in one hut. They set fire to the grass."

I didn't dare ask if they were our soldiers or terrorists. I knew that both sides had their own methods of dealing with the rural population and it was the village people who suffered most.

I didn't want to intrude and after glancing at him from time to time I turned to watch the honey.

"What happened then Mkava?"

"All dead."

"How did you get away?"

"I wasn't there. I was visiting my wife's family."

"And so who is left in your family?"

"No one."

I then understood why he'd not wanted to talk about it before.

From a tap at the bottom of the drum we filled sterilised jars and stuck labels on them. Working quickly we replaced the destroyed combs by melting wax sheets of pre-imprinted cells onto hot wires and returned them to the frames. By now it was near midnight. I couldn't imagine what Mkava must be feeling – relief at having told me? Or was he reliving the pain? In silence we drove back to the bee house and replaced the freshly made up supers in their hives.

71

11

Although there was always plenty for the children to do on the farm I also wanted to be able to take them swimming and when, over sundowners one evening, I mentioned it to Tim he got up and dragged the hosepipe onto the top lawn twisting it into a random shape. "What do you think of that?" he said. It wasn't bad, a few tweaks and it turned into a graceful free-form design. The next morning, just after Roll-Call, a team of farm labourers turned up with shovels and began digging. They paid no attention to me and they kept digging until Tim came in from the dairy and told them to stop. We now had a lovely big but unusable hole. Tim rang a company in Bulawayo and persuaded them to measure the interior and make a fibre glass lining for the pool and eventually they came out and installed the finished product with a pump, filter and drainage systems and laid down an attractive slate surround. It changed our lives out of all proportion. We now had somewhere to cool off, several times a day if necessary and, when it wasn't safe to go for walks outside the fence, the exercise helped relieve stress and relax tense muscles.

On shopping days to town we noticed bright orange and beige posters beginning to appear in public places – in shop windows, pinned on trees and telegraph poles.

"COME HOME your land awaits you," they implored. Addressed to "My brothers and sisters" and signed by "Bishop Abel Muzorewa, Prime Minister" ("I speak to you as a man of God") they beseeched those who had left the country, presumably to train for fighting the white farmers and government, to return. It promised that: "You will be fed and given clothes; have comfortable living quarters and your own bed; helped to find education and employment and see your families again." It went on: "All you have to do is: Hide your arms and ammunition; take off your uniform and wear civilian clothes; bring this paper with you... you will be greeted in peace and joy..."

Oh yes?

72

A new call sign had been added to the Agric-Alert list and we were curious to know who they could be. Who would want to move into the area in the prevailing uncertainties of drought and war? No one knew.

"Perhaps they'll be at the club on Saturday," John said. Having recently married and brought his wife out to live in the New Farm cottage, he was conscious that Sheena didn't know anyone locally. "I think we'll go too. I would like to introduce Sheena to the tennis club."

On Saturday afternoons, after the farm workers had been paid their wages and given their weekly rations of meat, salt, dried beans, dried fish and mealie-meal, all carefully calculated according to the sizes of their families, they returned to the compound to brew beer and bring out their drums. And it was then that the farmers themselves gathered up their families, tennis racquets and swimming costumes and headed for the Farmer's Hall next to the Police Camp in Nyamandhlovu, to relax and to be with friends. It was an opportunity – a rare one – for the children to meet with a few other children and we decided to go as well.

About thirty miles from Bonisa, the Farmer's Hall stood surrounded by its own high security fence topped with a barbed wire overhang. A few indigenous trees grew up through the otherwise barren soil and one, a thirty-foot Ichithamuzi with its pale-grey bark and sprays of pale-pink pea flowers, had been fenced off. It was important not to damage the Ichithamuzi. The slightest wound caused it to exude a sticky, red sap, like blood, which was perhaps why the Africans associated it with bad luck and witchcraft and named it 'destroyer of homes' in the Ndebele language.

As we arrived, energetic tennis players were running around on hard courts, others played with their children in the pool and some, escaping from the punishing sun, had gathered inside with their drinks, and were sitting on low chairs gathered around low tables. We went in to join them. As we passed one table Old Mrs Beale looked up and asked about Monica. She and her husband had known Monica well. Their ranch was not far from St Thomas' Mission, but since Monica had left and come to Red Bank Siding they'd not seen her. "It's as if she's gone to ground," Old Mrs Beale said.

As we were talking, Bronco Greaves got up from a small group and strode over to the bar, thumping his glass down. Ticky, standing behind the bar, automatically picked it up and refilled it with Castle beer. Bronco leaned his large, thick-set body against the bar, turned and surveyed the room.

"Hey," he called, raising his glass. The hall paused. "The Woods were mad, of course. Bloody mad. In fact, I'm telling you, they started it all." Clutching his foaming glass he walked more or less in a straight line towards his target. Jack Ehlers pretended not to notice 'Mr B' as he called Bronco (Mr Belligerent) and continued to sit, staring at shiny pools of spilled drinks on his table. But Bronco was not to be put off. He swayed a little, staring down at Jack.

"You're bloody mad. No wonder it was going cheap. You must have known the story when you bought the place!"

A flash of deep-pink anger flew into Jack's cheeks.

"Of course I knew," he retorted. "But it's alright, the priest said he'd sorted it out. It's not a problem. It's our turn to hold the Trek Church[11] next month. He can do it again then if he wants to. It's called exorcism or something."

The farmers exchanged glances. It was not that they were personally superstitious. Hell no. No, it was just that, as men who had been on the land most of their lives, they had an understanding of bush lore and a deep respect of local traditions. But they also knew Bronco's ways, and several, led by John, got up, stubbed out cigarettes in overflowing ashtrays and went outside.

A few of the older ones remembered way back when Jack's newly acquired ranch had been scrub land – all sands and dongas with occasional patches of shade trees providing shelter and camouflage for game. But then, in the early 1910s, Mr Wood, a store keeper from Bulawayo had bought the land – unfenced virgin bush – and named it Mimosa Park after the large number of native mimosas scattered over the property.

---

11 Once a month, according to a rota, clergymen from Bulawayo came out to hold a communion service on a host farm.

Parts of the ranch were well forested, mainly with hard woods such as teak, Mukwa and a few Ichithamuzis, one of which stood on a small rise overlooking a beautiful valley – on the very spot Mr Wood had decided would be just right to build his house. But the Ichithamuzi obstructed the view and Mr Wood instructed his boss boy, Msipa, to take the labour force and clear the land.

"You can keep some of the wood for yourselves," he had said.

But Msipa did not move.

"Well?" Mr Wood asked, "What's the problem?"

"Boss can not build his house here. It is not permitted."

"And Msipa," Mr Wood had stopped listening. "We'll use some of the teak for doors and floors."

But Msipa was adamant.

"No Boss! Tokalosh of Ichithamuzi very, very powerful. If it is cut down is mtagati. The spirits will be very, very angry. And then – then they will not rest."

Mr Wood, not accustomed to having his orders questioned, snapped back at him.

"It's only the Rain Tree, Msipa."

˙ "No, Boss. For you is the Rain Tree, but for us Ichithamuzi is also many other things. It must only be chopped down when the tribe are moving to another place. Then it is to tell the ancestor's spirits that their stay was over, they are now moving on for good. To chop down when not departing for good will bring down mtagati."

"OK, push off, I'll do it myself."

"No Bossie. No, the mtagati is too strong. Better you find somewhere else."

But Mr Wood had insisted that this was where he wanted his homestead and this is where it would be.

Not long after that, in 1914, he joined the Rhodesian Army to fight for Britain, King and country.

He was the first Rhodesian to be killed in action.

The Africans nodded. It was because of the Ichithamuzi Tree.

It was also said that the roots of the Ichithamuzi yielded strong muti which protected against snake bites, and there were vaguely remembered rumours of another couple who, a few months after moving into the Mimosa Park homestead, were making their way to bed one night when the mother popped in as usual to give her baby a last goodnight kiss. She paused in the doorway. As her eyes adjusted to the darkness she saw something move. Something independent of her son. Something in his cot. Later she could not bring herself to talk of it except to say that it was her husband who killed the cobra but it was too late; within fifteen minutes the boy was dead and shortly afterwards they moved away.

After some time, in about 1924, Mr and Mrs Tennant Thompson from South Africa bought Mimosa Park and lived in the house with their four children. Their eldest son, Hector, married and built himself a house fifty yards beyond and moved in when his wife became pregnant. But Hector quarrelled with his parents until, after a while, he invited them and his sister Muriel to dinner. His parents were unable to go but the next day, when there was no activity around the house, they went to Hector's cottage to check that everything was in order. They found a note pinned to the locked door. It read: "I cannot stand this life of strife." Inside, amongst the chaos of blood and overturned furniture, lay the bodies of Muriel, Hector's pregnant wife and Hector himself. It was so terrible that Muriel's suitor, Syd Longden, writing an account of it seventy-two years later said: "No one wanted to talk about it even in those days, and no one seems to have heard of it now."

The local Africans were not surprised – it was the curse of the Ichithamuzi Tree. Mimosa Park became known as 'The Voodoo' farm and for a number of years it lay unoccupied.

R.A. and Pat Fletcher who were surveyors married to two sisters had invested in land which they held jointly in undivided shares until one day R.A., seeing an opportunity, bought Mimosa Park without telling Pat. When it was discovered, the two families fell out, never spoke to each other again and the ranch was sold again.

After a while Ian and Isabel Forbes bought the ranch. Ian and Bronco Greaves did not get on with each other and they were not often seen at the Farmers' Club. But Ian did well, he made money and was well-liked in the district. He stayed on Mimosa Park for many years with his son growing up to learn about farming. And then one day the boy was encouraged to learn to drive. As he was driving the car back into the garage he accidentally stepped on the accelerator instead of the brake, pinning Ian against the back wall, breaking both his legs and leaving him in a wheel chair for life. Ian went on to lose a lot of money growing tobacco and, in need of constant attention, he fell in love with Anna, his carer. His marriage fell apart.

"It was the Ichithamuzi Tree, of course," they said.

About two years later, when the government promised more land for Chief Sigola, and met the Cumming's price for their home farm, 'Duncal', they accepted, and bought Mimosa Park from Ian Forbes' estate. Harry Cumming died in 1963 and his wife, Lynette, and son, Dick, took on the dairy and ranching enterprise. Aware of the 'Mimosa Curse' which Bronco, amongst others never failed to impress upon them, Lynette arranged to have the farm exorcised by an Anglican priest. After that, although Dick had a near death experience due to electrocution, he survived and everyone began to wonder if the curse had indeed been lifted.

By 1977 Dick began to see 'one man, one vote' was not far ahead. He had observed other African countries, noting that none had managed to retain its white population after their independence and he'd come to the conclusion that whites would be squeezed out of the country. He was thirty-five with a wife and two small children and it seemed sensible to go and make a new life and a new career sooner rather than later. Everyone was sorry to see them go and later he and Mary separated and eventually divorced. "What did the Africans say?" he asked. "I doubt they knew. It was the whites who enjoyed perpetuating the story! Anyway," he went on, "look at the number of Nyamandhlovu families who had their share of tragedy – perhaps they all chopped down an Ichithamuzi Tree!"

As we listened to the stories in the Farmer's Hall that afternoon, little did we know how, in years to come, Bonisa and Mimosa Park were to be tragically linked.

12

Changes in the country began happening quickly. By December 1979, negotiations at Lancaster House in London had culminated in Rhodesia/Zimbabwe reverting to British Rule and Lord Soames being sent out as the interim governor to oversee elections and the transition to black rule. He was the first British Governor since Humphrey's retirement ten years earlier and we reflected on the memories and the 'might have beens'. In September 1965 Harold Wilson had asked the Queen if he could send Lord Louis Mountbatten out to be governor of Rhodesia if Humphrey resigned, but Lord Louis was unimpressed, later saying to the press: "Gibbs stayed on, so luckily I was spared that one, other wise I might still be out there. I might die out there – and what sort of a funeral would I get in Rhodesia?" Asked whether things might have turned out differently if he had gone out there he chuckled and replied: "It's silly to ask me that. I suffer from over assurance and conceit." And now he was dead. Only a few months before Soames was appointed Lord Louis had been blown up in an IRA bomb.

In what some described as a final act of defiance, Mr Smith did not attend Lord Soames' official welcoming party at Salisbury airport because, his spokesman claimed, "He is away." But a few days after his arrival Lord Soames invited Humphrey to lunch with him at Government House. Although unenthusiastic about flying up to Salisbury for lunch, Humphrey appreciated the courtesy. He decided it would be impolite to refuse, particularly in the light of Ian Smith's snub, and he arranged to catch the early flight from Bulawayo the following week. Tim, also due in the capital the same day to attend a national farmer's meeting, had booked to fly up on a later plane. As he was leaving the house the phone rang. It was another sweltering day and I hoped it was not to say the plane was grounded, as happened very occasionally because of the high altitude and temperatures which thinned the air, causing delays.

"Tim!" Humphrey said, speaking loudly as if addressing him from Salisbury without the benefit of a telephone, "Just call at Little Bonisa on your way to the airport and bring my teeth from the bedside table if you will."

There was no opportunity for diplomacy when they met. Tim had intended to wait for the right moment and quietly palm Humphrey's dentures to him but Humphrey unselfconsciously put out his hand, received his teeth, popped them in his mouth and resumed talking with Christopher Soames.

It was a difficult and demanding time for both Christopher and Mary Soames. The anti-British diehards (who nevertheless jumped at invitations to Government House) regarded them with suspicion and didn't make things easier, but for others they were a breath of fresh air; an injection of the British ways they understood and believed in. The social highlight during their term of office was a large reception at Government House in honour of Princess Anne who came out to Salisbury on Save the Children business. On a glorious, balmy evening the great and the good, black and white, rich and poor, came together in the cool of the garden for what was, at that stage, the first time we had encountered such a large and diverse social gathering. A few people circled each other but by and large prejudices were set aside; no one mentioned 'the situation' and the evening went a long way to soothing troubled waters between friends. I overheard someone say: "The Soames' may not be too bad after all," and someone else added: "It was Harold Wilson and his British Government that were rotten to the core." Molly and Mary Soames began an enduring friendship that night and they kept in touch for years.

For us, the atmosphere of uncertainty evolved into apprehension about the future, and the arrival of a Christmas card from Bishop Abel Muzorewa, the interim Prime Minister of what was now known as Rhodesia/Zimbabwe, proclaiming Love, Peace, Prosperity did little to convince us these sentiments would come to fruition in the days ahead.

The day after Christmas, some of the terrorists, or 'guerrillas', (depending on your point of view) flew back in to the country and on 27th January 1980 the exiled Robert Mugabe returned to fight the election scheduled to take place in March.

A lot of people were appalled and fearful when Mugabe's ZANU[12] party won 57 of the 80 available seats in the 100 seat Assembly (twenty seats being reserved for whites) in a somewhat dubious election. Many made plans to leave the country fearing it was doomed. In his first address to the nation, Mugabe called us all, black and white, to put the past behind, to unite and develop together a new and prosperous Zimbabwe. He continued to broadcast speeches of hope and reconciliation, and appeared to do all he could to reassure the whites and the opposition blacks by including Joshua Nkomo in his cabinet, which persuaded some to stay on, to give him a chance and see how the situation developed. By reputation he was more educated, devious, ruthless and brighter than Nkomo. But I remained uneasy, wondering if this leopard, who had been involved in so much death and hatred for so long, could ever change its spots, and I tried to persuade Tim at least to make contingency plans in case we needed to leave in a hurry; but he was more confident than I was and didn't see the need.

In a way, when black majority rule arrived, it was a strange, almost perverse, relief. The boil of pent up feelings during a long and bitter bush war had been lanced – not necessarily the way any of us would have chosen, but at least a new direction was forced on us all.

We were tired. Tired of the uncertainties, tired of wearing sidearms, of observing curfew, of springing out of bed in the middle of the night when the fence alarm went off, of keeping the wireless volume low so as not to drown out suspicious noises, of closing the curtains before turning on lights, of never sitting with our backs to the window, even during the day. We were bone weary of anticipating trouble, planning our movements ahead, varying our travelling routes, watching for signs of land mines or ambush, of the disruptions when reacting to emergencies and, to some extent, being deadened ourselves by loosing friends and neighbours.

---

12   Zimbabwe African National Union

Independence Day was set for 18th April 1980 and, as serving members of the para-military Police Reserve, we were instructed to meet at the Tjolotjo Police Camp for the Raising-of-the-New-Flag ceremony. It was also a day for awarding campaign medals and Tim and I were both due to receive the Zimbabwe Independence Medal which was, we were told, making world history by being the first to be awarded to combatants from both sides of a conflict. I was glad that the terrorists had not yet come in from the bush to join us on this occasion; it would have been too soon, and I asked Molly if she would look after the children while we were away for the day.

"I think I could," she replied. "I'll ask Dot to come and help."

Dot rang from their farm deeper in Nyamandhlovu and agreed more enthusiastically. With no children of her own she doted on other people's.

"Is it alright if Bill brings me to Bonisa and stays with us, dear? You know I don't drive. We could be there by eight o'clock. Can I bring anything? She's in an awful fuss..."

Dot had never lost her American accent or the air-hostessy, eager-to-please manner honed during her years with TWA. She was devoted to Molly if somewhat in awe of her. But, despite their forty years of friendship and strong urgings from the rest of us, she could never quite allow herself to address Molly in terms more intimate than Lady Gibbs or, latterly, Dame Molly.

"Molly's bought herself a new pair of shoes," I told her. "Rubber soled ones, which she said wouldn't slip if she has to run over cement floors after the children! Manka and Peter will be here too. Just try and keep it all calm until we return, probably mid afternoon."

Soon after Molly, Dot and Bill arrived at the Big Bonisa we drove to Tjolotjo and stood, with about fifty or more other guests, under a spreading acacia tree in front of the Police Camp Office where we were handed a programme printed on yellowing butcher's paper. From 9am until 11.30am we were entertained by Traditional Dancing and Singing followed by the arrival of District Administrators, chiefs and other officials. After prayers and blessings, someone ran the New Zimbabwe flag up the pole and someone else read out messages from the Queen, from the President of Zimbabwe, from the British Prime Minister, and a reply from the Prime Minister of Zimbabwe. To round off the day, after yet more Traditional Dancing and Singing, there was a soccer match which we didn't stay to watch. The morning's formal ceremony had turned out to be curiously moving and our hope was that it would mark an end and a new beginning – one that included peace for all, but especially for the farmers.

A similar, but much grander ceremony took place in the newly named Harare in the presence of Prince Charles, Lord Carrington and President Banana amongst other dignitaries. Molly and Humphrey stayed on Bonisa and went to bed before midnight, before the British National Anthem was played and Union flag lowered for the last time. The raising of the new Zimbabwe flag followed with a twenty-one-gun salute and various parades and then as April 19th dawned there was a weird feeling of 'lostness'. Lost identity and still uncertain of the new, lost purpose and uncertain what form the replacement purpose would take, lost divisions and enemies but uncertain about the stability of the new unity and 'friends'. It would all have to work itself out in time.

One of the first changes after Independence Day came when security forces withdrew our automatic weapons. We were permitted to keep our sidearms, shot guns and hunting rifles, all of which were privately owned. Although I'd hated carrying G3s everywhere for so long, I now felt naked and vulnerable without them. Over the next few weeks the ex-ZIPRA combatants assembled in designated bush camps in preparation for their disarmament and being re-introduced into civilian life. Most complied and although a few melted into the bush with their AKs, opting to live the life of bandits, there were no further incidents during this time and the curfew was temporarily lifted.

As April became May the lingering summer heat was far more intense than usual for this time of the year, or so it seemed to me one morning as the corrugated iron roof of the dairy, relentlessly absorbing the rays of the African sun, converted the corner office into an oven, and I stood there wondering if I was being unwise.

"Stay in the house all day," Tim had said after receiving a telephone call the night before.

"Barricade yourself in there until it is all over." And there was some sense in this; after all, the house was inside the security fence. But I also wondered if it wasn't also a bit obvious. And in an obvious place what barricade could possibly afford protection against the unanswered questions of... who and what exactly was coming? Alastair Monson had given little in the way of hard facts, perhaps because of the party-line, perhaps because he didn't know them himself and his few well-chosen words had been loaded with meaning.

"Everything alright?" I'd asked Tim when he put the telephone back on the wall.

"There's something fishy going on," he replied. "Alastair was too damned cagey for my liking."

"Yes, well," I reasoned, "he has to be wary. Probably why he didn't put it over Agric-Alert."

"Mmm, even so..."

I could imagine Alastair, O.C. of the Police Camp, holding the telephone, eyebrows clamped together, carefully weighing both every word he spoke, and the spaces in between.

I glanced around the now disused dairy office. The ugliness of the utilitarian furniture was partially camouflaged by a film of red sand, borne in on the west wind through the broken windows, to settle on every surface – a legacy from the Kalahari.

Apart from where the glass had disappeared, it was not easy to see through the dusty windows and I considered the possibilities of concealing myself, and the three children, in there. On the southern wall the window was intact except for one of the small panes at the bottom which was now nothing but jagged shards of glass glinting where the sun caught them. This was encouraging. It would be possible, I thought, to hide behind the filing cabinet and to watch, silently and unseen, through the gap. The position of the room was ideal. The farm track rose up over the steep incline of the escarpment, fifty yards away, and wound around two sides of the dairy office on the corner of the building and it would afford an unimpeded view across the plains for miles in both directions. It also had a disused look about it, one that did not invite further investigation. Perfect.

The nursery picannin appeared suddenly at the office door, clicking his tongue, bringing me sharply out of my reverie and then stood silently waiting to be noticed.

"Yes?" I said.

"Manka say children ready. Boss say hide. Quickly he goes now. Cook say he has worms in the beans, what we have for our dinner instead?"

"Run to the house Aaron, tell Manka to make sure the children have books, Mazoe orange and biscuits. I will come and collect them in ten minutes. Tell Peter spinach. Run now." He took off like a spring hare along the track which led to the homestead, a few hundred yards across the plateau, leaving little puffs of dust where his bare feet hit the ground.

I glanced around the office, repositioned some of the furniture, decided that would have to do and set off along the same route back to the homestead.

There were a few difficult moments with Manka who objected violently and then sulked when told it would be better if she didn't come with us, but I was resolute and bore the children off to look for somewhere sensible to hide the Land Rover.

I told them that this was a sort of game, one that grown ups play, but one which would also be fun for children who followed the rules. We tucked the Land Rover behind a clump of bushes and two large anthills, made sure it could not be glimpsed from the track, and walked more or less backwards to the dairy, sweeping away our tracks in the hot sand with twigs.

Once inside again I sat down without bothering to wipe the dust off a chair and lit a cigarette. It tasted hot, dry and dusty. With proper packaging no longer available, cigarettes were stale before they even left the stores, and I vowed again to remember to pack them in the fridge with cut potato. I stubbed it out, wishing I could give up.

The children were absorbed in their books, cool drinks and biscuits and I thought about Tim and hoped he'd had time to get to the farm entrance near Monica's cottage in time to put the grain sack over the plough share identifying us. I was glad that Ticky had gone with him. She may not be much protection but she was an adoring companion and had provided a measure of comfort since we'd been disarmed.

The increasing heat was trying. Through the glass the sun's rays branded my skin and I moved further back inside the room. Rivulets of perspiration glued strands of hair and stuck our shirts to our backs. There was a tension in the air which was only partly explained by the build up to an electrical storm. One of the children was becoming restive and I had to curb my irritation.

I looked through the splinters of broken glass in the lower window. The clouds on the distant horizon were becoming thicker and darker, perhaps the Congo was sending us some rain after all. But there was also something more. A long snake of rising dust was approaching across the northern plain. The wind was blowing in the other direction, the silence eerie. The head of the snake vanished below the edge of the plateau for a moment and then we heard it. A low rumble of heavy, straining engines labouring up the escarpment. The wind changed. Dust billowed over the lip of the ridge, engines groaning louder pulled their burdens up the hill. Suddenly, out of the wall of red dust loomed the first vehicle, a Russian Jeep with a photo of Joshua Nkomo in the front window, followed by a seven-ton armoured troop carrier bulging with the terrorists coming in from the bush. Then another, and another. On and on they came, rolling menacingly towards us, in two batches – forty-eight in all, a tide of six-wheeled vehicles, a few towing field guns. The black masses, more than eight hundred of them, were hot, sweaty, gleaming like wet tarmac. They were rowdy, undisciplined, drunk – and armed. AK47s stuck out at all angles and there were other things – a few howitzers, 122mm recoilless rifles, RPG's, and anti-tank weapons which I recognised from my training.

The children stood silent and motionless. I was transfixed. The convoy, led by Tim, was now only a few feet away, moving slowly, circling the dairy. In the pitiless heat, the hot smell of diesel fumes combined with dust and the noise of grinding engines and drunken shouts.

Suddenly, a screaming of metal, of brakes cruelly applied. The convoy stopped. A confused tangle of black bodies, thrown off balance, dropped their weapons clattering to the floor, and were momentarily wrapped in a blanket of red dust.

A brief moment of stillness as the dust drifted away.

The sea of black faces regained their balance, and focussed in the same direction. They picked up their weapons and pointed them at a target outside the office door. I turned to whisper to the children.

They were gone.

I swivelled back to the office door. My eyes registered the target but my brain refused to accept the information. I began to enter another dimension. From somewhere above me came a voice. "Wave," it demanded.

Silence. Clicks from the guns.

"Wave!" The disembodied voice more urgent.

Young hands rose, tentatively, in stiff obedience trying to wave.

A few more clicks.

An eternal moment – the sort that splits atoms in the mind, decides futures – and then, from the top of the nearest troop carrier, a black arm threw an empty beer can at the children. Someone else copied and, in quick succession, they all threw down their arms, pointing fingers, laughing and jeering. What happened? Perhaps someone remembered the war was supposed to have ended.

Engines revved, two stood up and peed off the side of the nearest vehicle, then fell as the convoy jerked into motion once more. The others laughed at them and lost interest in us.

The children dived in the door and clung to me, speechless. Numbed, we stood there, watching the last vehicle disappear down the track to the back gate of the farm and beyond, where a camp had been set up to receive them on Khami prison land. When the final rumbles died away we collected the remains of the picnic, made our way back through the hot sand to the Land Rover and drove back to the homestead to face Manka and await news of Tim's return.

13

Tim returned home nearly two hours after the convoy had passed the dairy and he came out to join me for coffee on the verandah. He had, he said, arrived at the place he was due to meet the convoy near the farm entrance just in time to slip a hessian sack over the ploughshare proclaiming H.V. GIBBS. BONISA in white paint when he saw the convoy approaching down the strip road. Ticky gave a low growl and, as a precaution, Tim shut her in the Land Rover and walked over to meet Nkomo's returning forces alone.

Brigadier Mike Reynolds was the coloured ZIPRA Commander, which surprised us. We'd thought all ZIPRA forces were black and that only the Rhodesian Army had white, black and coloured soldiers. He jumped down from the lead vehicle, an open jeep displaying a picture of Joshua Nkomo in the front windscreen, and held out his hand.

"Hello Mr Gibbs, how are you? And how are your old Mum and Dad these days?"

"My parents are very well thank you," Tim had replied, shocked.

So much for disguising our identities – ZIPRA clearly knew exactly where they were and whose property they were crossing. During the previous few years there had been many indications of their presence on the farm, and I had thought, as I watched the convoy slowly winding its way around the dairy, that some of these may have been part of the group that had come looking for us one night. Maybe amongst them were those responsible for setting the booby trap in the fence – the anti-personnel mine – that Tim walked into just before we were married. He'd been lucky. Although the surgeon was unable to remove all the shrapnel, after a few days in hospital he had been able to return to normal life – unlike the two African police either side of him who died instantly that day.

The Brigadier continued: "Where are they? Your parents. They up at the house now?"

"No, my parents are in England," Tim replied coolly.

"Ah, yes. In the current circumstances that is wise of them." And, after issuing orders to the vehicles behind, he'd climbed back into his Jeep and indicated for Tim to lead on. Tim's instructions had been to take them along farm tracks beyond the dairy, down past New Farm, and as far as the back gate of Bonisa which led to the Khami Prison estate. There the convoy was to rest up before being taken further to an especially prepared camp deeper in the bush where they were to be demobbed.

Tim said he hadn't seen us as he led the convoy around the dairy. I was glad he hadn't known we were there. He'd wondered why Ticky became agitated but not growled and he'd not noticed that the convoy further back had stopped, perhaps because it was going so slowly in the first place. At the back gate of the farm he'd once more shaken hands with Brigadier Reynolds in a businesslike manner and parted, relieved.

That afternoon another convoy arrived and waited at the front drive, to be taken to their base camp along the same route. But this time we were prepared. As originally asked, I kept the children out of sight in the homestead and Tim led them through the farm without any further questions. A total of 1,800 ex-ZIPRA fighters passed through Bonisa and I wondered how many there were still in the bush. How many had retained their arms and refused to come in?

Despite declarations and hopes of peace we continued to live the way to which we'd been conditioned. We raked the cleared area outside the security fence each evening and checked it again for human spoor at 5am the next morning when Tim opened the gates to let out the milk-tractor to begin its trek to town. After he left each morning I lay in bed, waiting for Roll-Call to begin at 6am and, through the low window, watched the fish eagle judging the right moment to unfurl his wings and launch himself off his perch half way up in the jacaranda, into the first hunt of the day. Amongst the roots at the base of the jacaranda, a family of resident mongooses emerged, stretching in the early light, bouncing about with each other in the cool fresh air until the blast from Agric-Alert sent them scampering back to their holes. Manka also waited until she heard Roll-Call begin, and took it as her cue to bring in the early morning tea tray, while the children sat bleary eyed on our bed, until everyone in the district had been accounted for and then went off to dress.

We continued milking three times a day (although Tim rarely attended the midnight milking any more) and when the sixty or so sterilized churns were full of milk, they were submerged in water and cooled by convection currents from ice along one side of the pool until the start of the morning milk run. It worked well and Tim was proud that, after being tested, it was always accepted by the Milk Marketing Board in Bulawayo. The dairy prospered, disease rarely struck, and so it came as a surprise one day when two of the cows began slobbering. After a few more days they stopped eating, refused to drink, isolated themselves from the herd and gradually paralysis set in. It was rabies – a worrying and dangerous situation for all involved in the dairy.

More cows were soon identified and quickly slaughtered, decimating a large part of the herd, but for the fourteen workers the treatment turned out to be prolonged and gruelling. Acting on instructions from Mpilo hospital, I administered excruciatingly painful injections into their abdomens over a period of ninety days. As they lay in a row on the billiard room floor with midriffs exposed, I went down the line injecting each as quickly as I could. None of them flinched but I hated doing it and admired their courage and pride.

As time went on the injections were given less frequently but the pain didn't diminish. Tim decided to give his injections to himself. I don't know how he reacted. He did it in private and he never said.

Over the next few months international press reports of an improved political and security situation encouraged several friends from England to come and visit. They brought new horizons and conversations; they were fun, stimulating and brightened our daily lives. Quite a few came intending to visit Humphrey and Molly and were surprised to find they were actually staying with us. It made sense. We had the spare rooms and Molly hated cooking. Her cook, Lavu, was Manka's father and, although he'd been with the family since the early days, when the children were young and he was the nursery picannin, he had never quite got the hang of cooking. Now he was old and, despite his love of alcohol and other short comings, he'd been a faithful servant as I reminded Humphrey one night.

"Next year Lavu will have been with you for fifty years Pa," I said.

"Really?" he replied. "That's forty-nine years too long."

"Nevertheless, you must do something really special for him."

He thought for a moment.

"Yes. I will. I'll sack him!"

He didn't of course but, when the time came for us to part, Lavu retired and was given a house in the townships of Bulawayo and a good pension.

Molly and Humphrey always joined us for dinner when there were guests; they enjoyed company and the evenings were fun for them. I was grateful Peter had become reasonably competent in the kitchen. Using anthracite (which came from Wankie Colliery and recently, in the spirit of the New Zimbabwe, had been re-named Wankite) he had mastered the inconsistencies of the *Esse* stove. Guessing at oven temperatures and ignoring the soot, he deftly juggled hot dishes in and out of the five ovens with his bare hands.

In the evenings Molly wore long-sleeved, long dresses left over from Government House days when every night was a black tie occasion and, as we sat on the verandah sipping sundowners, she plunged her legs and skirts into a yellow plastic fertilizer bag, took out a ball of string and tied it around her knees. By the end of the evening she was the only one not covered in mosquito bites.

Local people still visited during the daylight hours and one day George Errington, an old friend who farmed in Plumtree, popped in bursting with his news. A veteran of the British Army and immensely pleased he'd never had to work because he had 'Private Means', we'd first met years before, when, soon after I'd arrived in Rhodesia, I nursed him in the Bulawayo Hospital. With one of his visitors, he'd debated, in a loud voice, what he thought my blood stock might have been. He decided it would probably be Lipizzaner. A compliment in his view, in fact the highest accolade imaginable, he said. He had an absolute passion for Lipizzaner horses, he insisted, and the visitor nodded in agreement. George refused to allow the indignities of hospital life to diminish him and regaled me with stories of his lineage and his early life in England.

"Of course one didn't have to work before war broke out in '39. One had sufficient private means. One was very fortunate," he said.

And now, sitting on the verandah at Bonisa several years later, it seemed one had been very fortunate again.

"A few nights ago," he said, "as I lay stark naked on my bed listening to the BBC World Service, and waiting for the dinner gong, this bloody gook burst in firing an AK. Tat, tat, tat, tat." George jumped to his feet re-enacting what happened. "He sprayed the bedroom. My bedroom. Can you imagine? His gun jammed. Ha! I grabbed my FN and followed him running down the passage. Shot the bugger dead." A satisfied grin spread across his face as he went on. "Know what? One shot. I haven't lost my touch. And the best thing of all. . . not a drop of blood on the carpet. How's that?"

"Unusual for there to be only one, George."

"Well, there were four actually. The others buggered off down the drive to a car and got away."

I'd hoped to introduce George to Monica but as usual she was reluctant to join us and meet new people and she may have been right this time. They lived in different fixed worlds. Ones that didn't even compliment each other.

"She isolates herself like one of the rabid cows," John murmured.

And then, one day, Monica had a visitor of her own. She sent a brief note up with Jack which Peter brought out to the verandah. It read:

"I'd like you to come and meet my sister. We'll be here all day. Monica."

She must have been watching the road because as I drove down she came out to meet me, followed by a wizened little twig, shuffling along, so stooped I could see the top of her head. She was nearly bald.

"Jane, this is Sue Gibbs. Sue, meet my sister Jane MacKenzie."

The wraith held out her hand, straightened up as much as she could and sank into the dust in a deep curtsey. Pale blue eyes looked up at me adoringly.

"No! No!" I protested, "You don't curtsey to me!" I cast wildly around for support from Monica but she was intently studying the flowers on a Christ Thorn. Jane held her position and gave an appreciative little giggle at my modesty. She knew I was special, Monica told me later, probably royalty.

Alas, she was senile and her perceptions were not perfect.

Monica turned back to us. She thanked me for coming and made it plain that, as she had invited me to meet her sister and I had now done so, I could go. I gently eased Jane upright again, kissed her on the cheek, turned and drove home.

14

During the early days of the transition to majority rule the practicalities of daily life didn't change much for ordinary people, black or white. The greatest adjustments were mainly ones of attitudes ranging from regarding 'the boys from the bush' as terrorists or gooks, on 17th April, to accepting them as 'brothers' on the same side a day later. Past allegiances of the 'war of liberation' of previous years were to be forgotten, new loyalties forged; commitment to unity the order of the day. And all of Mugabe's broadcast messages were to this end.

But in the upper echelons change of government and the armed forces came more swiftly. Immediately following Independence the three fighting forces from Robert Mugabe's ZANLA[13], Joshua Nkomo's ZIPRA and the Rhodesian army had to be integrated. Their disparate bunch of 'soldiers', some highly trained and motivated, a few not much more than rabble, had to be brought together and merged into the New Zimbabwe Army. A Joint High Command (JHC) was set up under Lt General Walls with the heads of the Rhodesian Army and Air Force and Major General Rex Nhongo (ZANLA) and Major General Lookout Masuku (ZIPRA). Other countries began moving into the New Zimbabwe revitalising embassies in Salisbury, now renamed Harare, and distributing aid. A British Military Advisory Training Team (BMATT) arrived to assist in the training and amalgamating of the separate forces and by July several new battalions were being formed each month.

At the beginning of 1982 Major General Shortis took over BMATT his first objective being to form a good working relationship with Ministers and senior officers of the ZNA[14]; but it didn't take him long to realize that information regarding the true situation in rural Matabeleland was consistently withheld. This could have been

---

13 Zimbabwe African National Liberation Army.

14 Zimbabwe National Army

deliberate or because they knew little themselves. Although we'd not previously met General Shortis, within a few weeks of his arrival he wrote a cleverly worded letter inviting himself to stay on Bonisa and asking if he could also bring his ADC. A stranger reading it could have received the impression that we were old friends and I was both curious and delighted. I hoped he would reveal something of the 'inside story', but it was not to be like that. Colin was a professional.

There were no apparent security problems in the area on the afternoon they arrived and, jumping out of their vehicle, they introduced themselves and shook hands with us. Manka carried their bags through to the guest rooms across the courtyard while we took the visitors through to the verandah.

We had tentatively assumed that this was a courtesy visit and, as we sat looking out over the lands, Peter brought tea and we talked in generalities, cautiously sizing each other up, not presuming to ask certain questions and waiting for Colin to take the lead.

His not very tall, powerful body oozed energy and as I watched him sitting there in uniform, I sensed an inner steel and thought I would not want to be this man's enemy. It emerged that John Gaye was not his ADC after all but an old friend from their days together in the Devon and Dorset regiment, who was here on a private visit. By borrowing the uniform of a Lieutenant Colonel he'd passed himself off as Colin's assistant for the purpose of travelling to Matabeleland and was obviously enjoying himself hugely.

"The only way to approach a road block is with Colin in uniform," he said putting out a hand to receive his drink. "He ran up the British flag, wound down the windows, waved like mad and drove on. It worked too, except at the one near Bulawayo, when, not stopping he barked at them, and bulldozed his way through. Scared the hell out of them."

Glancing at Colin's impassive face I could well imagine it.

As the sun edged towards the horizon, we went to our rooms to shower and change for dinner and Manka took the children off for their baths. Much of the oppressive heat had gone out of the day when we returned to the verandah an hour later; the disappearing sun streaked the sky with long red and orange ribbons and smoke from cooking fires in the compound was rising in the middle distance.

John drew gifts from a canvas bag. "For you," he said. "For good cheer." Out came Grouse Whisky, Floris soap with matching perfume, tins of biscuits and tea from Harrods and real chocolate (which I immediately hid). Almost forgotten luxuries. And he was right, they were of immense Good Cheer.

Clinking glass in the courtyard heralded Peter approaching from behind with a drinks tray. He was nervous of all combat uniforms and, although I felt sorry for him, my heart positively ached for the Waterford Glass wedding present and I willed him to make it to the table without catastrophe.

Much of Colin's career had been spent in areas of conflict, particularly in Northern Ireland, giving him a sound understanding of terrorism and the problems facing those living in our sort of situation. There was so much that didn't have to be said. He knew. We soon realized that he was also sharp, intuitive and didn't tolerate anything less than honesty and integrity from those both under and above him. He'd wanted the truth and he'd not been given it.

After breakfast the following morning, Colin and John went off to talk with the local people – to herd boys, fencers, a teacher from the farm school next door, the caretaker at Red Bank Siding beer hall, and to our own informants, setting up ground-cover – a network of information for the future. The locals had experienced the 'other side' of both ZIPRA and the Rhodesian army but they trusted the British, they respected them and they talked.

From then on Colin made regular visits to Bonisa. After dinner, in winter, with the cold seeping through the gap where the top of the walls did not quite meet the thatched roof, we rugged up around a large log fire in the drawing room and discussed anything unrelated to security. During these evenings I became aware that the steel I'd noticed in his soul was shared with a spirituality and a deep knowledge of, and love for, poetry which, when pressed, he recited flawlessly. And therefore I was only mildly surprised when he told us, one night, he'd been confirmed, by the Bishop, three times.

"Why?"

"Because the first two didn't stick. Why else?"

During summer visits we took our sundowners sitting on the darkened verandah smothered in citronella oil – which made cigarettes taste revolting but did help keep insects at bay – and occasionally, on the warmest evenings we swam in the unlit pool after dinner.

Colin usually came alone, but one blisteringly hot October afternoon he arrived with another, this time unannounced, visitor whom he introduced as Robert Adams.

He apologized. "I had very little notice myself and did not want to give information over your party-line." But beyond saying that Robert was here on a visit from Whitehall he offered no further explanation.

Robert looked uncomfortable in his jacket and tie. Dust stuck to his sweat-dampened collar and, although obviously not a lover of the bush, he was meticulously polite and did his best to show interest in everything. But he was genuinely intrigued with the super-enlarged map of Nyamandhlovu district on the verandah wall and the story it told, but looked uneasy when I pointed out the latest pin, stuck into a neighbouring farm, which I'd added two days previously. It was a green one. The colour I had chosen for abduction.

Andrew Johnson's farm, marched with both Bonisa and Khami Prison beyond New Farm. It was not a working farm, more of a smallholding with neither homestead, Agric-Alert, nor farm hands and Andrew used it for camping – for his weekend bolt hole where he could sit and commune with nature. As an absentee landlord he was not regarded as a full member of the farming community and nobody really felt they knew anything about him beyond the fact that he was a quiet, middle-aged accountant who kept to himself. But two days ago his company in Bulawayo reported him missing. Police Reserve went out to do a recce and returned none the wiser. Security Forces followed up with a sweep, or so they said, and insisted there were 'no gooks' there, but both Sharp's informants and John's said there were definitely about eleven of them hiding on Pilossof's land next door.

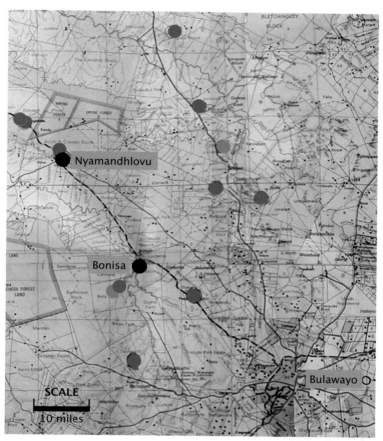

Nyamandhlovu

Bonisa

Bulawayo ◖

SCALE

⊢━━━━┥
10 miles

The map from the Bonisa
verandah with the pins showing
farms attacked: Blue for Attack,
Green for Abduction and Red for
Murder.

Nyamandhlovu is a district of the
province of North Matabeleland
lying north and west of Bulawayo.
Nyamandhlovu means 'meat of
the elephant' in the Ndebele
language.

Duncan Fleming and his
parents, MG and GG.

Big Bonisa.

Little Bonisa.

Above: Wedding of Susan and Tim Gibbs with MG Fleming and The Rev. Jonathan Siyachitema.

Below: Tim and Susan Gibbs.

Clockwise from top:
Sarah, Caroline,
David and James.

ZIMBABWE

Murders, fuel shortages, drought: could things be worse?

A community battered from three sides

The violence in the troubled Matabeleland province of Zimbabwe has reached levels this century. Judith Matloff reports from Harare.

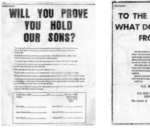

WILL YOU PROVE YOU HOLD OUR SONS?

TO THE KIDNAPPERS WHAT DO YOU WANT FROM US?

P.O. BOX 4487 HARARE
OR
P.O. BOX 37109 JOHANNESBURG
SOUTH AFRICA 2000

The parents of KEVIN ELLIS
BRETT BALDWIN
JAMES GREENHILL
MARTIN HODGSON
TONY BAKELI
WILLIAM BUTLER

Some of the newspaper reporting of the period.

Spectrum
PICTURE FOCUS

Even at playtime, a gun for mum

Sue Gibbs, wearing a pistol, enjoys a more joyous moment with her daughter, Sarah, on their farm in the violence-ridden Matabeleland where more and more women are carrying guns to protect themselves from armed dissidents of disgraced Joshua Nkomo.

Pistol packing mum

Zimbabwe housewife Sue Gibbs clutches her child in fear — and is prepared to shoot from the hip if necessary — after roaming rebels killed five whites, including two boys, near her home in Bulawayo, Zimbabwe's second largest city. Killings and kidnappings have been blamed on gangs of armed bandits, believed to be ex-guerrillas loyal to Opposition leader Joshua Nkomo. — UPI picture

Weapons training.
Top: Susan Gibbs in white shirt.

Below from left: Molly, Instructor, Humphrey, John.

The three-stamp
mill at the gold
mine.

Below left:
Mary Buxton.

Below right:
Antonia Gibbs.

It was too much for Colin. Curiosity outweighed our protests and he left Whitehall (as we referred to Robert) with us and went out in the Land Rover on his own. Two hours later he returned restless, burning to 'go in there' and flush out the group of eleven 'gooks' ground-cover swore were still there. But with curfew almost upon us, and no back up, to begin tracking would have been madness, and common sense won. For the rest of the evening we watched him pacing around and fidgeting and I thought he probably wouldn't get much sleep that night.

In the event, none of us got much sleep.

The dogs barked incessantly, Koki whined and scratched at the bedroom door, fence alarms went off frequently, and the guards on night patrol were more jumpy that usual, knocking on the bedroom window several times, reporting unusual noises. The call of a nocturnal bird wafted through gauzed windows of the sleeping verandah: "Good Lord deliver us. Good Lord deliver us," and as I lay there trying to sleep I thought, wryly, that the Litany Bird should have been made our National Emblem.

A shot rang out – an accidental discharge from one of the guards. I hoped the children hadn't heard any of this but they slept on unaware until the early hours of the morning. About 4am a huge explosion propelled us all out of bed. An unnerving quiet followed but by now we were all wide awake and we instinctively gathered on the verandah and sat there debating what to do next. I went off to the kitchen to make tea but, when offered, Robert said he would prefer something stronger.

For us to venture out to investigate was out of the question. We knew that security forces would not react at night and as neither the homestead nor Little Bonisa cottage had been hit and the blast, we agreed, had come from somewhere between us and Monica's cottage, we came to the conclusion that it must have been before the bee house on the line of rail. There was no point in having the whole district disturbed by using Agric-Alert with nothing specific to report and nothing for anyone else to do and, at Colin's suggestion, we returned to our rooms and lay wakefully waiting for dawn.

Peter burst in before first light, running up from the compound, breaking curfew, breathless with the news.

"Not just the rails!" he exclaimed. "The whole train. Poof! But no people. It was a goodis train only."

"No people, Peter? There must have been. What about the engine driver? the coal tender? the guardsman?" No, he didn't know about them.

Nyamandhlovu security forces refused to react. They didn't have enough men and they didn't have transport. It was a shame they said, but there it was.

Mkava's routine morning check of the area raked around outside the security fence revealed human spoor.

"Many footprints," he said. "Sometimes they are carrying heaviness. Deep footprints."

Robert looked as if he wished he was somewhere else. Perhaps behind his desk in Whitehall. Colin, incandescent, rang through to headquarters. No, Army Headquarters didn't think there was anything they could do from Harare. But Colin pulled rank, insisted on help, and eventually help arrived.

Later that day, just as Colin and Robert climbed into their vehicle for the return drive to Harare, a picannin from Andrew Johnson's property ran into the yard saying he'd discovered his boss's body stuffed down an antbear[15] hole. He didn't know how he'd died. It was one of those things.

We were pleased that Whitehall had been with us, that he had been shaken up and we hoped that, whatever his brief had been, he would present an objective first hand report to Whitehall.

---

15 Common name of the African Aardvark

15

Until now we had kept loaded pistols belted-on, and full magazines for our G3 assault rifles on the curtain pelmets in each room, but after a few months the government claimed that, although there were a few dissidents left over in Matabeleland, they were nothing to worry about. The bush war had now come to an end, they said.

But from time to time alarming reports of Zimbabwe appeared in the international press and I was amazed at how many people were still prepared to come and visit. Over a three year period more than two hundred names had been added to the visitors' book, mostly men, who in some ways were easier guests to occupy than women. There was always something needing to be built or repaired and if that didn't appeal men found themselves with a hunting rifle in their hands and instructions to 'go out and shoot for the pot.' Organised shooting parties had stopped a few years before and with numbers in the compound now tipping two hundred and sixty there was a constant need to replenish the five deep freezers, mainly stocked with venison, for the weekly rations.

But one man I did not look forward to having was the French Ambassador. Tim had met him on a business trip to Harare and invited him to stay on Bonisa for the week of the Central African Trade Fair held annually in Bulawayo. But I protested.

"I don't know him, a week is a long time and I'm not feeling well," I said somewhat ungraciously.

Nausea rose up again and I couldn't bear the smell of make-up, but this time I recognised it for what it was. Cravings for youngberry pancakes flambéed in rum had me up at night again and left me feeling unfocused and floppy during the days. 'Benignly Bovine' was how GG Fleming described my mood as I drifted through the days, and she was right. And then things began to go wrong.

"If you don't rest you'll lose this baby," Paul Fehrsen said. "No fussing, and put your feet up." I told him I couldn't. Stress was part of life. The French Embassy had rung to ask if the Ambassador could bring with him an entourage of five when the Trade Fair began next week. I really had to prepare. Outraged, Paul rang Tim.

"If you don't put these people off I'll put Sue in hospital for that week and everyone can cope without her."

They didn't come. But others did – the Flemings and old friends from Bulawayo took advantage of the end of hostilities and brought companionship and pleasure. But since being disarmed I was feeling insecure, more apprehensive than ever about the future, almost as if some hidden part of me knew something I didn't and it showed in little ways. I paid less attention to the kitchen and garden and was sharp with Monica when she came up to use the telephone, and I had to apologise.

Manka understood. She hovered around more than necessary, making decisions without consulting me and quietly removing the children when I threw up.

But despite the all-day morning-sickness David and I continued the schoolroom routine as best we could. Lessons were going well and with his natural curiosity and enthusiasm he learned quickly. The hours I'd spent gluing simple words to the outside of fifty match boxes and their corresponding pictures inside was paying off, and he could now recognize and name most of them.

It was Friday 13th of February 1981. The *Bulawayo Chronicle* informed us that Julius Caesar, Joan of Arc and Charles I all died on Friday 13th and it was the first anniversary of when Mount St Helen's blew its top. This was so interesting we abandoned formal lessons and were discussing volcanoes when Peter knocked on the door.

"Egalandi is here, Nkosikasi. He is sick."

Egalandi had never been sick before, or if he had he'd been cured by the witch doctor. It sounded as if Egalandi himself thought the answer to his problem was beyond my small clinic in the back yard, and I asked Peter to tell him to pack a bag and I would take him into the hospital after school. As we sat down at the desk again I glanced out of the window and noticed the fish eagle hadn't returned to his roost in the jacaranda. Manka was sitting on a rug underneath the tree, intent on her weekly task of silver-polishing but that didn't usually keep the fish eagle away. We looked more closely and listened. Every thing was strangely still. There were no other birds or bush noises, the only sound a distant rumbling to the south. This was odd. A storm perhaps but storms, when they did arrive, most often blew in from the north, from the direction of the Congo. Sporadic rumblings continued for sometime and David's attention drifted back to the match boxes.

Suddenly he sat up. "That's not thunder. That's big guns," he shouted.

Explosions and muffled booms erupted from the background rumblings.

"That one's a rocket," he exclaimed triumphantly.

It was impossible to continue. We abandoned match boxes and volcanoes to go in search of Tim. As we strode through the courtyard, Peter was on his hands and knees with a tin of Cobra Wax polishing the verandah floor.

"It sounds as if there is a war going on Peter," I said. He looked up briefly.

"Ah, yes Madam," was his matter of fact reply and lowering his head he resumed polishing. We found Manka in the dining room packing silver in baize lined draws.

"It sounds like a war Manka."

"Yes, madam, it is Entumbane. It is burning. Mkava told me."

Entumbane, an African township on the opposite side of Bulawayo from the white suburbs and said to have been built to take account of the prevailing wind, was ablaze, and in the far distance we could see a dark plume rising above it.

We found Tim in the workshops trying to repair an old tractor with, due to sanctions, the frustratingly few spare parts available.

"Egalandi needs to go to hospital, but Manka says Entumbane is burning. You can just see the smoke from here," I said.

Standing up he said, "Let's try anyway. We'll all go. It may not be that bad, we might get through."

101

As we approached Bulawayo the sounds of battle became louder, sharper, and the smoke and smells more pungent. We stopped just before the Luveve Road entrance to the townships and asked one of the soldiers manning the road block what was going on.

"We are here to prevent ZIPRA dissidents from entering the city centre," he explained. "They raided the armoury at Ntabazinduna barracks and stole weapons."

"And then?"

"Then they killed thirty-six ZANLA soldiers at Connemara and fled into the bush. Then they came in to Glenville and killed eleven more."

"But you are not ZANLA or ZIPRA are you?" I said.

"No, we are National Army. We are here to stop the dissidents. They are rubbish. Now they are entrenched in Entumbane. They are killing each other. We are killing them. Everyone is killing each other." He shook his head and laughed.

I hoped we hadn't been foolish bringing the children with us but John was away and we could not have left them unprotected on the farm.

"We want to go into Bulawayo," I said.

"No. You can't. It is forbidden. Bulawayo has been put on a war footing. Even for journalists. The airport road is closed. But you can stay here if you like."

A helicopter clacketting overhead hovered for a moment and then flew off towards the west, directing mortar fire on ZIPRA positions in the townships. Billowing smoke continued rising from Entumbane and hung in the air, a Stygian cloak of gloom blackening out the sun and refusing to dissipate. In the murky light green phosphorescent tracers arced through the sky like comets between the dissident forces of Nkomo and Mugabe.

We sat in the Land Rover watching the battle raging; watching the three armies slaughtering each other; feeling as if we had somehow strayed into the wrong life. From the smoke and dust, a few people emerged, running towards the Falls Road, their black faces lacquered with sweat as they escaped, empty handed, from the townships.

I turned back to the guard on the road block.

"We have a sick man in the back and want to take him to Mpilo Hospital."

"No. You can't. It is forbidden. Mpilo is full, full. They are even turning away dead bodies. Hundreds of them. No room. Not even in the mortuary."

"Oh Hell! Well, can we go to our friends in Kumalo?"

"No. It is forbidden. They are there too. In Kumalo, in vehicles. They knocked down a senior liaison officer. Then they ran over him. So we are fighting them there too. Is better you stay here. We are the oldest regiment. We are Rhodesian African Rifles. We will win."

"That's alright for you. What about this sick man?"

"I can do nothing Madam," he said, shrugging his shoulders.

We sat for a short while longer watching ZANLA attacking ZIPRA... Mugabe against Nkomo.... Shona fighting Ndebele. The bush war had come to town.

Egalandi didn't seem surprised. He agreed that there was nothing we could do and that he would accept treatment from my backyard clinic and we turned around and drove back up the Victoria Falls Road. Little did we know we had just witnessed the battle that would change everything in Matabeleland. The one that would bring Mugabe's North Korean trained Praetorian Guard, into the area — the brutal, undisciplined, unpredictable Fifth Brigade; the ones with a blood lust which would kill tens of thousands of Ndebele and eventually drive many of us out of the country.

Back on the farm I took Egalandi to the clinic I'd set up in the kitchen courtyard where I treated eye infections and skin diseases and other minor ailments with iodine crystals, Mercurochrome, gentian violet, embrocation, and liniments. Patients were dosed from the store of large brown bottles made up by Pioneer Pharmacy in Bulawayo and labelled 'Coughs', 'Sickness', 'Diarrhoea' and 'Constipation'. Antiphlogistine poultices, treatment for burns, gauze and crepe bandages stocked the shelves along with Fitzsimons Antivenin snake bite serum which claimed to be effective against Cape and Egyptian Cobras, Ringhals, Puff Adders,

Night Adders, and the most dangerous of all, Gaboon Vipers and Mambas, although I doubted anything was helpful against bites from the last two. I'd also added a tourniquet, a packet of razor blades and later a breast pump which worked wonderfully for sucking poison out from a cut down wound which eliminated the necessity of taking it into one's mouth. Mkava monitored the queue each morning and had his own ideas on who was genuinely sick and, with no medical knowledge at all, weeded out the ones he deemed to be 'ama malingerer' before herding the others into line.

I gave various mutis to Egalandi who seemed to recover quickly and enjoyed telling Peter all we had seen and heard. Following a short rest after lunch I took the children swimming. It was late afternoon, although still quite hot, and we were all feeling the after-exercise languor when Peter came out to the pool, walking quickly and carefully averting his eyes so as not to look at me in a bathing costume.

"Mkava, he want to see you Madam."

Leaving Manka in charge of the children I quickly dressed and went to the back yard, where Mkava, clearly agitated, spoke rapidly:

"Nkosikasi, we have many visitors. Come and see."

"Visitors?' I asked. "What visitors? I didn't hear a vehicle Mkava, Are you sure? How many?"

"Plenty."

"Well where are they?"

"Come quickly," is all he said, pacing off towards the Land Rover and climbing in. We drove half a mile down the track to the railway line on the far side of the dairy and were met by a group of about twenty grubby and dishevelled children, most of them barefoot. Behind them came more, eighty or ninety in all, shepherded by three young teenagers. All dirty, exhausted and frightened.

One of the older ones, who looked about fourteen, stepped forward.

"Today we come from Entumbane. All day we walk. No water. No food. Please, you help us."

They must have walked some fifteen or twenty miles and just stood there, hot, dehydrated and pitifully mute, not knowing if their families were still alive, knowing only that hundreds were dead.

Tim instructed the dairy foreman to fill milk churns with water and have the rest of the labour force meet him at the old, disused dairy behind Monica's cottage at Red Bank siding. After cleaning and sluicing out the few rooms, they went in search of blankets, hessian sacks, mugs and plates to turn the shed into a make-shift shelter for the night.

When I returned to the house Manka was bathing the children.

"Where's Peter?" I asked.

She shrugged. "Ungaaz. Don't know, Madam."

Annoyed, I told her to hurry, to find Peter, to gather up Ben the gardener, and the workshop boys and meet me in the kitchen garden. We picked cabbages, carrots, parsnips (which Peter, unable to say 'parsnips' called 'carrots aziku gaz' – carrots without blood) and a green, fleshy creeper with no name but which passed as spinach and had become known as 'Peter's Green Soup'. We went on to plunder the ration stores for dried fish and beans, packets of frozen venison and a large bag of mealie-meal. The resulting stew didn't look very appetizing, but it smelled good, was nourishing and the children wolfed it down in a way that made me wonder how long it had been, even before setting out on their trek, since their last meal.

Many of the children were unwell, some suffering with festering sores and eye infections. I raided the clinic stores to treat some of the minor ailments, stuffed them in a bag and returned to the shelter. When I came to the group with coughs I noticed behind them crates of Coca Cola in glass bottles stacked against the walls, some of which were still full.

"Where did you get these from?" I asked the young spokesman. "You said you didn't have any money."

"No, Ma, we haven't," he replied. "But your cook, he gave us a present."

So that's why I'd not been able to find him. He'd gone to the beer hall. The barman didn't stock much in the way of soft drinks and

Peter had bought up their entire supply spending a great deal of his wages. Several of the women from our compound turned up to take charge of the young ones during the night and, after reassuring us that they had all they needed, we returned to the house before dark. Although curfew had been lifted when we were disarmed, most of us still stuck to it, partly out of habit and partly because we still didn't quite trust the newly declared peace.

I immediately went in search of Peter. He was back in the kitchen making unnecessary mountains of butter balls with wooden pats – a sign of distress, which always showed itself in frenetic activity.

"Peter, about the crates of cokes. That was generous of you," I said. He shrugged.

"But," I went on, "you are a Shona and they are Ndebele. In Entumbane your people and their people are killing each other. And now you do this very kind thing."

He worked faster at his butter balls, shaking his head as if the whole thing was beyond reason.

"Ah! Nkosikasi. Is no good, this fighting; this war. Is no good and they, they are only children."

"Well, thank goodness it's all over," I said.

But it wasn't all over. It wasn't all over at all. It was only the beginning of what was to become known as "The Situation" in Matabeleland.

16

A few weeks after Entumbane we received a telephone call from Xan Smiley. He'd visited Bonisa on previous occasions and we knew he was the editor of the prestigious *Africa Confidential* (to which we subscribed) which did not use by lines for its correspondents, who happened to write extraordinarily well-informed articles. It seemed to us as if many of these articles could only have come from 'insiders' throughout Africa, frequently involving countries with repressive regimes.

Although he had visited us before, we knew little about Xan – a state of affairs he seemed happy to maintain. Although we felt Humphrey knew more about him, to us Xan was something of an enigma. He'd deftly picked our brains for local (and any other) news and useful information, any contacts we'd had, any approaches made to us, for instance by the South Africans?

We had in fact been approached by the South Africans soon after independence. They wanted us to pass information to them from our knowledge of events, especially security activities, in the area, from information from local ground-cover, and also anything we might be able to discover from our political and diplomatic contacts in Harare and elsewhere. We said no. But they applied greater pressure, making increasingly generous offers, should we have to leave the country for whatever reason, of a decent house in South Africa with a good car, education for each of the children, passports, and an annual income it would be foolish to refuse. We refused. Although not enthusiastic about Comrade Mugabe, nor, in my case, optimistic about the future, to pass information to another country still felt very much like treason and eventually the South Africans left us alone and I did sometimes wonder who, if anyone, had agreed in lieu of us.

But this visit from Xan was different. He remained just as reticent to talk about his own activities, about where he'd come from and where he was going after leaving us, but he was generally more open and brought with him Jane Acton, who was to become his wife, which fleshed out more sociable subjects. They'd arrived late having been stuck behind a tractor pulling a tree along behind it in order to grade the dirt road which had been left in an awful state after the recent rains and, following a quick cup of tea on the verandah, we all went down to the dam.

It was the hour before sundown and as the sun moved towards the horizon, its pink and yellow swags draped the sky – a brief, magical time of the day – and we sat on the bank watching the game come down to drink. Kudu cows, tentative and shy, edged slowly out of the bush and made their way towards the water in small groups. A herd of water buck waded in the shallows. Smaller buck, monkeys and masses of birds arranged themselves around the dam, and then my favourite appeared – the stately, glossy, black Sable, the national emblem of Rhodesia/ Zimbabwe – holding its head high, its long scimitar horns curving over its back. It stood majestically, like a victorious emperor, watching us watching him. The animals, although cautious, were not nervous – a good sign – and we relaxed and chatted.

"You know Africa well," I said to Xan. "Could you live here? In the bush?"

"I sometimes feel I do!" he said. But that was all.

I turned to Jane. "I hope you know more about Xan than we do. He's so secretive, it could lead you into trouble."

They both laughed and changed the subject.

The latest issue of *Africa Confidential* had contained an article about Robert Mugabe, his thoughts and his lifestyle when he was conducting his war from the bush, in neighbouring Moçambique. It could only have been written by someone who had been there with him and Tim wondered where the information might have come from.

The next day, just before they left, Xan offered to sign the Visitors' Book and, as he signed his name on the open page in bright red, I felt that something had changed. As we watched them drive away from Bonisa, Tim said it was as if Xan was signing off from a mission accomplished and I looked at the disappearing car and wondered.

So much was changing in the country, different journalists came and went but we didn't see Xan again on Bonisa.

Nick and Carola Mangnall, who were also staying with us at the time, took one of the vehicles and a couple of weapons and left for a few days at Victoria Falls. I was sure Nick was experienced enough to know all the necessary precautions but just before he left we'd shown him the *General Advice to Motorists* issued by Security Forces:

"Do not stick to a routine. Where possible take a different road, at different times, on different days. Drive fast in rural areas. In the event of a collision with a pedestrian, a cyclist or another vehicle, don't stop. Continue on to the nearest Police Station and file a report."

This was all very well but we only had one road between the farm and Bulawayo and so we decided to acquire The Leopard.

No one quite knew why it was called The Leopard — it didn't resemble anything feline. The overall impression was more of an awkward, and somewhat ridiculous, praying mantis. The armour-plated body, painted camouflage green, was cylindrical at the bottom, and topped by a green canvas roof, stretched over hoops which served as roll-bars. Lengthwise inside the 'cylinder' two benches ran down the sides on which a total of four passengers could be strapped, uncomfortably, facing each other, as if in choir stalls. A pair of thickly-plated back doors went half-way up the back with an open space above them which, we presumed, was to ensure that all possible dust was sucked in to smother the passengers in the dark, furnace-hot interior.

It looked like a joke, but it wasn't, and it did at least give some peace of mind when I drove David, and later Sarah, to the Hebrew-English Nursery School in Bulawayo, several times a week. The children hated it. But the biggest challenge was for the driver. The vehicle had been purpose built in Zimbabwe around a 1600cc VW engine kit which, for some unknown reason, and extremely inconveniently, did not include a petrol gauge. Occasionally a top speed of 50mph could be attained but it was unbelievably heavy, difficult to steer and had vastly reduced visibility. Narrow slits of thick, bullet-proof glass either side of the driver provided a begrudging concession to, slightly distorted, peripheral vision and the front 'window' of the same glass stretched from side to side but was only a few inches high restricting forward vision. Anything high, low or close up was out of visual range making stopping at traffic lights hazardous unless I remembered to do this several yards too soon, before they disappeared out of sight.

The elongated, armour-plated front of the vehicle sloped steeply forward, doubling the length of the vehicle, in a manner intended to deflect bullets. Front and back wheels protruded inelegantly from both ends and stuck out to straddle the road and were designed to take the impact and fly off instantly should we hit a land mine. If this happened, shear-bolts protecting an exposed petrol tank between the back wheels also stripped off and flung the petrol tank away from the vehicle, lessening the effects of the blast and risk of fire and leaving the roll-bars to take over.

But usually, when travelling alone, I preferred to use my car which is what I foolishly decided to do on the day James had a doctor's appointment in Bulawayo. A few years before he died Duncan had won a white Renault Caravelle in a competition and generously given it to me. I loved it. It was my pride and joy – fast, and nippy, it held the road well and I liked to drive at speed, usually with the roof off, my enormous, pink, silk scarf streaming out behind like a comet.

It was after breakfast and the air was still fresh and clear as James climbed on to the small bench behind the driver's seat. I gave Manka a few last minute instructions for the other children, while Mkava put a paper bag of flour on the dashboard, before we drove off down the dusty farm track to where the strip road, which serviced other outlying farms, turned right towards Bulawayo. The two parallel strips of tarmac, snaked away into the distance. Once I felt both sets of tyres had a purchase on the strips I drove as fast as I dared. Unusually, an oncoming vehicle appeared a few hundred yards ahead and I slowed briefly, manoeuvred to the side and turned up the windows. Nikki Bates from the farm next door and I waved and gave the 'road clear' sign as we passed each other and I drove on into the blinding wall of dust.

After several miles we came to the straight, full-tar of the

Nyamandhlovu Road and turned east towards Victoria Falls Road leading to Bulawayo.

James had been unusually quiet. At four years old he was not yet able to play 'I spy' and I tried, without success, to encourage him to sing nursery rhymes with me. He was not interested and just sat, preoccupied, staring out of the window with his mouth open as he'd been taught. I was uncertain how much he actually understood the reasons for this and I opened my own mouth, wondering if in the chaos of an emergency, I would have enough wit to remember to follow the further army instructions. This, the precautionary part, to prevent blast damage to ear drums, was easy if unnatural, and I mulled over the rest, while scanning the bush and trying to watch the road.

Suddenly James shouted.

"Guns!"

Too late. We were in it. I glanced to the right. A line of AKs bristled from the bush, fifteen, maybe twenty, from well spaced bases. Each aimed and traced us as I stamped on the accelerator, willing more speed. Flour, flour, my mind whirled frantically. I grappled for the paper bag and flung it out of the open window. It burst and a fine white cloud floated down spreading over the tar, covering the verge and soil and settling into becoming a stark land mark, impossible to remove or, more importantly, to disguise from aerial reconnaissance.

But the guns remained silent.

We rounded a bend in the road. Shaken, and contrary to all training instructions and common sense, I pulled up a few hundred yards further on and turned to reassure James. His face was white, bloodless; his mouth still open, silent. I started to say something.

Then all hell broke loose.

Back from the road we'd just driven down automatic fire splattered through the silence. Tyres screeched on tarmac, harrowing, sickening sounds, of bush being ripped through. Jubilant, over-excited voices, army-type boots running, ringing out on tarmac. Somewhere a grenade exploded.

There was nothing reassuring to say. I slammed into gear, steadily flattened the accelerator and raced for Bulawayo.

17

The safest time to be in a 'hot' area was said to be just after an 'incident'. Terrorists, knowing the place would be crawling with security forces, made a hasty get away; nevertheless I was uneasy about having to take James along the same route home later that day. But as there was only one road, there were no other options. By the time we arrived at the site of the ambush the mess had been cleared up and anyone unfamiliar with the significance of the small signs of some flattened vegetation and a fine coating of white flour marking the spot would not have suspected anything untoward had taken place. The road was deserted and we had a clear run.

But James didn't speak and, although attentive and unquestioningly obedient, his quietness disturbed me, and I was sure it had something to do with living the aftermath of his experience. He wouldn't talk about it and I decided to single him out, to do with him more of the things he enjoyed. We took Koki and went for interesting walks outside the security fence and a hundred yards or so down the well-worn path to the upper dam, tracking spoor of small animals on the sun-baked red earth, guessing how long since they'd passed that way and stepping superstitiously over the tracks left by snakes. We stood for a long time watching the busy, orderly lines of ants bearing heavy burdens to their nests.

"We call them anthills," I told him. "But they are actually termites and very clever. Deep inside the temperature is always the same."

"They're big," he said.

"Some are even bigger, taller than you."

"Why did Mkava break one and take it away?"

"Because it's just right for making the floor inside his hut. He packs it down hard," I said. "Some farmers even spread it on their lands – it helps to hold water. And do you know that sometimes tiny bits of gold are found in them."

"Wow," he said, impressed.

At these moments he was completely absorbed in all we were doing and I hoped it would help restore his concept of normality, but at other times he remained withdrawn and I felt impotent to reach him. A dust-devil got up, half blinding us with sand and fine dust and we ran behind the dam wall to shelter for a while.

Perhaps because of the deadening effect of the wall, perhaps because of the wind, or a combination of both, we didn't hear it coming. Suddenly, skimming the dam wall, with a deafening, clackering, a helicopter gunship appeared, paused and hovered over our heads. The noise changed – thwop, thwop thwop from the giant twin rotas tore at our hair and, trapped, we ducked. James, wild-eyed rooted to the ground as I shouted "Damn you. GO." But unhearing they waved, stayed a few more moments, then flew off in the direction of Nyamandhlovu.

It was a long time before James spoke again.

I talked calmly to him, explaining that these ones were on our side, they were good and they were hunting out the bad ones who were nowhere near us – if they had been the helicopter would have landed. I persevered, trying to interest him in other things. I bought him a black plastic motorbike from South Africa which he loved, propelling it along the ground by his feet, and for some reason stripped naked apart from a hat. We didn't know why he didn't want to wear clothes, he said he liked the sun on his skin, but he continued to insist on a hat. It didn't matter what sort of hat – police hats, fireman's hats, any hard hats, he adopted them all and wore them constantly. But he would not wear clothes and we dubbed him 'Knickerless James' but he thought we were calling him 'Nicholas' and preferred to be known as just James as he'd always been, so we dropped it.

It was a few weeks before he seemed to be himself again, at least on the surface, but I didn't quite trust the reality of the outward appearance and sensed that some of the shock and fear remained buried in some deep place.

"If you're not going to wear clothes don't go near the bananas and paw paws," I warned him. "There's a new wild hive in there and they're cheeky ones."

113

The swarming season was underway. Good rains had brought the veldt into bloom, providing abundant foraging for bees, and the wild hives thrived, expanded, produced new queens and then split off into dense, dark clouds dipping and diving almost poetically over the land, like small flocks of queleas, looking for places to colonise. We'd already had to remove one swarm from the chimney – vicious brutes which I'd transferred to outside the kitchen garden where they'd settled down well and behaved themselves.

Ken Mappin's elderly mother hated bees. Since developing an allergy as a young woman, Mrs Mappin's fear of bees was extreme and she demanded that Ken remove the three newly established wild hives from the trees in their garden. Knowing that I ran a small business selling honey to the Indian store keepers in Bulawayo, Ken rang me.

"If I can get them boxed up tonight could I bring them over to you?" he asked. "They're in our garden. Can't come at night of course but I could be with you in the morning."

The next day Ken arrived at Bonisa soon after sunrise, bouncing along the farm track in his Land Rover, heedless of the effect on the seething contents of the boxes which had already endured the best part of twenty miles.

"Morning," he called cheerfully, briefly tipping his tatty, old bush-hat as he began off loading the first of the boxes. "You will have to be careful of these, they are one hell of a lot of ferocious guys."

"All African bees are ferocious," I said.

"Yup," he grinned, "But these are something special!"

As if to prove themselves, a dull humming emanated from inside the containers and uncertainty began to form in me. All the hives in the bee house were healthy and I did not want to risk introducing any disease from the wild ones nor did I fancy mine mingling with what could be a more vicious strain.

I'd risen before Roll-Call that morning, assembled three new wooden hives, filled the supers with frames of waxed combs, stuffed newspapers in the entrances and placed them in readiness under the Pawpaw trees a reasonable distance from the other wild hive, behind the kitchen.

"Over to you," Ken said, dumping the final box on the ground.

"Could you stay a moment and give me a hand?"

"Nope, sorry. You're the expert. You'll be OK. Nothing will get through that kit you're wearing." He gave my veil a cursory tug. "Well, must be off." And clambering into the Land Rover with a hearty, "Good luck!" he tipped his hat again and drove off in a cloud of dust.

"The age of chivalry is dead," I thought.

Peter, who had been watching from the kitchen window came out to join me.

"Aaah Nkosikasi," he said. "Listen to them. These ones are cheeky. Too cheeky. Is better you leave them until tonight."

But I couldn't. I knew that by evening they would be dead. The day was already warming up, they'd been shaken up in Ken's's Land Rover and, although the growling had died down to a dull hum, it would be dangerous to delay. I sent Peter back to the kitchen with instructions to keep everyone, including the dogs, indoors until the bees had been transferred.

I put a match to the cow-dung in a puffer and when it was smoldering pumped gusts of smoke into the first box. The undertones of grumbling died down and then stopped. Moving quickly, I lifted the lid off the first hive, up-ended the box and tapped the mass of sleepy bees down on to the combs below. Rapidly replacing the lid I moved on to the next two boxes. The transfer was complete and, encouraged, I unplugged the entrance holes, gave a few extra bellows of smoke for luck and began walking away.

From behind me I heard a low protest begin to vibrate inside the hives, swelling rapidly to a furious throaty crescendo. Stunned, I hesitated and stopped. Suddenly the first hive erupted. A stream of angry bees poured out like a thick, dark liquid.

Pain shot into my neck. Sharp. Searing. Another and another. A murderous frenzy of enraged bees hurling themselves at me were suddenly inside the veil. *How did they get there? Was it Ken's tug?*

I ran, yelling, through the orchard, around the side of the house, to the front lawn. Peter took a shortcut through the courtyard and, standing in front of me, he brandished a hosepipe drenching us both in powerful jets of water. It didn't help. Running further across the lawn, he grabbed my arm, pulled me into the schoolroom and slammed the door on the boiling mass outside. He ripped off my veil, swatting and stamping on bees speaking soothingly to me.

"Too sorry, Nkosikasi, aagh, too sorry." Finally I looked at Peter. Bees crawled through his black, curly mat of hair, his lips and hands were swollen and distorted. But he didn't flinch, his only concern was for me.

"It's alright Nkosikasi. I'm alright. Don't worry. They will die."

A few spasmodic buzzings came from dying bodies on the floor as the swarm still outside threw themselves against the window. With my whole face on fire I could no longer see through swollen eyes.

"Peter, where's Manka?"

"She hid James and has gone to get the Big Boss Madam."

A few minutes later Humphrey's firm voice came from the doorway. "You're coming with me!" Peter refused to come with us. I urged, almost pleaded with him.

"Is alright, is nothing," he said. His swollen face had turned grey. I knew he must have been in pain, but he was adamant. And as Pa led me through the courtyard to his car out the back I told Manka to give Peter some analgesics and antihistamines and to keep the children safely indoors until Tim came home.

The staff at the hospital, although sympathetic, gave me a good talking to – How long had I been keeping bees? I should have known better than to work them in the heat of the day, they said, as they further punctured my skin with injections. I returned home, chastened. Peter smelling strongly of carbolic soap (his answer to all afflictions) seemed to be almost back to normal and was in the kitchen happily making bread.

"David has gone back to school," he told me. "The boss took him, but he rang on the telephone. He say: 'Peter, is Mummy still that funny shape?'"

The next day I went to check the hives under the Paw Paw trees. They stood empty, the bees had gone. I wondered briefly, but didn't dare ask, if they had returned to the Mappins.

18

During the following days Fifth Brigade came and went throughout the district at will. Agric-Alert buzzed with reports flowing in of sightings and incidents. Although most encounters were relatively minor they left in their wake heightened vigilance and increasing tension.

Mrs Rankin's age and widowhood made her particularly vulnerable and her troubles seemed to be never-ending. One morning, at 7.30am, she indignantly reported over Agric-Alert that: "Four girls have been taken out of my compound and raped *before breakfast*."

John Barry, Severine's husband, followed saying: "They must have come on to M'Pandeni because Red Berets are currently beating up Marion Rankin's workers at Hilda's Kraal. It's chaotic but no one has been killed so far, I am thankful to say."

A few hours later, from his farm next door to Bonisa, Tony Sharp, notified that Fifth Brigade had come on and 'thumped' one of the women in his compound, "But it's alright because her husband thought this was justified as she was being 'cheeky,'" he said and then added, "a picannin who tried to run away impaled himself on a bayonet sustaining a small wound. But, that's alright too because the Fifth Brigade medic dressed the wound and altogether I think they behaved rather well," he concluded.

We decided the time had come to employ armed guards, to patrol around both houses, inside the security fence, particularly at night. Ray Fawcett ran his own very successful security company in Bulawayo and when we told him our needs he supplied two to cover night patrols. "One to keep the other one awake," he said.

"Which is which?" I asked.

"Both," he said enigmatically.

Tim didn't have a problem sleeping but since coming on to the farm I did, and since Ray's guards arrived I slept marginally better.

John went down to Red Bank Cottage and made another attempt to persuade Monica to accept an Agric-Alert set but again she refused.

He came back stammering with frustration and I decided to go down and reason with her myself.

"Monica, this is silly. Without a set you have no idea what's going on in the area, and besides it's not fair on the men who may have to put their lives on the line for you."

"It's alright, they won't have to. The Lord will look after me."

"Yes, I know that, but He also gave us the means to help ourselves. Listen Monica," I went on, exasperated, "I had a 'Road to Damascus' experience a few years ago. I believe, I have faith, I pray. Every night we pray with the children for your protection, along with ours. But we have also been given common sense and brains to be practical and do whatever we can to help ourselves."

She threw her head back holding my eyes with a look of – was it regret, or was it pity? I didn't know. But she said nothing. Then, wordlessly indicating that the interview was over and that we clearly did not draw water from the same well, she moved towards the door. I left, acutely aware that, in her view, Jesus probably hadn't called me to be one of his sunbeams and I knew that we would never speak of it again.

When I arrived back at the homestead Jack Ehlers was sitting on the verandah drinking coffee with John. He stood up, flung his trademark Stetson on the coffee table and held out his hand.

"Just popped in to invite you to my wedding," he said.

"Thank you – that's very kind of you," I replied, knowing he'd made wedding plans but surprised to find ourselves invited, and I wondered why. We were not particular friends; perhaps it would be a large wedding with the whole district invited. That Joy was a highly regarded, middle-aged widow from Mashonaland I knew, but not much more than that. I'd wondered if she could have been aware of his reputation. Perhaps not. If she did, would she marry him? At the Farmer's Club his social manner was unfailingly courteous but he guarded his private life and rumours of a darker side persisted.

John cut in on my thoughts. "Have you had any trouble with Fifth Brigade on Mimosa Park?" he asked. "We haven't heard you on Agric-Alert."

"Ya, man, a small thing. They got in at 8 o'clock on Saturday, locked my cook in the bathroom and stole all the booze. We were in town. But it could have been worse."

"I trust the curse isn't at work Jack." John shot me a mischievous look.

Jack knew about the Ichithamuzi tree and the subsequent catastrophes that befell successive residents before he bought Mimosa Park. But being Afrikaans by birth and by nature neither he nor his first wife had been easily intimidated by stories of curses.

"That was just bad luck and anyway nothing much happened to the Cummings before they sold it to me," he scoffed.

"Everything's relative – they didn't have a perfect life there and then their marriage broke up and what about Beryl?" John reminded him. "She left you sometime after you bought Mimosa."

But Jack laughed it off saying: "Trees... curses... all that was a long time ago."

As John and Jack talked about cattle I reflected on that first day Jack and Beryl had come to the Nyamandhlovu Club and the murmurs of disbelief when Jack casually announced that they planned to gut the lovely old Mimosa homestead and re-design the interior around a large indoor swimming pool. Even so, the only time I'd visited Mimosa after that, I'd been unprepared for the interior opulence of what had been essentially a Matabeleland farm house. Now, transformed by the entire central area having been turned into a swimming pool with free-standing Grecian columns marching down either side and, at one end, an oversized ornamental Venus standing naked, sensuously gazing out over the pool, with a fan shaped fountain at her feet gently splashing into the water below. Reclining loungers and small tables were scattered invitingly around the edges. Beryl drew my attention to the galleries surrounding the pool.

"Jack and I couldn't agree on a bar theme and so we decided to use all our ideas," she said, leading me through five alcoves lining the walls. Each alcove formed a three-sided sitting room facing the pool and individually decorated – there was an English pub, a Moroccan Tent, a Moulin Rouge, a Wild West and an African safari camp. Each contained a themed bar stocked with every kind of exotic liquor, all of which, unobtainable in Zimbabwe, had to have been imported. To my mind the whole thing in itself seemed like the outworking of a curse.

"You see," she went on triumphantly, "our guests never get bored."

At the weekends the house was filled with visitors – 'townies' the district called them and speculations about the 'goings on' in the 'Pleasure Palace' outdid each other in imagination and luridness. Jack and Beryl were aware but didn't let it bother them. They had everything they wanted they said – the friends, the lifestyle, and the house to accommodate both.

I got up and poured more coffee.

"We haven't seen you at the club since Corrie died, Jack. You must miss him. Who is running the clinic now?" I asked.

Dr Corrie de Kok, had befriended the Ehlers after they took over Mimosa Park and had quickly become a regular weekend visitor. An Afrikaans GP from Bulawayo with a reputation for being an astute diagnostician, he'd set up a weekly clinic on the ranch for the 'boys' and their families from surrounding areas. But Corrie ran his clinics differently from others – he charged his patients. Jack had first taken Corrie to the Nyamandhlovu farmers' club soon after they met and a momentary hush fell over the room as they entered. Jack introduced his small, dapper friend to a few of the men and Corrie, with much aplomb extended a limp hand to each stunned member.

"Good God! One of 'those'," Bronco said as embarrassed murmurs broke out and covered whatever else he said.

The arrangement between Corrie and the Ehlers appeared to suit them all, but after a while we began to notice a change in Beryl. She looked strained and became withdrawn, living behind a smile-screen, deflecting enquiries if she was alright. And then one day, without warning, Beryl took herself off to South Africa for a holiday and didn't return. Some thought she had joined a religious group and moved on, but whatever happened to her Jack showed no distress. When Corrie moved permanently onto the farm no one assumed that it had anything to do with the clinic, and the rumours started up again. And then Corrie died.

"I closed the clinic down when Corrie passed on." Jack startled me back into the present, "But Joy said she would set it up again after we're married." Mimosa Park had thrived under Jack's management. Despite his attempts at elegant debauchery, he turned out to be a good farmer, building up an impressive herd of pedigree Brahman Cattle and successfully growing sugar beans and summer maize. But he was a hard, and some said occasionally aggressive, task master. The bush telegraph informed us that although the labour respected him it was out of fear, not affection.

"Just look at all that. You won't get that anywhere else. Hey man, the veldt looks good this year," Jack said, indicating the view from the verandah. "So many have left, but me? I'm here to stay. It's about time everyone forgot who lost and who won the war. It's over. They won, we're the vanquished. So what? We must just get on with it. Hell, man, if I went down south there'd be some white man telling me "Hey, it's eight o'clock. Start Work!" He paused for a moment before adding: "I'm telling yous ous I'd rather be slotted by the munts[16] than live like that." It was a joke. Only a joke, but then he didn't believe in the curse. If he had he might have guessed it hadn't yet worked itself out. But he didn't know that.

"Anyway," Jack went on changing the subject back again, "I thought I'd invite Monica to the wedding. Could you bring her?"

"We could, of course, but she may not come. Don't be offended if she doesn't, she's not keen on social occasions. You know she won't even have Agric-Alert."

"Hell man, Monica and Marion Rankin, two old biddies who shouldn't be living out here. They're a liability."

I flew to Mrs Rankin's defence. "She battles on here alone, fighting disease, the elements, and security problems, keeping her labour going and patching them up when she has to. She does have Agric-Alert, she's armed and she constantly keeps us

---

16 Muntu: the African word for their people.

121

all informed. It may not be wise but you have to admire her guts and tenacity."

We sat in silence for a moment listening to the throb of the Lister engine pumping water from the dam. John lit another cigarette and got up.

"Well, must get on. Work to be done." I knew he'd had enough, he was stuttering.

Jack walked over to the edge of the verandah and gazed out at white clouds clotting together in the purest of blue skies and the lush, tall stands of maize waving gently at us from the lands.

"By the way, you ought to make your kids keep their shoes on Eh? The nasty bugs are out at this time of the year," he said.

"I know."

"Ah man, you've got a lekka place here. Beautiful Bonisa eh? If ever you think of selling up let me know."

How dare he even think it! Jack Ehlers living in my home? Taking over our farm? Never.

But then I wasn't to know what lay ahead.

19

The morning sickness passed off and, as winter approached, the days became cooler, my energy returned and I took over the afternoon walks from Manka again. The children had a short rest after lunch before we put on vellies[17] and strolled down the two hundred yards or so to the dam. It was a place of gathering, a sort of village pump for humans and wild life. Water birds – waders, plovers and herons – pottered around the edges, unconcerned by game coming down to drink or by women coming up from the compound, bringing their picannins, to fish for Barbel. Africans didn't mind the dense mass of bones, nor the muddy taste of catfish which feed off the bottom and are of no commercial value, and they regularly landed ones large enough to feed a family.

Spreading over 250 acres, Bonisa Dam was comprised of two dams. When antbears burrowed through the wall of the first dam causing it to burst through, Tim constructed another, all encompassing one, around it until it formed the largest stretch of water between the Zambezi and the Limpopo; an oasis in an otherwise dry, dusty veldt, attracting birds and wildlife from miles around. In the early 1960s Sam Rabinowitz, a prominent Bulawayo Jew, sent Tim to Israel under the aegis of the Jewish National Fund to live on kibbutzim and study fish farming. On his return several months later he stocked the dam with Tilapia (or St Peter's fish as it was also known on the Galilee). A successful enterprise grew up, regularly providing the Bulawayo Club and later Bulawayo supermarkets with fish which, following UDI, became even more sought after, when international sanctions prevented the importation of seafood, and we became virtually the sole supplier.

While the children busied themselves modelling mud huts thatched with spikes of grass, and dug shallow holes to explore for

---

17   Abbreviated form of veldschoens, a desert boot.

buried treasure, I sat on the bank idly watching monkeys grooming each other with black leathery hands, listening to the distant voices of chattering women and picannins drifting across the water as they fished with hooks and lines attached to short sticks. Sometimes Luka, the workshop supervisor had to use his pliers to take the small fishing hooks out of eye lids or ear lobes, but today there were no injuries. Basking in a warm, timeless peace, it was as if the future had somehow been postponed. Always different, yet always the same, I appreciated every moment knowing it could all end in an instant. Sitting there I thought about how we had arrived at this situation. We all cast blame on politicians, on the British Government – and on China and Russia for supporting, supplying and training terrorists groups. We also blamed the Zimbabwe government for perpetuating Ian Smith's censorship of the media, claiming it was 'in the national interest' and 'for security reasons' but we were sure the real intention was to keep us all insular and ignorant, allowing for greater government control, and my annoyance knew no bounds as day after day the newspaper arrived with large blank columns and, on at least one occasion, a totally blank front page.

As time went on, aware of my increasing frustrated hunger for information, Tim had given me a subscription to *The Times* of London. The airmail edition often arrived in two days, three at the most, and on one occasion it came out on the milk tractor in the next day's mail bag. Having up-to-date international news made all the difference and, after we'd both devoured it, we handed it on to others who also read it avidly and then likewise passed it on to their friends and neighbours. The first copy, having been delayed by an industrial strike, didn't arrive until 4th January 1983. In full-blooded enthusiasm I ripped the flimsy paper in half while tearing off the wrapper. Piecing the bits together again I spread it out on the verandah table and stood looking at it, stunned.

There on the front page, above the caption 'pistol packin' momma' was a photograph of a woman, a pistol on one hip and her young son, looking distraught, on the other. I remembered the moment Alexander Joe, the freelance photographer, had taken it.

James was upset. He'd just collided with Sarah at the bottom of the slippery-slide. It hurt. He was in tears. The later edition carried our names under the caption and news agencies sent the photo around the world. In the coming weeks other copies arrived from Australia, Norway, Japan and other countries bearing captions such as 'Fear Grips Whites in Zimbabwe', 'Matabeleland on Fire', and 'Gun-toting Farmer's Wife'.

I shouldn't have been surprised. Since Fifth Brigade began their campaign in Matabeleland journalists had arrived at the farm with increasing frequency.

As the afternoon wore on I lay back on the bank scanning the skies, for signs of the fish eagle. My Fish Eagle, as I thought of him. He came in from the direction of the homestead, circled low over the water and plunged, braking against extended talons, as I watched enthralled. Then he arced away grappling with his catch, spraying droplets into the air like shards of shattering glass, and I willed him not to drop it. A small herd of waterbuck waded into the dam. Although more docile than the other antelope we rarely saw them during the day until late afternoons brought them down to drink and cool off. The children giggled at the white rings, like loo seats, painted on their rumps and made up rude stories about how they got there.

Sarah slipped a few seashells into my lap. They were definitely seashells but we'd no idea how they got so far inland and I decided to take them on my next trip to the museum. The air cooled rapidly and the evening melded into the brief minutes of golden calm before darkness descends. We suddenly realised the monkeys had gone, and the women and picannins were packing up their fishing rods. Reluctantly the children stuffed the still-wet mud huts they had made into their pockets and we made our way back to the homestead for bath time and supper.

I'd been trying to be sensible and Paul Fehrsen was pleased when I next went for a check up.

"For a thirty-nine-year-old you're doing alright," he said, "but you must have a Caesar. You couldn't manage it the good old-fashioned way last time, you're less likely to do it this time and with the security risks in Nyamandhlovu we'd better book you in a week early… that will be in four weeks time."

"I'd like to have the baby on 14th June," I told him. "It's David's birthday. It would be fun to have the oldest and youngest birthdays on the same day."

He flipped the calendar.

"Nope, no chance of that. You can't have a baby on a Sunday. We only run on skeleton staff at weekends. Sorry," he added cheerfully.

While the receptionist tried to contact the gynaecologist and make a booking with the Lady Rodwell Hospital, I re-joined David and Sarah in the waiting room. A large notice on the wall behind a row of chairs read: 'Please knit for our troops. Patterns below.' The fingerless gloves looked too difficult and I picked up a half finished, green balaclava and began knitting. Looking around the other patients sitting there busily clicking needles or unwinding skeins of wool between them, my mind went back to when I first met Julia Painting. At the beginning of the war The Rhodesia Party, in which both Duncan and Tim were involved, held a knitting competition to raise funds to oppose Ian Smith and I was on duty when Julia walked in. The first thing I noticed was her youthful beauty and elegance. The next thing I noticed was she only had one arm. She read my thoughts, which were probably obvious, and explained that she'd parted with her arm when she was taken by a shark off the South African coast, however knitting wasn't a problem; in fact, she claimed, nothing defeated her. She was an overcomer with a technique. When some seemingly impossible task presented itself she went to sleep that night, concentrating hard on the problem, and woke the next morning having received the solution in a dream. In night visions she'd been shown how to put curlers in her long, thick hair, how to drive and how to knit.

"Look," she said, and wedging one needle between her knees she deftly wove stitches with one hand.

Sister put the phone down and handed me the hospital booking arrangements.

"Have you heard about Peggy Francis?" she said. "She died this morning." Sarah looked up. Startled. "Who shot her?" she demanded.

"No one. She just died."

"How? How did she die?" she persisted.

"Very reluctantly," the nurse glanced at me – we both knew Peggy Francis, she didn't like not being in control.

Shocked, yet again, by the childish assumptions of the normality of death by shooting, I resolved again to try and persuade Tim of the need, not to leave, but to make contingency plans to leave, or, at the very least, to take a flat in the relative safety of town. But, apart from boarding schools in Mashonaland and then Cape Town, Bonisa had always been his home. He had a sense of permanence about it and he couldn't imagine that the current situation was anything more than a temporary phase which we could 'ride out'.

Driving home I thought about what plans to make for the three children during the time I would be in the Lady Rodwell. I knew the Flemings would willingly have them in to stay in Burnside but MG and GG were getting older and, although they would never say so, I wondered if it might be too much for them. With a couple of weeks left to think about it I put it to the back of my mind and turned instead to planning a list of items to move into town for safe keeping: passports, birth certificates, citizenship and other important documents, photo albums, recipes, some jewellery and a few paintings – articles which would be difficult to replace if a tracer set fire to the thatch. The Flemings would be happy to store those too.

That evening I broke with routine and went out hunting with Tim. I'd hunted regularly when living in the low veldt but since shooting a leopard that had been killing calves, only to open her up and discover furry twin cubs inside, I'd been unable to pull the trigger again. She'd had to be shot. She'd been caught in a wire snare and all but chewed her paw off trying to release herself, but somehow it still haunted me. However, shooting for the pot was a different matter, a way of life for farmers, and by the time we returned at sundown we'd bagged several guinea fowl, a brace of partridges and a good sized impala which Peter hung and eventually turned into an excellent curry which, a few nights later, he presented for dinner before our weekly game of bridge with Molly and Humphrey. We'd agreed that, rather than play for money, losers would take the winners out to dinner in Bulawayo at the end of the year, although how this would be accomplished we didn't know. We would have to spend the night in town and not everyone would be thrilled at the thought of having eight extra to stay for the night. Humphrey's deafness during dinner didn't interfere with his game afterwards and he was on a winning streak when a sudden stab of pain made me wince. He stood up, alarmed.

"It's time to go home Molly," he said throwing his cards down.

I laughed. "Indigestion. That's all. It's Peter's curry. It's not the baby, if that's what you're thinking. Not yet." But his hearing was no longer acute and he vanished through the door with Molly hurrying after him. Soon after midnight it was obvious that Humphrey had been right, the baby was not going to wait until morning. When Tim rang her at 1am Molly got up, bravely struggled through the kitchen garden in her nightie and, half asleep, climbed into a bed next to the night nursery. It couldn't have been more inconvenient for everyone. As we raced for Bulawayo, praying for a clear road, Paul managed to catch the surgeon who was packing his car to leave for a holiday in Moçambique and by the time we drew up at the Lady Rodwell they were both already there, scrubbed up, waiting in theatre. Familiar hospital smells of antiseptics and, was it ammonia? assailed us as I overheard Eric say to Paul.

"It's rather premature but we can't wait."

"Well please don't you do anything premature – make sure I'm asleep!" I feebly joked before the relief of drifting off under anaesthetic.

Suddenly I felt pain but was unable to move. I heard a voice far off.

"She's waking up," the anaesthetist said matter of factly.

"Don't worry, we're nearly finished," Eric replied.

There were only a few stitches to go and I felt every one of them. All along I'd been certain this baby was another boy, there were no doubts, I wanted another boy. Another boy would be perfect. The nurse leaned over me. I knew she was going to say: "You have a lovely brother for David and James."

She said: "Mrs Gibbs, you have a lovely baby girl." *What? What did she say?* Joy, quite inexpressible came in like a flash flood. I had no idea I'd wanted a girl. This girl and no other – tiny, yellow and beautiful. A boy would not have been perfect at all. This was.

Paul was the first to put his head around the door.

I grinned at him. "It may not be the 14th but it is the 7th and it's still a Sunday!"

20

Caroline spent her first days in a Humid crib under blue fluorescent Bili lights to reduce her jaundice and, although physically small and frail, her spirit was robust and we knew she would make it. Paul and Paddy insisted, just to be certain, that we stayed with them in Bulawayo after leaving hospital until she no longer needed her oxygen cylinder near by. But, despite the warmth and kindness of the Fehrsens and their staff, I longed to take Caroline home, to return to the family and to the familiarity of the bush. I even missed Peter's breakfasts of burnt toast and vulcanized eggs, but it was three weeks before Paul eventually allowed us to go back to Bonisa.

It was a lovely fresh sunny morning when we collected the other children from the Flemings and drove home to be greeted by an overjoyed Manka, and a curious Peter. David, Sarah and James doted on their new sister and I was glad we still had a few months ahead to be together on Bonisa before it was time for David to begin boarding school in Bulawayo. We were delighted when both Simon Rhodes and Nick Mangnall agreed to be Godfathers to Caroline and, although Nick and some of the other Godparents were not able to be present, it was a special service conducted by The Rev Jonathan Siyachitema, who married us, and had also christened James marking his first white baptism.

Caroline wasn't the only new life on the farm that month. One morning some time after our return Peter burst into the schoolroom.

"Nkosikasi, come quickly. Koki she's having babies on the sofa. James is helping her. Come very quickly."

We ran to the drawing room. Although Koki looked pure Rhodesian Ridgeback she also had Alsatian blood – not much, but I didn't trust it. We reached the door just in time to see her third pup begin to emerge, watched by James standing to one side. Then he lent over, took hold of the slippery little body and began pulling. I leapt forward but Koki got to him first. Swinging her head around, she opened her mouth, clamped her jaws over his face and slowly, deliberately and very gently, pulled him away leaving the half delivered puppy hanging from her. I grabbed James and although he clung to me, bewildered, there was not a mark on his face.

"Good girl Koki," David said as he came in and strode over to pat her.

"Leave her alone," I bellowed.

"Is very good dog," Peter stood in the doorway, watching in amazement. "But too sorry for the sofa Madam."

I could not have cared less for the sofa, in fact I was secretly pleased having looked for several months for an excuse to have it re-covered.

Over the following days Koki made it known she regarded our babies as being of equal status. She took my arm, leading me to her basket to admire her puppies and in exchange she took every opportunity, when she thought no one was watching, to lean into Caroline's basket and lick her.

The day MG, GG, Paddy, Paul and Peter and Jill Baker came out for lunch Monica drove up from Red Bank Cottage, unannounced, with a card for Caroline and to use the telephone. The curfew, re-instated after the battle in Entumbane, remained in place and although there had been an uneasy lull in reported incidents, visitors still preferred to come out in convoy when possible. Monica knew our visitors slightly but refused my invitation to join us for lunch, and after a lengthy telephone call followed by a brief glance at Caroline, she left leaving eddies of dust down the track in her wake.

John had received a report giving the 'all clear' in the area and I so took the Flemings, Fehrsens and Bakers for a walk down to the track, crisscrossed with game trails until we arrived at the dam. A welcome cool breeze blew off the water. The fishing boats had pulled up, their nets spread over the bank and although there weren't any game animals to be seen at that time of day, a flotilla of pelicans glided over the surface of the water between a sprinkling of mallards, white-faced duck and one lone Ethiopian snipe. We sat on the bank enjoying the coolness and peace, talking and speculating, as always, about 'the situation' and how it affected us all in different ways. Conversations everywhere invariably came back to the subject, occasionally new information came to light but solutions were never found.

Paddy said she had volunteered to assist in a soup kitchen for our troops. "There is so little we can do to help, other than that. It's very frustrating," she said. I asked GG if she would take back the parcel of important documents and photo albums I'd prepared for safe keeping: "Of course," she said. "You should remove precious things that would be difficult to replace, but as for anything else, well, take a chance. Don't even make a list. Enjoy living with what you have and then, if you lose everything an accurate inventory of what you did have might be considered unimportant and insurance won't pay." I'd been slowly learning during those days to hold on to an appreciation of my most loved (mainly inherited) material things while at the same time distancing myself more from them. It was a tough, deliberate discipline until eventually it became a reality.

As the sun climbed higher in the otherwise empty blue sky, scorching exposed arms and legs, we walked back to the house for a drink before lunch under the shade of the verandah where Tim joined us on his return from town.

"Sorry I'm a bit late," he said. "I stopped on the Nyama Road to help Betty Miller change a tyre. She was returning from Bulawayo with supplies for her father's staff stationed at Bembezi. They'd asked him to go out and pick up their families because the 'army' had shot twelve of their men. Apparently the victims had identity disks which included the word 'Rhodesia'. They're all dead. She's now worried about what on earth they were going to do with the surviving families."

We'd been hearing for some time about increasing numbers of orphans, of discoveries of shallow graves, sometimes containing large numbers of bodies, and we were sure there were many others we didn't know about. Missions and African communities took in survivors but it put a strain on their finances and resources.

As we went through to the dining room for lunch, Agric-Alert spluttered, and Bronco Greaves came through saying his herd boys had reported a 'sighting' of a large group down near Fountain Farm. It seemed to be heading in the direction of the Olds or Beales. "No idea how many of the buggers there are," he said. The Beales, Fountain Farm and the Olds on Compensation were all on the far side of Nyamandhlovu, but terrorists moved quickly through the bush and we advised the Flemings, Fehrsens and Bakers to return to Bulawayo in the early afternoon in case they decided to come this way.

That night I dreamt the house was full of people. Outside the security fence we were surrounded by terrorists, madness fuelled by smoking mbange, brandishing weapons, chanting ancient Shona war slogans of blood lust which, despite not being familiar with Shona, I could strangely understand. As they broke through the fence and swarmed across the garden I woke sharply, paralysed with fear, sweating. Unable to calm down I got up, weakly struggled into a dressing gown and, with clammy hands, strapped on my FN Browning. It was only a dream I kept telling myself as I left Tim sleeping soundly and tiptoed out of the bedroom. The sweet scent of the moonflower filled the moonlit courtyard and the stone slab paths were cool and reassuring under my bare feet. As I paused in the kitchen doorway feeling for the light switch a movement caught my eye. Something to do with the window opposite. Panic flooded through me and I pulled out my pistol.

Where were the dogs? Why were they silent?

A man, silhouetted against bright moonlight, a rifle slung over his shoulder, reached through the open window.

A shot sliced through the silent darkness. Dogs barking. *Did I do that?*

"No Madam! No! Don't shoot! Don't shoot Madam! It's me Madam! It's Sixpence!"

"Sixpence? You're Sixpence? What the hell are you doing?"

"Sorry Madam. I am stealing Madam. Too sorry Madam."

"Sorry? You're only sorry because you are still alive to feel sorry."

Tim appeared in the doorway. "What's going on?" he asked, then angrily turned on Sixpence. "Give that weapon to me. Where's the other guard?"

The second guard ran up behind Sixpence, wrenched the rifle off his shoulder and passed it through the window to Tim.

"I'll tell Fawcett's Security to take you away in the morning. You're sacked. Until then you will spend the rest of the night in the driver's room at the back. Understood?"

"Yes Sir, yes Madam. I understand," and hanging his head, he clapped his hands together."

21

It was sometime since I'd checked the bee house and, for no particular reason (apart from the obvious) I became unhappy about going out at night. And so one morning, several weeks later, after all farmers had been accounted for on 6am Roll-Call, I went down to check them before the heat of the day made them testy. Despite my temporary neglect they were thriving and I went on to meet David in the schoolroom. David's desire for learning seemed insatiable. Our correspondence school supervisor gave encouragement in every yellow bag and I had begun to look forward to our morning lessons in a way I'd not have thought possible. We were so engrossed in our work that morning we didn't notice the time and Peter had to call us for breakfast.

Tim came in with a basket of grapefruit from the orchard and had just sat down to join us.

Suddenly the crystal clear morning shattered.

Peter jumped when the first alarm pierced the air, and muttered something in Sindebele. Hot coffee poured from his tray down his white apron and khaki trousers and ran scalding on to his bare feet. The dining room fell silent. We looked at the each other.

Who now? hung unspoken, suspended, in the air.

Peter produced a cloth and stooped to mop the floor.

The alarm, sprang to life again – automatically over-riding volume controls, swelling through a crescendo, reverberating across the courtyard. We rose swiftly from the table and rushed to the Agric-Alert set in the bedroom, aware that every farmer in the district would be doing the same. Eventually the alarm died away, normal volume resumed and the familiar voice of Sunray from Camp Headquarters crackled through.

"Six Three, Six Three ... this is Control... Over."

Pause. No response. We scanned down the Roll-Call list.

Six one... Six Two... Six Three... *Oh God! The old Beales*.

135

"Six Three, Six Three, Six Three, This is Control... Come in please. Over."

The set spluttered. The voice again, more urgent this time:

"Control calling Six Three.... *Do you Read?*"

Silence.

"OK Six Three, will try land line. Stand by."

Silence. Endless, nerve stretching. Random thoughts. *Where's Monica? Dear God, please, not there with them.*

"Calling all stations... All stations... this is Control... PATU Sticks[18] mobilise immediately, repeat, immediately, proceed along green route into 63."

Turning from the set I saw that Tim had already discarded his khakis in anticipation and was dragging on his camo-kit. I snatched a green water bottle from the webbing, darted into the bathroom, filled it with water and returned just as he was buckling up his high, leather boots. The disembodied voice resumed.

"Four One... this is Control. Stand by."

I picked up the hand set.

"Roger Control this is Four One. Standing by. Over and out."

The Land Rover, supplied by security forces and known as 'The Friendly', stood operationally prepared in the back yard. Painted in camouflage, it was old, square and heavy to steer due to the additions of armour plating underneath, to protect against land mines, and roll-bars, fitted like ribs over the open back.

Racing through the now familiar procedure. Tim snatched up the G3 with spare magazines and grenades while Mkava grabbed rat packs and boxes of ammo. I stuffed a jersey in to a bag with Molly's fruit cake – just in case the follow up lasted longer than the rations (and also because by now there were several cakes stacked in the freezer and I didn't want to hurt her feelings) and handed it to Tim. With the Friendly loaded, Mkava ran ahead to open the security gates as Tim leapt in and took off in a cloud of dust and disappeared over the lip of the escarpment. Mkava slowly closed the security gates again.

---

18 Police Anti Terrorist Unit.

We exchanged glances but didn't speak and I walked back along the sandy track, now rapidly warming in the sun, to the homestead.

Energy pumped restlessly through me. I walked back through the courtyard, with a heightened awareness of the scents from the thickly planted shrubs, all especially chosen for their luxuriant foliage and soft colours in pink, white and green. From the fountain in the middle of the courtyard water plumed several feet into the air and splashed loudly down into the surrounding fish pond. Splash, splash, splash – I vaguely wondered if goldfish got headaches and threw them a handful of fish-food before wandering aimlessly onto the verandah and gazing out over the expanse of open plains. It was winter and spreading to the horizon was a sepia carpet of sand, dust, tufts of dry grass, and scrub with a few bare trees standing out as stark landmarks. The Kalahari making a bid to encroach. During the rainy season it was different. Then we would return to the verandah time after time anxiously scanning the skies for the promise of a dark smudge to drift, like blue/black ink dropped into water, from the Congo, on to our horizon. The days grew increasingly tense. Farmers became curt and irritable as, more often than not, the darkening clouds (and with it our hopes) dispersed, leaving us with only the wilting crops, brittle grass, short tempers and as the weeks wore on, despair. But when the clouds did develop and the winds blew the precious rain towards us, and lightning forked across the sky and the storm broke, all tension broke, the land refreshed, colours emerged from dust, and its vegetation washed clean.

I walked over to the map on the wall and stuck a blue pin on Beales Farm. The colour I'd chosen for attack. It would take Tim and his recce stick a long time to get there and I hoped it would not be too late.

The Agric-Alert fussed again from the bedroom but no one spoke. It was kept there partly because it was easier for me to answer when the first Roll-Calls began each morning, partly because it would be at hand in the event of a night attack and partly because, being in a fairly central position, reports and sit. coms. could be heard, blasting across the courtyard and throughout the homestead.

137

More crackling. The Member in Charge spoke:

"Four One, Four One… Control."

I stabbed a finger on the speak-button.

"Control, this is Four One; Go.'"

"Right, Four One, proceed to Base Camp asap. Copied?"

"Copied Control. The road? Over."

"Clear as far as known."

"Roger, thanks. Over and Out."

There was nothing for it but to take the children. Manka and Mkava had anticipated and were already prepared. We scooped up the children, with pre-packed books and toys. Mkava clutched my medical kit as I picked up my G3 and one spare magazine.

Mercifully the road was tarred, the only one in the district that was, and we covered the thirty or so miles in record time, singing children's songs and playing 'I spy', in reasonable confidence that, in the bitumen, any land mines would be easily spotted.

A guard, immaculate in his khakis with shiny brass and gleaming boots, held the gate open to the Camp. As we drove through with a wave, a broad white grin slashed across his face. We parked near the rudimentary building which served as both Nyamandhlovu Head Quarters for the Para-Military Police and also as the Joint Operations Command (JOC) Post.

Sunray[19] emerged on to the verandah from one of the two rooms to greet us.

"It's not good," he called. "The Beales are being casevaced… should be here any minute."

I settled Manka and the children on a rug under a sparse acacia several yards from the building and, leaving them to unpack their toys, followed Sunray into the office. It was a small cluttered room dominated by the large control board on the back wall. Call-sign numbers for the Agric-Alert systems of each homestead ran down the left hand side of the board, each with its own tiny light bulb and their corresponding name. Many of the numbers had been crudely

---

19 Sunray: the designated name for the Member-In-Charge

crossed out – testimony of a shrinking community. The light next to 'Six Three... Beale' still glowed red.

"Coffee?" Sunray asked, gesturing vaguely in the direction of a PC standing on duty in the doorway.

"No thanks," I replied. "Where's Tim?"

"Don't know. They've started the follow up – reckon there were about ten gooks."

By now it was mid-morning, the sun had risen higher and the chill given way to increasing heat. It was stifling in the little corrugated-iron roofed office and the combined smells of B.O., gun oil and leather drove me out onto the verandah again. Sunray followed and we stood together talking and occasionally waving to the children, who were happily making animals out of a roll of wire.

At last, beyond the security fence two vehicles, recklessly driven, came into view and skidded through the security gates. The first, an open Land Rover, pulled up sharply in front of the office enveloping us in a suffocating cloud of dust. We stepped off the verandah and looked over the side into the back.

"Shit!" exclaimed Sunray.

Old Mr Beale's body lay uncovered where it had been thrown, contorted and beaten to a pulp. His face, no longer there, was a seething black mask covered in gathering flies. The only thing recognisable about him was the awful green shirt he loved to wear and a surge of affection for it coursed through me.

A few Africans in camo stood around wondering what to do and Sunray, furious rounded on them. "Cover him. Damn it, man!" He rasped at no one in particular and turning abruptly he strode over to the other Land Rover, a covered one this time, which had stopped fifteen yards behind. He wrenched open the back door and held it open for me to climb inside.

Old Mrs Beale had been placed in the recovery position, her head wedged against the cab. She was an enormous woman and Mkava and I crawled over her with difficulty.

Although cold, clammy, in shock and deeply unconscious, she was still alive. The beatings to her head and upper body had left her face mottled and misshapen. Blood seeped from one ear. Livid, purple and black bruising marked the otherwise colourless skin of her body and from the blood encrusted wounds fresh blood still oozed.

An automatic check list ran through my mind: Airway: clear but could do with some assistance. Not a tracheotomy, I hoped. I'd not done one before and, although I would if necessary, the thought frightened me. Mkava helped me push an airway tube down her throat. No reflex. Well, at least she wouldn't be spitting it out and it may even hold her for a while. Pulse: rapid, thin and thready, typical of shock, but could also indicate internal haemorrhage. My mind raced, frantically trying to recall the army training on war-specific injuries. The sickly, sweet smell of blood mingled with acrid urine and the sweat of fear, was overwhelming. I had to concentrate not to faint. Or vomit.

Think... Replacement fluids for shock but may increase pressure in head injuries.

One eye, so swollen that I fleetingly wondered if it was still there, steadfastly refused to be prized open, making it impossible to compare pupils and assess brain damage.

The vital signs were weakening. Without a drip she would soon die from shock. Even with one would she make it? *Would she want to live? Had she seen her husband killed? Who had been first?* The possibility of rape flashed through my mind, but that, thank goodness, was irrelevant for the moment and for someone else to determine later.

Mkava found the drip and held the bag high. I applied the tourniquet and unsheathed the needle.

Her veins collapsed. *Damn!* The only option now was to do a 'cut-down' of the vein.

Sweat streamed down our faces into our eyes and a nauseating stench filled the interior of the Land Rover. I turned to open a widow. It was stiff and curtained with dust on the outside. Mkava gave it a thump and, as it flew open, horror spiralled up through me into a frozen panic.

David had broken free from Manka under the acacia and was running towards the other Land Rover. Trapped inside, I shouted at him to stop. He ran on, out-pacing Manka and pulled himself up to stand on the wheel hub and look over the side of the open back. In seconds Manka was behind him, wrapping her arms around his small, rigid body as she gently peeled his fingers off the edge. She lifted him down, holding him close, rocking him and making little crooning noises.

I began to scramble out over Old Mrs Beale, but Mkava was holding the scalpel in his out-stretched hand – a steadying look in his eye. As I attached the blade ready for the first incision, a low, endlessly long sigh, came from somewhere deep down inside Mrs Beale.

It took a moment to realise that it was her last breath. She was gone.

Bastards, inside me shrieked. *Bastards*.

Mkava rapidly re-assembled the medical bag and crawled out of the Land Rover. I followed.

Hot, thick tears of rage and grief blinded me and he extended an arm to support me down the step.

"Aach... Too sorry Nkosikasi," he said, "Too, too sorry.'"

And he turned his head away, ashamed.

22

We had driven back from the Police Camp to Bonisa in silence. The younger children slept while David and Mkava stared out of their windows. I tried to talk with David but he just looked at me blankly and when he'd gone to bed I returned to the map on the verandah, removed the blue pin on Beale's farm and replaced it with two red ones. It was another day before Tim came home. He said they had caught up with some of the group and engaged them in a fire fight but, if they'd inflicted injuries, there were no signs that they'd had a kill.

Over the coming weeks and months I tried to draw David out, to persuade him to talk over the incidents at the Police Camp but despite my efforts he locked the memories inside, covered them over, and never referred to the events of that day again.

It was 1981 and as his seventh birthday approached we began making preparations for him to begin school in Bulawayo. Whitestone School was re-opening following a period of closure during the early years of the bush war and it gave great pleasure to MG and GG that their own grandson would be in the first intake of pupils. It also provided boarding for boys from the outlying areas, and had been a success from the beginning. Pupils were drawn from all over Matabeleland and beyond. Seretse Khama, President of neighbouring Botswana, had caused a commotion in South Africa and amongst the tribal elders of the Bamangwato by marrying a white English woman, Ruth Williams, and, as Rhodesia remained largely unconcerned, Bulawayo seemed the obvious place to educate their sons.

Spread over the veldt along the edge of their Mzinzini Estate six miles south of Bulawayo, MG and GG built schoolrooms, dormitories and a small thatched chapel complete with custom-made Mukwa pews. They added a swimming pool, tennis courts and sports field with cricket pavilion. Substantial houses for staff nestled privately amongst the rocks of surrounding kopjes and, in order to make a professional start, they recruited a headmaster and teachers from England. And now, after several years, it was re-opening.

"You will be safe here David," I assured him when we took him there on the first day.

"But you're not safe," he shot back, clinging to me weeping. "And anyway they don't kill children."

We were not to know then how wrong he was, and I reminded him that we were constantly vigilant, we took every precaution and couldn't be more cautious. Mrs McIntyre, the house mistress, gently peeled his arms off me, wrapping him in her own, and held him tight. Over his shoulder she mouthed imploringly: "Go! go quickly."

"It's not the end of the world, it's only a new stage in life," Tim said as we drove away. But I was bound up in David's anguish, aware that, since Duncan's death and S'iponono's forced return to her tribe in Botswana when her own beloved son was mistreated by her husband's second wife, I had been the only constant factor, his security, in life and as we drove home I wept on the inside.

We arrived back in time to hear the sound of Sunray's voice blasting out through the gauze bedroom door into the courtyard.

"Calling all stations; all stations. This is Control."

Several call-signs answered:

"Come in Control. Reading you strength 5."

"Roger. All stations, a group of Fifth Brigade reported in the area, estimated to be eighty strong. That's Eight Zero. Be vigilant. Report any sightings asap. Over and Out."

I asked Peter to bring tea to the verandah and as I sank into a chair and lit a cigarette Yvonne Sharp's voice came on.

"Control. My labour force are running away in all directions. The herd boy said it was Fifth Brigade's doing." No one else responded.

Oh Hell. The Sharps, our nearest neighbours, were just across the Khami on Whinburn Farm. I hoped their unwanted visitors were going the other way.

A few minutes later the land line rang.

"You might like to know," Yvonne said, "they came to the house and asked for cold water. I told them where the tap was but they insisted they wanted very cold water, so I had to give them some from the fridge. They were OK, but they did say that anyone who ran away would be shot." I went and told Peter to tell the other house staff, if Fifth Brigade turn up, don't run.

An hour later she rang again.

"They're on their way over to you, probably through Thorn Valley. This lot don't have vehicles, they're coming on foot. At least that's what the herd boy says." I asked her to ring JOC in Nyamandhlovu and report it while I got the message to John who, after quickly alerting the dairy, the workshop boys and the outside labour force, drove down to the compound to warn the women and children. We hoped for the loyalty of the two hundred and sixty people living on the farm, but couldn't guarantee it; after all, they and their families were also in danger and, if any of them were beaten, threatened or killed some may capitulate, tell of our movements or lead them to the house, and who could blame them?

It didn't take the Red Berets long to cover the distance between Whinburn and Bonisa. They stormed into the compound, brandishing AKs, kicking over cooking pots, scattering scrawny chickens and emaciated dogs and sending women and children scurrying for cover. But after hitting one woman, and making gestures with bayonets, they calmed down and announced that they wanted to talk. And talk they did, Mkava reported later. They bragged about killing people in the Kezi and other areas in order to extract information. They asked questions about dissidents, and laid down ground rules for the dairy workers, commanding them to only work the hours that they, the Fifth Brigade, would dictate. They would remain in the area, they said, and, apart from the direct route to and from work, there was to be no movement after dark. Especially there was to be no movement around Red Bank Siding. Any one seen there would be shot and so would anyone who ran.

After a while John, who had returned and joined me on the verandah, became uneasy about Mkava's safety. There was nothing specific, he said, just a feeling. He went back to the compound and politely explained to the Red Berets that Mkava was needed up at the house, that something had gone wrong with the honey extractor which only Mkava knew how to put right. Slightly bewildered, but grateful, Mkava returned with John who locked the security gates behind them and insisted that Mkava slept in the back quarters, behind the kitchen, that night. And so, at 2am, when the soldiers returned to the compound looking for him, he wasn't there. Angry and frustrated, they 'thumped a few women', including his wife.

"Aaah, is alright Madam," he said later when I commiserated. "They only hit her once."

Although the compound was only as few hundred yards from Red Bank Cottage, Monica was miraculously ignored by Fifth Brigade, and remained unperturbed. I was glad, although, looking at the state of her cottage and 'garden', I privately thought a visit which resulted in a good thumping for Mpofu wouldn't go a miss.

David was never far from my mind and it was a great relief when, a few days after school began, Mrs McIntyre rang to assure us that he was fine.

"He's interested in everything, doing well and enjoying lessons, and although he misses you all, and Koki, he's already made friends," she said. "There's Stephan, Rowen Elmes and the two little Tavenor girls, Tammy and Candy. Their grandparents live on Secret Valley Farm, which can't be far from you. It's just off the Nyamandhlovu Road."

"I know Rowen but not the others," I told her., "Is David still concerned about us?" She avoided giving a direct answer.

"He'll be fine. It's always difficult at first, but they settle down and he's also friends with Ian Khama, a nice boy – they compete with each other in Ndebele lessons." I hoped she was right and that he was being kept so busy he didn't have much time for his imagination to dwell on fears about us.

With David settled in to weekly boarding it was time to turn my attention to teaching Sarah. I set about making a few changes to the Bonisa schoolroom to make it more personal for Sarah and once again the tractor began arriving back from town with the heavy, waterproof, yellow correspondence school parcels in the mail bag. Sarah proved very different from David. She would sometimes turn up for lessons clutching a small posy of flowers for our work table; she arranged the more attractive items on the nature table in the front and put the jars of snakes to the back and she was less distracted by tractors on the front lands than David had been. Her interests were different too and it took a little while for me to adjust to the feminine approach.

23

Dissident activity and the sporadic appearances of Fifth Brigade kept us vigilant. Increasing for a while, then dying down, only to erupt again in unexpected places, in Matabeleland if not always in the Nyamandhlovu district. At Filabusi, Harold Hilton-Barber was gunned down as he went to pay his workers; Richard Trotter took a hit when he stopped to open a gate to his emerald mine in the same area, but survived; Dr Peter Gradewell and his niece Donna Clark were murdered at a cattle dip near Plumtree; and further north, Phil Ellmen-Brown was shot at his homestead in Lupane.

The numbers of visiting journalists also increased, both English speaking and foreign. They came from Europe, Asia and Australasia but, strangely, none at all, that we knew of, came from America. The government reacted by issuing a banning order against all media planning to visit Matabeleland. Press and television journalists found themselves stopped at the airport and relieved of their cameras and films. But a few of the more tenacious ones managed to slip in, and I admired their imagination and courage. They came quietly on back-tracks, across farms and through river beds; or disguised as fertilizer salesmen or irrigation consultants, or vets; and to support their covers they drove down the Nyamandhlovu Road from Bulawayo with a few pipes or sacks of grain thrown causally into the back of their open pickups; or books on animal husbandry lying on the front seat. One especially innovative crew, when stopped at the road blocks, claimed to be old friends of the family and to prove it produced photos of us spliced together with photos of them, although those with access to the international press may have recognised the recently published images.

At first I refused to talk to the media. I worried that exposure would make us vulnerable, but Tim said they were our secret weapon and went out of his way to make himself available for interviews. When he was quoted in both South Africa and the UK as saying: "In

Matabeleland it's worse now than it was during the seven years of war before Independence." I was apprehensive of a backlash. But it didn't happen and gradually I came to see that although there may be risks of repercussions, the risks in 'normal' daily life were great anyway, and there was no other way of revealing the full extent of the hidden evil of the massacres and violence. Most media visitors proved to be thoroughly honourable, reporting accurately, disguising their sources and, when speaking with the local people, taking only first-hand accounts of atrocities. It was this that finally won me over. A few other farmers also spoke out. Broncho Greaves spoke recklessly, I thought, but others were too cautious. One was quoted in the Cape Argus as saying: "Trouble is with so many people running around with guns you don't know who is a bloody dissident." Which was true, but he failed to mention Fifth Brigade who carried out so much of the torture and murder and then blamed it on the dissidents. Other farmers clammed up completely, prompting the Rand Daily Mail to claim that Nyamandhlovu had developed a 'laager mentality', and in no time at all the media crews knew who would co-operate and who to avoid.

Tim had been spending more time in Harare on the Trade Development business between France and Zimbabwe, in partnership with a Frenchman named Jacques Schwartz and Senator John Shoniwa. During his time away John ran the farm efficiently and kept a constant ear to the ground regarding security matters. The workers liked him, and brought any information or rumour they could, leaving John to determine the relevance. I felt safe having John around. With his canny perception he kept an eye, not only on his own family but on ours and on Monica who, although she annoyed him, he regarded as part of his responsibilities.

And then we bought a gold mine or, more accurately, we bought a hole in the ground fifty miles south of Bonisa in the Tribal Trust Lands of Esigodini. The area breathed hostility. Hilly, rocky, arid terrain made desolate by over-grazing and deforestation by tribesmen who felled trees to build their kias and cooking fires. Little top-soil remained in which to plant crops beyond a few mealies and what was there was taken up by the wind. In summer months unbearable heat radiated from the surface rocks, but underground, tunnels, cool and inviting, contained seams of gold. They were thought to be the remains of abandoned ancient workings from the days of King Solomon when, thousands of years ago, the land was known as Monomotapa.

More recently, our 'hole' had been mined successfully by German partners, but they were interned during the Second World War, their equipment looted and many of the tunnels blown up. All that remained now was a hole, five feet in diameter and a hundred feet deep, which didn't look promising.

Knowing nothing at all about mining, except that it required abundant water, and having established that this was available from nearby bore holes, we bought the 'hole' and renamed it Ngede – the Honey Guide, the bird which was said to unerringly lead those who followed it to wild hives dripping with golden honey, and we hoped the name would also evoke some form of guidance to find the line of lode, dripping with seams of gold!

The Department of Mines offered a great deal of help. We would need a mill, they said, several cyanide tanks, and a crucible for smelting the ore; and they told us how to go about finding most of these necessities secondhand. One day they rang and said they had information regarding a three-stamp mill, abandoned but still standing, on an unnamed farm at Turk Mine east of Bulawayo, but they couldn't help us more than that. "Just pitch up at Turk Mine and ask someone if they know of it," the helpful clerk said, and with less than even vague directions we set off hoping to locate both the unnamed farm and unknown mill.

Heat shimmered off the tarmac and in the distance a donkey cart approached, seemingly floating above the road out of the mirage. We stopped and asked for any information the driver might have.

"Just follow the dirty road," he said. And we did, for miles and miles, through dry scrub-land, assailed by hot dust, until eventually we arrived at what looked as if it had been a small, attractive homestead long ago, but was now little more than an unkempt hovel. The equally unkempt and wary looking owner emerged on to the veranda. He didn't offer refreshments, which immediately labelled him as either mean or an outsider, but he did say he would sell us the three-stamp mill for very little on condition that we paid cash, now, dismantled and removed it ourselves, and did it soon. I had a curious feeling that, although he probably did own the farm, he may not have actually owned the mill; but it had obviously been standing there, disused, for a long time and all we could do was take his word for it. No paperwork changed hands, only bank notes.

From where we stood, looking up at the enormous structure, it did not seem as if it would be possible to take the huge, thick and heavy timbers apart, let alone transport them, with their conveyor belt, to our 'hole' – the best part of a hundred miles away. But somehow, with the help of Mkava and one or two locals who had climbed into the pick-up hoping for a ride into town and were unfortunate enough to find themselves involved in the hot, dirty work, we managed it and, taking the curfew into account, we eventually set off for home, instead of Ngede, by mid afternoon. With the wide, dangerously swaying load, we hoped for a clear run and that any other transport we might meet would know and observe the rule that said vehicles going into a town had precedence over those going out. We were lucky. Other than a bus bearing a large placard across the front reading: "SORRY NO GOATS", and a low cart pulled by Africaaner-looking cattle being encouraged by a driver with a long pointed whip, the road was deserted and we arrived back at Bonisa exhausted, wondering if the farmer had been right and we were, after all, mad.

The next day we left early taking a few of the farm workers to help to transport the mill to Esigodini. Esigodini, previously named Essexvale, was the birth-place and home of the Reverend Canaan Banana – an Ndebele appointed by Robert Mugabe (who considered him to be more malleable and therefore a safer pair of hands than Joshua Nkomo) to become the first President of the New Zimbabwe. It was also Mugabe's way of paying lip service to the tribal balance of power. Canaan Banana, a quirky, liberal theologian promptly, and with much approval, adapted the Lord's Prayer, to say: 'Teach us to demand our share of the gold and forgive us our docility' and his many sons still lived in the hills and villages around Esigodini. Canaan Banana held the Presidency for seven years. As the problems in Matabeleland increased, he made himself popular by negotiating hard to have the Fifth Brigade removed. Even those who regarded him as a stooge figure-head applauded him.

And then one day he walked over the border into Botswana and vanished. The first we knew of it was on opening the *Bulawayo Chronicle* one morning to headlines screaming: "Yes! We have no Banana!" But why he'd done it remained a mystery until he was eventually found, and brought back to public pronouncements of lavish praise from Mugabe who lauded him as "a very special gift to the nation" and then promptly had him arrested, tried, and convicted, on eleven counts of sodomy.

Arriving at our 'hole' we realised the enormity of the task ahead and how little we were prepared for it. All of a sudden, from behind a kopje, several local tribesmen appeared, arranged themselves in a semicircle around us and stood silently watching.

What now? I'd been feeling jumpy since Tim Sutton, an Esigodini farm manager, had been shot dead recently.

Then an old man spoke. In good English he said: "We are gold miners. We are all experts. We want jobs."

Despite their tatty, dusty clothes, their gnarled hands and leathery faces, to me they looked like a heavenly host of angels, answering our need for help… and so they turned out to be.

Having conferred with the others, the old man stepped forward again.

"I am Solomon," he said. "And some of these ones behind me are Bananas. I worked this mine when I was a picannin and the Germans were here. I will work it again, if you would like, but I only work if I am 'Boss Boy'."

He looked so dignified and ancient as to appear to be a contemporary of the original Biblical Solomon, his face bearing witness to years of living under harsh conditions. But his eyes were deep and steady and I sensed something trustworthy in this upright old man, something in his natural pride and humility.

We agreed to Solomon's terms and under his supervision the work team showed themselves to be every bit as experienced as he'd claimed. They made erecting the three-stamp mill look effortless, and turned to constructing a pulley system over the shaft to which they attached a rope with a tin bucket on the other end. It was a small bucket. There was just enough room for one foot to stand tippy-toed on the bottom, and it was rusty. John was horrified when he saw it sometime later and he cut a milk can in half, welded a firm band to it and attached it to the rope. As it lowered us one at a time, bouncing from wall to wall down the shaft, we clung to the rope, in terror. From the first platform a tunnel went off along the seam and then plunged down another hundred feet, following the line of lode, in which tiny glints could be easily seen.

Solomon gave his heart to the mine with the strength and energy of a much younger man, and he appeared impervious to both heat and fatigue. Under his instruction the blasted rock was brought up in the bucket from deep underground and tipped onto a table to be crushed under the hammers of the three-stamp mill. The resulting ore then travelled by conveyor belt out to one of the thousand-gallon cyanide tanks, where it was tipped in and joined the sludge.

Solomon took us to one side and spoke assuredly. "It is better you smelt the gold away from here," he said. Although we trusted Solomon we were less certain of other, younger ones living in the Tribal Trust Land, or for that matter their visitors, and so, recognising it would be foolish and unfair to put temptation so blatantly in the way, we took Solomon's advice and once a week loaded up the sludge from the cyanide tanks and took it to the crucible set up behind the kitchen in the Bonisa backyard. As the fire got hotter, the ugly grey sludge heated up, and slowly silver and gold separated out and sank to the bottom. The heavier gold formed a button on the very bottom and above it settled a shiny layer of silver. We were not, by law, permitted to keep the gold, which had to be assayed and sold to the Reserve Bank, but they weren't interested in silver and over time we accumulated many ounces of it. I wanted to do something with it – perhaps make it into some sort of keepsake for the children one day. I mentioned this to a friend who said he had the franchise for making medallions in Botswana and he offered to design and turn all the silver into attractive one ounce coins. I gave him all we produced and we were delighted with the result. On one side of each coin he stamped a profile of David Livingstone and on the other, he put my favourite antelope, the Sable, standing majestically aloof on a small rise and very obviously male.

Tim spent quite a lot of time at Ngede, but I didn't go there as much as I'd have liked. Caroline was too young, and I felt it was important for Sarah to keep to the routine of spending each morning in the schoolroom. So James sometimes went by himself with Tim. He especially enjoyed Solomon, who looked at him gravely, treated him with respect and engaged him in serious conversations, consulting him on the condition of the stamps and the merits of purchasing a new bucket. Solomon stated that as James was only four he was still too young, but that when he grew up he, Solomon, would work for him, James. With equal gravity, James agreed.

24

Red Bank siding stood at the bottom of the farm track, about a mile from the homestead, and at night I loved lying in bed listening to the puffing and chugging of the old steam trains as they worked to gather speed for climbing the low hill before the straight run into Bulawayo. Since the bush war began, and we had come under curfew, the goods trains mainly ran at night. They travelled without lights, for security reasons, which was hazardous, but each engine had been fitted with a huge 'cow catcher' on the front — more like an 'elephant catcher' we thought and they did very occasionally run into elephant, but that was usually further north, nearer the Zambezi Valley.

The parcel we were expecting had not arrived yesterday and we decided to see if it was on this morning's passenger train from Victoria Falls which would have been unusual, but you never knew these days.

Mkava moved further down the platform and squatted on his haunches a short distance away from me. There were a few other people on the platform, perhaps eight or nine, also waiting patiently in the expectation that a train would eventually arrive, and I wondered how long they had already been there, for time did not mean much here. I recognised most of them. They often visited our farm workers, coming over from Stratford's farm, usually at weekends, to join in our compound's weekly beer-drink on a Saturday night. They were all typical Ndebele — tall, rangy, proud and content. Secure in their identity as 'the warrior tribe', they did not much aspire to material things which was just as well, for chances of gaining worldly goods were slim. They chatted easily amongst themselves with the familiarity of families and old friends, and from time to time one would separate out, stroll to the edge of the platform and, with a hand shielding his eyes against the scorching sun, scan the horizon for the first tell-tale plumes of smoke.

Several years of drought had all but turned the veldt into a dust bowl. Heat and dust pervaded everything, bleaching the colour out of the bush during the day, and producing spectacular sunsets in the evenings.

Off to the right a small herd of impala grazed peacefully on the little grass there was, largely ignoring their exuberant young, frolicking energetically around them. The adults were used to the trains by now and rarely showed more than mild interest, briefly lifting their heads to watch, while continuing to chew on tufts of dry grass dangling from their mouths.

At last a dark smudge appeared in the distance. Everyone stared, concentrating on the rhythmical puffs of black plumes coming closer and closer until the familiar chugging of the engine could be heard and it came slowly into view. The straggly group began gathering up their few belongings, checking they had everything, gripping onto young hands and preparing to board.

As the train approached I waved a greeting to the driver. His white, coal-streaked face stared straight ahead, deliberately ignoring me.

That's odd, I thought, he was usually the one to wave first.

There were few carriages behind the engine today, only three plus the guard's van at the back, each one a dark brown with Rhodesia Railways emblazoned in yellow above the windows. Slowly, fussily it drew into the siding, let out a long sigh and came to a halt.

Then... nothing happened. Nothing at all.

After a brief moment of uncertainty I suddenly became aware that Mkava had stood up and moved closer to me. Very slowly his hand came up and rested on my arm.

Why was he touching me? He never touched me.

A sudden gust of wind whipped up dust and drove a small whirlwind towards the platform. The edge of it caught us, enveloping us in the smell of dust and hot fresh dung but there was also another smell.

Almost imperceptibly Mkava tightened his grip on my arm. I turned to look at him but he was looking at the impala. The entire herd stood facing the train, heads raised, sniffing the air. They had stopped chewing. Even the young ones were still.

Something was wrong.

What was that smell? I faintly recognised it but my confused mind struggled to identify it. *Why hadn't the driver waved? Nor the coal tender for that matter. Where was the guard? Why hadn't he appeared before now? He always did.*

A baby strapped by a large green towel to its mother's back became restive. Little beads of sweat were glistening on the tiny black face, and the persistent flies darted around its eyes and nose making it fretful. The mother absentmindedly jiggled it up and down without effect. Finally she untied the towel, slid the baby around her side, brushed away the flies, and gave it her breast.

The guard leaned out of the van at the back, barking orders, in Shona, to the little group.

"Get back. No passengers today, train full."

Shona?

In spite of not understanding Shona the message was unmistakable, and the little group fell back a few paces, bumping into each other, looking bewildered.

Then it hit us all. He was not a Rhodesia Railways guard. He was in battle fatigues and on his head he wore the Red Beret of the Fifth Brigade.

Despite the heat, my blood turned to ice.

Oh God! No! Please not.

Several more Red Berets jumped down from the guard's van onto the platform, brandishing AK47's with fixed bayonets and gesticulated aggressively at the Ndebele who stood in front of them, paralysed.

Rooted to the spot I turned to Mkava again. He was not paying attention. His eyes were scanning the carriage windows – no sign of faces or full carriages – he looked at the doors and I followed his gaze to the bottom.

In frozen panic I began to understand.

That smell.

Waves of nausea washed through me. From the bottom of each carriage door oozed thick ropes of blood. Bright red. Gooey, sticky, sweet-smelling blood. Rapidly congealing and turning dark.

A cold evil dropped over us all, like a shroud.

Mkava abruptly released his grip on my arm and moved away. He suddenly appeared completely relaxed, almost confident. The rest of us watched in astonished horror as he sauntered nonchalantly towards the Red Berets. He called out something in their native Shona. They laughed and replied. A good natured banter struck up. He continued moving towards them, holding their attention. From the few words of Shona I did understand it seemed they were trading insults about the Ndebele – 'The Warrior Tribe' they scoffed – but now everyone would know that they, the Red Berets, were superior. They were invincible and they waved their weapons in the air to demonstrate it. Mkava joined in their smug laughter. They clearly assumed that he was one of them, not an equal of course because he was not in the Fifth Brigade, but a Shona nevertheless and therefore a friend.

After a few minutes the now all powerful Red Berets turned their attention back towards the group of Ndebeles.

They'd gone.

In that moment the laughter died. Silence fell and a wariness rose up. They looked uncertainly at Mkava.

Oh God. What now?

Everything was utterly, ominously still.

From the corner of my eye I saw the watching engine driver, his face grim. He turned away as if in slow motion and reached towards the whistle. It shrieked obscenely through the stillness. He did it again. The tension and, it seemed, the world, shattered.

The self-proclaimed warriors scrambled frenetically towards the guard's van, roughly pushing each other aside, knocking off berets and shouting abuse in the ugly rush not to be left behind.

Puffing and grinding, the train began easing itself out of the siding, trying rapidly to gather speed, ostensibly for the hill which was still some distance away, hauling itself up the incline.

It was only then that the driver waved. Leaning out of the engine he blew the whistle again – this time triumphantly.

Mkava remained silent and still. Again I turned to look at him. His face, no longer black, but a dirty grey. He was gazing at the globs and threads of blood now bubbling on the hot ballast next to the tracks, to the swarms of flies gathering, attracted by the stench.

I longed to reach out and put my hand on his arm but something warned me not to.

"Mkava?" His eyes met mine, but he said nothing. "Well done, Mkava."

"Nkosikasi", he said, "Come, mange wena chia telephone lapa Bulawayo Station."

And turning, he led the way back to the Land Rover.

25

It had been several weeks since Colin Shortis last visited and we were beginning to wish he would come again. We wanted to talk to him about Fifth Brigade. The web of ground-cover he'd set up worked effectively and, although he said he didn't use his information overtly, it did give him the advantage of knowing the right questions to put to Rex Nhongo, and for that local knowledge was essential. But Nyamandhlovu covered a huge area and from their training bases just over the borders of Botswana and Zambia, the ZIPRA terrorists had covered vast distances both during the war and now. Since they had been officially disbanded, it became obvious that as dissidents they were continuing the pattern. We needed to spread the net for gathering wider information. And so, when eventually Colin rang to say he would be visiting again we offered to take him down and introduce him to people we knew on the far side of Nyamandhlovu on one of the last cattle ranches before the Tjolotsho Tribal Trust Lands.

"How much have you told them?" he asked.

"Not much," I said. "Not on the party-line. Compensation is a ranch owned by the Olds family and run by Martin, one of the sons. It's about three-quarters of an hour from the Botswana border. There's no road and no border post there so the locals move freely from one side to the other."

"Sounds as if it might be helpful," Colin said. "We're not currently getting any information from that area."

"Martin also runs a butcher shop in Nyamandhlovu," I said. "It's the only one in the area and it's a magnet for locals, strangers and gossip."

We knew Martin and his wife Kathy better than we knew some of the other farmers in outlying areas. Since Kathy had married Martin and moved to Nyamandhlovu they'd become firm friends with our farm manager. They were all much of an age and occasionally, when they got together at the Zurnamer's cottage in New Farm, John and Sheena brought them up to the Bonisa homestead to see us.

When I rang Kathy I was careful not to say too much but I quickly realised I didn't have to – she immediately understood, and without asking any awkward questions invited us all to lunch the day after Colin arrived.

The long drive to Compensation took us west along a road of meltingly hot tarmac shimmering with an unreachable mirage. As we passed through Nyamandhlovu there were few signs of life apart from a shabby little building, surrounded by red dust, with women trying to sell water melons and men sitting drinking beer in the middle of the morning.

No vehicles waited outside the Farmer's Hall and even the Police Camp looked deserted. A little further on one straggler hung around the small clinic, and, apart from a few scrawny underfed dogs cowering around Martin's butcher shop, a small white building standing on the side of the road at the turn off, it looked deserted, the heat apparently having driven everyone in doors.

The signpost at the turnoff announced 'Silver Streams', Martin's parents' farm but there was nothing to indicate that Compensation lay next door to it, almost as if Alfie and Gloria Olds regarded Compensation as an appendage. As we turned off on to the dirt road the vegetation thinned to scrub bush. Heat haze, mingled with dust, hung over the track and we were glad we were driving west and not into the morning sun. A small Egyptian Cobra slithered off to one side of the road but other than the occasional bird nothing else moved.

The land around Compensation was low, flat and comparatively featureless. The house, a small square, whitewashed bungalow under a corrugated iron roof, looked exposed and vulnerable, particularly to rocket attack, and as we approached the security fence I was struck all over again by how much extra natural protection the Bonisa homestead provided, spreading, as it did, high on a plateau.

In a paddock to the right of the house, Martin's beloved horses stamped and shook their heads sending small clouds of flies

160

streaming into the air only to settle again as if playing some unkind and relentlessly unbeatable game.

Martin emerged from the front door, opened the security gates and waved us through indicating to us to park at the side of the house.

"Good to see you," he held out his hand as we climbed out of the Land Rover. "Come inside. How was the journey? No road-blocks?" A large, powerfully built man with most of his face covered by a bushy, black beard, he had seen a lot of action while serving as a Grey's Scout – one of the mounted units of the Special Forces – during the years of bush war. He didn't talk much about those days, but sometimes it was in his eyes.

He led us around stacks of sandbags piled up outside the windows to the front door.

"This is your secret weapon," Colin whispered to me inclining his head towards Kathy's battered wheelchair standing to one side. "The media would love this."

In the small sitting room the air hung still and stifling, imprisoned by the sandbags which prevented any breeze from circulating, and as our eyes adjusted to the darkness I noticed Colin observing every detail, paying particular attention to several cheerful paintings on the wall, all clearly done by the same hand.

"I did those," Kathy said appearing from the kitchen and negotiating her way around the furniture. "It's my hobby but since the security problems escalated we don't meet as a group as often as we used to. I do miss it." She moved towards the front door, pushing a small table out of the way with one of her crutches. "It's so hot in here, we'd be cooler outside under the trees."

"Is that thing yours?" Colin asked indicating towards an assault rifle propped up next to a baby's crib. "How ever do you manage it?"

"Both the baby and the G3 are mine," she said laughing.

Martin said. "She doesn't manage very well. But thankfully she hasn't been put to the test yet." And calling to Flora to bring a drinks tray outside, he led us out to chairs spread beneath a large shade tree in the garden.

"She was nearly put to the test," Martin continued, "a couple of weeks ago at a bloody nightmare of a road block. A Fifth Brigade one this time. We were going in separate cars to Bulawayo and Kath was following behind."

Kathy interrupted. "When we got to the road block, I was stuck, and just watched from behind as they surrounded Mart. Red Berets everywhere. One of them put his bayonet to Mart's throat. All I could do was immediately lock all my doors and thank goodness I did because then I was surrounded by the rest of them – yelling threats and insults they peered into the car, jabbed at the windows and jeered at Martine asleep in her carry cot on the back seat. 'Mafuta, mafuta... Fat baby,' they shouted. I thought they were going to kill us."

"They were drunk of course," Martin said. "Or high on dagga, or both. But then their O.C. appeared from the bush and amazingly they all beat a hasty retreat."

"I don't suppose there was anything you could do under those circumstances. Grovel?" Colin said.

"It was quite extraordinary," Martin grinned, "the O.C. apologised profusely! He said 'The bastards are drunk. Because of the pouring rain they've been shut inside drinking all day.' I'd never have thought a Fifth Brigade commander would have apologized for anything. Must be a first. But what he didn't know was that under the army poncho I was wearing because of the rain I had already drawn my sidearm – and was ready to shoot," he laughed. "It was a bit tight for a while. But then they let us go." He shook his head at the memory.

Colin looked thoughtful. I was curious but didn't like to ask what was going through his head and he changed the subject. "Do you get elephant down here?"

"Not for a while. A herd came through about three years ago but they didn't like being shot at and they scarpered," Martin replied. "We get a few leopard, but most of the big stuff has gone now."

After lunch Martin took Colin off to talk to some of the labour and other local tribesmen while Kathy and I stayed behind and talked. She was a realist. "I know that just because Mart has good labour relations doesn't necessarily mean we won't be attacked, and if we are I just hope Mart is here so there is at least one pair of legs between us."

"Was that worthwhile?" I asked Colin on the way home.

"It could be very good. We will have to wait and see what it produces," he said and glancing sideways at us added, "By the way, Rex Nhongo said you should be grateful to have Fifth Brigade here protecting you."

"Protecting us? They're creating havoc, they're doing most of the murders, and they're brutal. Did you challenge him about it?"

"He simply denies responsibility. You see Fifth Brigade doesn't come under the Army's jurisdiction – it is in the President's personal command. His Praetorian guard. It would take Mugabe's instructions to reign them in. That's not likely while he is determined to destroy Joshua Nkomo and his power base and there's not much we can do about that."

There was something warm and reliable about Colin that gave us confidence and when, a few weeks later, he made another fleeting visit, he came with a present for Kathy.

"We all know she can't possibly manoeuvre a G3, it's much too big and heavy," he said. "I've managed to get her an Uzi instead. Much better."

Where did he get an Israeli weapon from? We didn't know, but we were all glad that the shorter stock was easier for Kathy to control. Nevertheless the same hope remained – that she wouldn't be put to the test.

26

As Whitestone's exeat approached, David rang and asked if he could bring Rowen Elmes out to Bonisa for the weekend. Rowen's parents lived in Bulawayo, and although they spent much of their time in the bush, fishing on the Zambezi and hunting in the Valley, that was further north, where it had been relatively quiet. So I was surprised when they gave permission for their son to come out to Nyamandhlovu. Perhaps I shouldn't have been. They'd taken David with them on a fishing trip a few months before, and he'd returned bursting with stories about hippo wandering through the camp at night, of hitting crocodiles with paddles from the boat and, best of all, of sheltering behind anthills and shooting at unexploded land mines. The only thing he hadn't liked was the oranges injected with gin, which one of the men in the party insisted eliminated the need for lugging bottles through the bush with all the other katundu. He said very little about fishing.

I collected the boys from school in the Leopard at the end of the week and, as we rattled along the road, they chatted about the mixed doubles match they'd just played with the two Tavenor girls.

"They played quite well, for girls," Rowen pronounced.

I held Rowen in a sort of nervous affection. Wild now, but he showed signs of promise for the future. As GG's words came back to me regarding another situation: "It's a pretty feeble sort of woman who can't defend herself against a child," I steeled myself to be firm with him. The drive home went easily, and for the rest of the day they swam, and fished and competed to see who could take the most ticks off the dogs. Rowen displayed respect, and his good manners charmed even Peter and Manka. But by lunch time the following day things changed.

Peter came to me, agitated.

"Amos is here to see you, Madam. You must see him now. Straight away."

Amos, one of the reliable boys from the workshops, had never spoken to me before, answering only to Tim, and I followed Peter to the kitchen door where Amos stood gazing at the ground.

"What is it Amos?" I asked.

Amos was ashamed. He had not wanted to come to the Nkosikasi, he said. But he thought that if he didn't, the Nkosikasi would be very cross with him. And that is why he was here. He stood, head hanging, staring at the ground.

"What is it Amos?" I asked more insistently.

He shuffled awkwardly, intent on wriggling little craters into the dust with his toes.

"Well?... What is it?"

"It is the Nkasana, Nkosikasi... David, and his friend."

"What about them?"

Silence.

"Amos," I was becoming testy, "Tell me."

"They have taken the Master's gun."

"What gun? Why? Where are they now?"

"On the back road, near the compound."

"Doing what? Tell me Amos!" Alarm sliced through my bewilderment.

"They are shooting chickens Nkosikasi. It is hot, and the guinea fowl, they are resting now."

"Where's Mr Zurnamer, Amos?"

"Lapa workshops Madam."

He loped behind me through the back yard to the workshops. Overcoming his shyness, he bellowed over my shoulder, "Boss John, Boss John."

John's stocky body slid out from under a tractor.

"Chickens. Many chickens dead," Amos announced importantly.

John listened to the story, wiped his hands on an old oil rag and climbed into the Land Rover.

"Come with me," he cut Amos off in the middle of his third recitation of the dead chickens and indicated towards the passenger seat.

Everyone knew that, although only eight years old, David and Rowen had both hunted with their fathers guns, for small things... guinea fowl for the pot, or the occasional ververt monkeys which destroyed the crops. They were well trained and experienced in handling shotguns, but this! This they had done without supervision, without permission, without authority. It had also involved stealing keys.

The farm workers loved the children dearly. Naturally patient and understanding themselves, they often clucked disapprovingly when I exercised discipline. But as I walked back to the verandah I wondered if this would be a step too far, even for them.

John reappeared half and hour later, his face stern.

"Five chickens've been shot dead. There's uproar in the compound," he said. "I've checked the gun room, the guns are back and locked up again, but the boys have disappeared."

"Disappeared? Where?"

"What does 'disappeared' mean?" he responded. "Actually their tracks lead back here, to the house."

Suddenly I thought I knew. David's secret Den. We strode off towards the garden beyond the top lawn. There, a few yards away, four motionless white legs protruded from under the thick, green naartjie tree. John dragged the boys out one at a time.

"You won't get away with this," he said angrily.

I pulled the wooden spoon from it's permanent home in my belt where it lived, tucked in opposite the holster with the FN Browning, and gave them both two hard whacks on their legs.

David was contrite. He was very, very sorry. He would never, never, never, do it again, he said. But Rowen stood his ground stoically, refusing to flinch, and two faint red marks appeared just below his khaki shorts.

I looked at John and raised a despairing eyebrow. He took a flat, thirty-cigarette pack from his breast pocket and did a swift calculation on the back.

"Right. Come with me." He marched them off around the courtyard fountain, where that morning they had experimented and finally discovered just how long was too long for a frog to be held under water, and out to the back yard.

"I am setting you gwaza," he said.

It was with some satisfaction that I thought I saw Rowen wince, as I turned and went inside to telephone his mother and, with some trepidation, confess that I had whacked her son. I needn't have worried. She was delighted, she said; that boy was nothing but trouble; in fact she would be amazed if he survived into adulthood.

As Peter brought a coffee tray out to the verandah and put it on the table, I glanced at him. He obviously knew but his face was impassive, he didn't speak, and I let it go. When John reappeared a few minutes later we sat in the big Morris chairs. Spring was approaching, such as it was – never a very discernible time of year, and a series of dust devils swirled around the dry, sepia veldt. As we talked we subconsciously scanned the horizon for signs of late rain.

"What gwaza did you give them to do?" I asked.

John leant back, his hands behind his head, looking like a man in control who was beginning to enjoy himself.

"I worked out the value of the five dead chickens. Then I loaded the kids into the back of the Land Rover, grabbed some large hessian sacks and took them off to the camel thorn trees. You know the ones – at the top of the farm road."

"Cattle feed?" I said.

"Yep. They have to fill the sacks, sell them to the farm, take the money and pay the bereaved chaps in the compound." He put his cup down and glanced at his watch. "About time to check on them. You coming?"

At the top of the track, two splendid camel thorn trees towered up in the middle of a clearing. Full ripe pods hung like pale flags from their branches, dwarfing the two young boys gathering the windfalls underneath. Several bulging sacks leaned against the trunks of the two trees. John looked surprised.

"You'll be able to feed the whole herd at this rate... Rather quick work wasn't it?" he added suspiciously.

Punching the crown of his broad brimmed hat into shape, he slapped it back on his head and walked pensively over to the Land Rover. The track back to the homestead turned around the supplies store room and, as we drew near, John braked abruptly, got out fumbling with his keys and strode, wordlessly, off inside. Seconds later he emerged, exasperation with just a hint of admiration written all over his face and pointed at two broken windows.

"Four full bags missing from the store – damned kids – they won't get away with this." And after loading an arm full of empty sacks into the back of the Land Rover we roared back to the camel thorns. He threw the sacks on the ground and barked at them.

"Right. So that's your game. It's now double gwaza and you can add on two hours."

Just before sundown David and Rowen appeared, barefoot and exhausted, their khaki shirts and shorts stained with sweat. They stood before John, all rebellion drained away. He paid them in coins, fifty cents per sack.

"That's three times the total value of the chickens. Now we go to the compound where you will apologise – sincerely. You will grovel if necessary. You will hand the money over, all of it, with both arms extended, African style." And he drove them clutching the coins down to the compound.

The workers accepted both the apologies and the offering with dignity and with equal dignity and generosity extended forgiveness.

A week later the post bag came out on the tractor bringing a letter written in childish scrawl.

"Dear Mrs Gibbs," it began.

"Thank you for having me to stay.

I am sorry I took the shot gun.

I am sorry I broke the windows.

I am sorry I shot the chickens.

But I did enjoy myself.

With lots and lots of love,

From

Rowen."

27

The morning after David and Rowen returned to school I set aside time to encourage Enoch. Despite his years of experience he'd not developed into an instinctive gardener or a man of the soil, and when, as had happened recently, I neglected our routine after-breakfast tours of inspection, his motivation faltered until I again showed interest and appreciation of his efforts.

Once again the hottest month had arrived, but I loved it. I loved the way, at this time of the year, a soft blueish haze hung over the top lawn in the morning light – a mingling of giant agapanthus in full bloom and a mass of sweet smelling jacaranda blossoms carpeting the lawn where they had fallen from the over-hanging tree. Mauve, lilac and bright purple flowers of the bougainvillea climbing a nearby thorn tree framed the dry lands beyond.

Sometimes, before the household stirred, I would come out here and sit on the grass, listening to cockerels crowing in the distance, watching smoke from cooking fires wisping above the compound. As I absorbed the pink and yellow hour of dawn, drawing it deep into myself, I'd come to realize that it wasn't merely pleasure, I also needed it, depended on it. An awareness crept up on me that the uglier the circumstances in my life, the more I needed beauty – it nourished and healed.

As we went around the garden, Enoch drew my attention to everything; to the browning grass, stiff and sharp under bare feet, although neither he nor the children seemed to notice; to the parched soil and the way in which the plants and shrubs, chosen for their hardiness, thrived with few pests, because of his vigilance. I had known the dipladenia – the Bleeding Heart creeper – displeased him for some reason, and he tried again to persuade me to rip it out. Having refused to grow up the side of the house where I'd planted it, it now ran in happy abandonment down the rocky bank beyond the pale orange bauhinia.

"Is no good, this one. This one is bolshie", he insisted, but I suspected his real reason had less to do with what he saw as the aggressiveness of Dipladenia and more to do with colour. He assured me that Morning Glory also drew a veil over the rocks and wasn't as 'bolshie'. But to me it had been clear from the beginning that Enoch's preference was for all things blue and purple, and I suspected, if left up to him, they would be the only colours allowed to survive in the garden.

"The Bleeding Heart stays," I told him firmly, "It binds the soil together better than Morning Glory."

I no longer bought plants for the garden, but Paddy had given me a miniature white poinsettia which a friend had smuggled in from Kenya for her, and Enoch thought that the Summer House, heavily draped in Golden Shower, would provide an attractive back drop for it.

"I need more poles to mend Summer House. Shower Creeper is too heavy, the roof, it is buggared," Enoch said.

"No. Enoch. It is broken."

"That's what I said Madam. It is buggared."

As I dropped a stone to mark the spot for Paddy's poinsettia, it felt curiously portentous – as if it were somehow the future plunging, deadened, into the soil of Bonisa, and I wondered how much longer we would be able to stay here – if we would be here long enough to see another season of growth and maturity.

I'd inherited a joyously abundant garden, created by Molly in the early days from virgin bush. It was her passion. Whatever enthusiasm she lacked for cooking and domesticity she more than made up for in planning and planting, always finding room for 'just one more plant'. It fulfilled all her creative instincts, and when the beds filled up she added new terraces, lawns, borders, and found spots for flowering trees and shrubs, all selected with an eye for their colour and foliage and shade.

Walking on from the Summer House, Enoch proudly pointed out his efforts at pruning a large number of rose bushes. I complimented him on his initiative but privately vowed to make sure I did them myself next time.

"And now Nkosikasi, is better we go to the vegetables."

170

"Vegetables? Why Enoch?"

"Peter's Green Soup is dying. Maybe it has Haw Haws. Come and see Madam."

Enoch took particular interest in the kitchen garden, perhaps because he had permission to take from what it produced for his family. He lovingly tended the paw paws, mangoes, bananas, avocado pears and melons, but showed less interest in the citrus orchard, preferring instead to spend extra time on taming the prolific growth of loganberries and youngberries, especially when in fruit.

The sharp smell of lemons mingled with the faint sweetness from the frangipani as we rounded the side of the house, and before reaching the kitchen garden gate we could see Peter's Green Soup. The thick, fleshy, very green creeper flowed along the ground like liquid, crawling over, under and between other plants, threatening to take over the whole area. No one knew what it actually was. Some said a type of spinach, although it didn't taste like it, and having discovered it wasn't poisonous it had become Peter's favourite. When I drew the line at eating it as a glutinous vegetable, he made it into soup – frequently. As far as I was concerned it was a good colour, it was edible, and above all the children loved it. On the principle that all green vegetables are 'good for you', I encouraged it and hoped it really was 'good for them'.

There didn't appear to be anything obviously wrong with the plant and we were still examining it when Peter ran through the gate. He loved being the bearer of news and breathlessly announced:

"Nkosikasi. The milk tractor she is back. There is a boy on it. He wants to see you."

"Who is he Peter."

"Ungaaz. Don't know," he shrugged. "He say his name is Elias."

In the back yard, standing by the trailer, was a vaguely familiar, tall, very thin old man.

"Elias? Is that you Elias?"

"Yebo, Nkosikasi."

He had the same courtly manner I remembered when I'd met him in Suburbs two years ago. He'd been restoring a chair for Paddy

171

then and was in good health, but now his body was stooped and emaciated, his wizened skin clinging to the protruding bones.

"I'm very pleased to see you, Elias," I said. "I've been sending messages on the bush telegraph to find you for weeks, in fact since August. No one seemed to know where you were. Are you still in Chitungwiza?"

He dropped his eyes and stared at the ground. I wanted to tell him there was no shame in his suffering, that I knew he was a good worker, and that work had been difficult to find; but instead I pretended not to notice his frailty and glanced away, pointing at Koki.

"This one," I said, "gave birth to her puppies on the sofa, it made a mess, and now they need to be re-covered. Could you stay with us for a few days and do this?"

He looked up, unsmiling, and began talking rapidly in a language I assumed to be Chinyanja and he assumed to be English. I called Peter over. Speaking slowly and with a certain amount of gesticulating, we reached an understanding. Yes, he could stay now and yes, he would re-cover the sofa if it was still alright under the old, spoiled covers. He would live in the kitchen courtyard rooms reserved for drivers and nannies, and Peter would feed him from the kitchen. Although Elias was more accustomed to working on an old Singer treadle sewing-machine, he thought he could manage my old and very basic Harrison – an electric one and I set him up in the designated sewing room. A comparatively cool room on hot days, in the east wing next to the gun room it had the advantage of being next to the schoolroom on the other side so we could liaise when necessary. It was clear that Elias could do with a square meal, but was too proud to say so, and I took Peter to one side, told him to do what he could to put more flesh on the old bones and quietly hoped Elias developed a liking for green soup.

"Also make a box for him to send back for his family Peter. I presume he has a family?"

"Yes Madam. But they are far away and they are not strong. He can not send a parcel. They are too far from anywhere and too sick collect a parcel. Some of his children have died. His wife can't walk."

"There must be a way, Peter. See what you can find out."

Two days later Morden arrived from the farm next door. I suspected he'd been sent for by Peter, who regarded Morden, as headmaster of the local school, as the last word in knowledge and worldliness.

"Peter tells me Madam finds Elias difficult to understand," Morden said.

"Yes, Morden. The problem is he thinks he's speaking English."

"Aah, Madam. You see, he is speaking English. He is speaking King James English. Mission station English. He says Thee and Thou. But he also has an impediment."

"You should get Monica to interpret," John said when I told him. "She ran a mission and could make herself useful, for once." But John was wrong. Monica's interest lay in helping children, not old men, and in any case I didn't think we needed her.

Morden began appearing at the kitchen door each evening just before curfew, and about the time Peter produced food for them all, and they squatted together around bowls of steaming mealie-meal and stew, and talked until an hour or so after dark. Peter often spent the night there in the staff quarters with them and when, at 6am, curfew was lifted, Peter and Elias returned to work and Morden disappeared back to his school for the day.

Despite their different tribes, languages and education, the three formed a curiously strong bond and as the days went on Peter and Morden began urging me to find more work for Elias to do.

"He's very good Nkosikasi," Peter assured me.

"I know that Peter."

"And we need new cushions for the verandah chairs, they are finished, Madam."

"No, Peter not finished, just old and a little faded."

"Yes, Madam, they are finished."

But I gave in and bought thick green floral cotton and asked Elias if he could stay longer.

Other things were also brought to my attention.

"The day nursery doesn't have any curtains Madam."

173

"The day nursery doesn't need any curtains Peter. It's a day room."

"Manka says the children's beds would look nice with new covers," Peter informed me quietly one day.

"No."

"And Elias needs the work, Madam."

Although I knew I was being manipulated, I found I was enjoying both the transformation made by Elias' work and the transformation of Elias himself, as the dried out shell who first arrived blossomed into new life and energy, his eyes, no longer dull, his skin taking on a sheen.

"Madam needs nearly all her other chairs re-covered," Peter announced one morning as the day for Elias's departure approached.

"No Peter. That's enough for now. We'll ask him back another time."

"The sofa in the billiard room is bad, very bad," he said.

Making one last concession I bought heavy duty blue denim to cover the offending sofa and asked Elias to stay on another week.

A few days later I was teaching Peter how to make cream cheese from the small churn of cream brought over from the dairy each morning. I'd given up making butter because it always turned out unattractively white and waxy, reminding me of a man's sweaty, bald head and it quickly went rancid. We'd just hung the muslin bag from the rafters and were fighting off the flies gathering around the drips underneath when Manka ran in to the kitchen.

"Red lights..." she began and was cut off by the ear-splitting alarm screaming out through the house.

"Control, control this is Two Four."

We knew who Two Four was. We didn't need to check. Mrs Rankin. Again.

Since her husband died, of rabies, a few years ago she had battled it out on the farm alone through relentless droughts, disease and difficult labour problems.

"Two Four, this is Control. Come in."

"Control, Two Four." A body's been found behind the dairy. They say it's one of Pilossof's boys. Over."

Peter muttered something and shook his head.

"Copied that Two Four, we'll send a detail – go to landline for directions. Over and out."

Everything seemed to be in hand and we went back to squeezing whey from the muslin bag.

Ten minutes later the alarm rang out again.

"Come in Two Four."

"Another two girls have been abducted and soldiers are beating up my labour. Over."

"Describe, Two Four."

"They're in camo fatigues with red berets. I don't know how many."

"Roger Two Four, will react on green route. Over and Out."

We knew they wouldn't and I hoped Mrs Rankin didn't realise it. She didn't appear to be personally threatened at the moment and there was nothing we could do by ourselves without back-up.

We were fed up with Fifth Brigade. Nyamandhlovu Police, now under Ndebele control, were afraid of them and all our efforts to have them withdrawn came to nothing. No one in government wanted to take responsibility for them. It was constantly claimed that the head of Fifth Brigade, Brigadier Perence Shiri, also known as Black Jesus, was 'unavailable'. Managagwa, also never accessible, apparently spent all his time 'in parliament'. Likewise every other military or civil servant was either 'on leave' or 'in the bush', or 'visiting a very sick mother'. Our frustration, simmering below the surface of everyday life, was made worse by our being blocked from appealing to any higher authority.

The whole district felt the responsibility of looking after Marion Rankin – as we did for Monica Barrington. They were stubborn old girls, soft targets, sitting ducks; but there was nothing we could do without the rest of the stick.

Mrs Rankin came on the air again, using the speak button without resorting to the alarm this time.

"It's alright now. My workers are bruised, but fine, and they've returned to work. Apart from the dead ones of course."

I knew Elias would have heard it all from his sewing room and I was concerned that he might have felt apprehensive about an Agric-Alert.

"Peter, please go and find out if Elias is alright," I said.

But it was Morden who got there first and reported back.

"Elias says he is a very old man. He has seen fighting. He has been tortured. But here, inside the fence he feels safe. And, if not, then perhaps it is God's will. Don't worry Madam. He says today he has food and today he has work. He is alright. He is very happy."

Susan Gibbs, Sam Goodenough and Sarah ready for beekeeping duty.

John and Tim dipping cattle at New Farm.

Leaving Bonisa compound.

Fifth Brigade,
Troops at Entumbane
and one of the ZIPRA convoys
passing the dairy.

Dame Molly and Sir Humphrey Gibbs.

Independence Day at Tjolotjo.

The Leopard: used for trips in to town.

Clockwise from top:
'Knickerless' James,
John Zurnamer, Colin
Shortis, Paul Fehrsen,
Paddy Fehrsen

Farm staff visiting Sir Humphrey at Government House.
Egalandi (far left). Lavu (fourth from right).

Ben and David.

Last Christmas at Victoria Falls.
From left: Caroline, Manka, James, David, Tim and Sarah.

Big Bonisa after the fire.

28

Elias returned to his kraal in Chitungwiza with money in his pocket, parcels of food for his family and in better condition than when he'd first arrived on Bonisa – a pleasure for us all. As he left I decided the time had come to take the four children for a short break in a different part of the country, somewhere away from security tensions. And so we flew up to Harare to spend a weekend with Tim and Jeni Webb, parents of my Godson Phillip.

Tim didn't like leaving the farm and his parents for more than a few hours, and certainly not overnight if he could avoid it, but he accepted that I felt the need for a change and that it would be good for the children. Some of us living in the Nyamandhlovu area with young of similar ages did meet sporadically for an informal playgroup which, although better than nothing, was too infrequent to build friendships, and David especially barely had time to overcome his initial shyness before it was time to go home again. But in Harare whole weekends were spent as families and young friendships grew over barbeques, tennis, and around the swimming pool. The Webbs understood about having fun, of joining in together, and over time they became the hub of many relationships. Our friendship went back to when I first arrived in Bulawayo in 1963 and later, during the ten years of Duncan's ill health, they stood by us. When the doctors advised us to see a specialist in the UK, Jeni came to London with us, an arrangement GG secretly made with Jeni, and paid for before telling me. The idea was for Jeni to make sure I had an evening meal when I returned from Westminster Hospital each evening to our lovely penthouse apartment overlooking Hyde Park – also arranged by GG. Although food didn't venture very much beyond cornflakes, Jeni, witty, loving and buoyant, kept my spirits up – the perfect companion during an anxious and trying time. And then, a few years later, when on one hot October afternoon in Bulawayo, Duncan died, Jeni rang from Harare offering to fly down to be with me.

"No. Thank you, I'll be alright," I said not wanting to interrupt her own family life. But early next morning when I walked into the drawing room, there she was, sitting in an armchair beside the window. She looked up from her book.

"I'm not here," she said.

Later, when S'iponono told me that she had put a tray of coffee and two cups on the table next to Mum Jeni, pointedly adding that my new baby was sleeping, I went through to the drawing room.

"You needn't have come. You have your own children to look after."

"Don't be silly," she said, pouring the coffee. "We've been through too much together for me not to come. Besides, it's not only for you, I needed to come.

Life in Harare felt both familiar and strange. Nyamandhlovu and Harare, although in the same country, couldn't have been more different. It was more than the natural difference between town and country, our whole life styles had been driven apart. The expectancy here was of normality. Here there were no undercurrents of anxiety, no need to be constantly alert. But somewhere along the way I'd been conditioned to the more security-conscious life on Bonisa and felt no longer able to caste my anchors adrift and be instantly carefree. Without reason I still felt vulnerable and somehow no longer fully part of the tribe. It was different for the children, easier. For them, this was a place were there were lots of people who were kind and having fun and who obviously loved them. They sensed that even Luka, Jeni's house boy, was free from threat but even so there were still brief moments when it unnerved them to see me not wearing a sidearm.

Harare, being the capital city, had always been better off than Bulawayo. We called it Bamba Zonki... Grab everything (for themselves). Imported goods, not seen in Matabeleland for years, filled shops and supermarkets, and I crammed our bags with both delicacies and the mundane – tins of sardines, delicacies for Tim, olives for me, pickled walnuts for Humphrey, face cream for Molly and sugar, matches, light bulbs, loo paper and whisky for home stores. Wonderful as it all was, something had shifted inside me and I no longer had the capacity to fully relax and live like that for long. Perhaps one day it would return.

On returning to Bonisa, refreshed by the break and good company, we slipped back into the familiar ways of living. In the short time we'd been away Broncho Greave's son, Robin, and his wife Jean, had been attacked in their homestead on Fountain Farm, not far from Nyamandhlovu. Robin had taken a shot in the face, lost an eye and sustained other, multiple, injuries. We were fond of them both and relieved they had survived.

Shortly afterwards leaflets began circulating warning that the Agric-Alert network system was about to be dismantled. It was no longer needed, the government claimed, because everyone was now free and secure in the New Zimbabwe, and therefore they would no longer pay for it. We protested vehemently and, after a lot of dispute regarding the true situation in the bush, eventually a compromise was reached. Government reluctantly allowed us to keep our sets, but the farmers themselves would have to pay rent for it. The arrangement was fine by us and I wondered if Colin Shortis had been instrumental in persuading Government to agree. But he never said and, although longing to know, I didn't cross that line by asking.

In the meantime we received reports that both the dissidents who had been giving trouble, and the Fifth Brigade had moved further north. And that afternoon John came out on to the verandah for tea and announced he'd just heard that six white tourists had gone missing.

"Two British, two Australians, and two Americans," he said. "Bastards abducted them on the Victoria Falls Road, though what they thought they were doing there in the first place I don't know. Did they think they were exempt from violence because they came from abroad? That the Fifth Brigade would stop them in the bush, ask for passports and then wave them on? Bloody fools probably thought bush war is some kind of spectator sport? And now we've got to risk our necks and go looking for them." Full page advertisements with offers of substantial rewards appeared in the Bulawayo Chronicle, but the missing tourists were not found until three years later, when, up beyond Gwaii River, six shallow graves were discovered in the bush.

Reports of incidents kept coming in. In the virtually uninhabited Lupane forest area, two field hospitals were discovered, fully equipped with electric generators and radio comms, operated by ZIPRA, and supplied from rear bases in Zambia. Now a curfew was imposed on Northern Matabeleland, banning buses and private vehicles in the communal areas, and also, specifically, banning all reporters.

But still our visitors kept coming. Simon Rhodes, a young bachelor, had left Britain to study tobacco farming in Mashonaland and make a new life in Rhodesia shortly before Independence. He'd been referred to Molly and Humphrey by his cousin Robin, Lord Plunkett, who lived in Mashonaland but, being more of an age with us than with the parents, he subsequently came down frequently to stay with us and he eventually became one of Caroline's Godfathers. And then one day he rang asking if he could bring his mother down for the weekend.

"She's staying in the High Commission and although they are very kind, she longs for a time in the bush, a time of informality. Just two days," he said.

Just the right sort I thought, *I'm all for informality*. The two days planned for Margaret's visit stretched into three weeks. A wonderful three weeks, plucking me out of the routine of every day life. We hired a light aircraft and flew up to Chobe, just south of the Zambezi in northern Botswana and from there down into the Okavango. I was soon to discover she had remarkable stamina. Whereas the walking safari took all my energies, Margaret, although fifteen years older, thrived. She didn't seem troubled by the painful Tsetse Fly bites, and during the heat of the day when most sensible people and animals rested, Margaret took a guide, a gun, and went walking.

News reached us on the camp radio this first night that Sir Hugh Beadle had died. Margaret had met Pleasance, his widow, when she came out to lunch with us one day on the farm, and I told Margaret the story with which he'd regaled us sometime before over a camp

180

fire in Deka. He said he'd been commissioned in the early days to set off from the Zambezi to walk south with rudimentary equipment to chart a permanent boundary between Southern Rhodesia and the Bechuanaland Protectorate, as it was named before becoming Botswana. At the same time another party set off from the Limpopo with the same equipment to walk north and when they finally met in the middle they were only one hundred yards apart. He'd pronounced this "Pretty Good."

"It can't have changed much since those days," Margaret said. "It's still wild and untouched." And we both hoped it would stay that way for a long time. Hugh had also loved hunting and suffered constant back pain since being charged by a rogue elephant which, after knocking him to the ground, knelt on him, breaking his back in several places.

"Did someone then shoot it?" I asked.

"Sure they did," he said, "but the real hero was the wind. It blew my hat off, the ellie turned and went after it presenting them with a perfect shot."

Five days of following game through the bush, sitting at water holes, Margaret with a white turban and large blob of white sun cream on her nose, watching wallowing hippos, birds and various buck coming down to drink and crocodiles sunbathing, passed too quickly, and eventually, sunburnt and refreshed, we reluctantly flew back to Victoria Falls thereby avoiding the border crossing at Pandamatenga, and from there drove the two hundred miles down to Bonisa.

Being a country woman at heart, Margaret loved every aspect of farm life and everything intrigued her. The Nightjar amused her... "They're so odd the way their feet go along the branches, not at right angles like other birds. And their cry! It sounds so desperate!"

"It's known as the Litany Bird. It's calling: 'Good Lord Deliver us, Good Lord Deliver us,'" I said.

"Most apt," she replied dryly.

We also shared a love of the fish eagle and in the evenings we sat quietly with our drinks, Molly in her yellow plastic fertilizer bag watching him launch off from the jacaranda, and swoop down for his last hunt of the day on the dam.

I had to continue Sarah's lessons in the schoolroom and so in the fresh, clear early mornings Margaret and John, mounted the rather scruffy ponies, and went out following game trails in search of meat for the pot and labourers' rations. When meat was plentiful and the kill large she helped John cut it into strips for soaking, over several days, in zinc baths of salt and spices, turning it each day to ensure an even distribution of seasoning. Unflinchingly she hung the meat, dripping with blood, on hooks to dry into biltong.

She also, with the help of the children, threw herself into our annual ritual of soaking all the cut glass in a bath of warm water and pouring oil, to combat dryness and cracking, over upended wooden furniture on the lawn, adding constantly to it until it seeped through to the surface on the other side.

Margaret said she'd like to visit the gold mine; she'd not seen one before and would very much like to go underground. I did not think this a good idea but she insisted she wanted to do this, and so we left early one morning, when the mist had not yet burned off the valleys, and drove down to Esigodini. The day was becoming hot by the time we arrived, and Margaret was intrigued with everything we showed her.

"Shall I go down first, Margaret?" Tim said.

"Yes, but how? I don't see..."

"Like this." Tim put one foot in a small bucket attached to a pulley and kicked off from the side. "You have to make absolutely sure you hold onto the rope and remain upright. Otherwise you will have trouble." When he got to the bottom, one hundred feet down, he tugged on the rope and Solomon turned the pulley to bring it up again.

"The bottom of the bucket is rusty. It's not attached all the way around," she said in astonishment.

"Just put one foot in and remember to stay vertical."

She gingerly put one foot in the bucket, gripped the rope and I eased her away from the edge to the centre of the hole. As

Solomon slowly let the rope out Margaret leaned away from it, sending her feet skywards as she bounced off the sides of the hole until she landed bruised and scratched at the bottom on her bottom.

"That was an adventure," she called up to the surface.

"Gutsy," I called back.

We also noticed Monica responded to Margaret with unexpected pleasure and acceptance, appearing on the farm track more often than usual, always mid morning.

"Just popping in to use the phone," she called, giving a cheery wave, and later uncharacteristically wandering out onto the verandah to join us for coffee.

"You've made a coup and won a heart," I whispered to Margaret. But John was not impressed.

"Reading Monica is like reading tea leaves; only less accurate," he said. But I enjoyed watching the interactions, Margaret rising to the challenges of the moments together.

And then one evening while we sat on the verandah sipping sundowners dreamily watching the sunset, half listening to the news, an announcement leapt out.

"Security Forces regret to announce the death today of Mr David Stirling. Mr Stirling was ambushed as he returned home, from a hunting trip, to his farm, near Victoria Falls Road." I tried to understand the words. David, death, ambush.... All in one sentence? Today? Now?

Duncan had watched David Stirling growing up from childhood. "A fine young man," he'd said whenever David's name was mentioned. "Great character. He'll go far." He'd married a lovely girl named Genevieve, they had two children and a farm at Sun Valley and when our first child arrived Duncan wanted him named David.

For the first time in a long while I put my head down and wept.

29

It was Maundy Thursday. The seven months since we first dropped David at Whitestone School had passed quickly and now we looked forward to having the Easter Holidays together on the farm. The autumn bush colours blurred into a haze of burnished gold as I put my foot down and drove fast along the strip road towards Bulawayo, and as the chill of the early morning burnt off I felt at one with the glowing warmth of the day. Mrs McIntyre's regular telephone calls always gave positive reports. No, she said, as far as she was aware David hadn't talked about his experiences when the Beales were murdered, and there was nothing in his manner to suggest he suffered lasting damage. But I felt less certain. His denial of any memory of it, and his reluctance to talk, constituted lasting damage in my mind, and I feared it may show itself in other ways in the future.

He was ready, bags packed and standing outside the dormitory with Stephan and Tammy when I arrived. On the way home he chatted happily about school life, about his friends, about the kudu bull that came down from the kopje and passed his dorm each morning on its way down to drink from the Matsheumhlope River at the bottom of the valley, and he talked about the Night Ape Stephan kept inside his shirt who was called Willie because it peed on its hands before launching itself on to a branch.

"Pee's good and sticky, Mum. He gets a better grip."

"How are classes going?"

"They're fun. I'm top in Ndebele."

"Do you know what today is David?"

"Yup. At R.E. this morning Mrs White told us about the crucifixion. Do you know what they did to Jesus, Mum?"

"Yes," I said. "I've told you about that."

"They lied, they beat him and spat on him and *then* they squashed thorns on his head. And *then* they hammered him to a cross with big, thick nails."

"Yes, I know, David. They were a cruel lot and they were brutal to Jesus."

He thought for a moment and then burst out –

"*Oh boy* ... Just wait until God finds out!"

"It was God's idea!" I said. He looked at me incredulously.

"I told you, remember? He could have got out of it. He did it for us."

"Oh."

As we turned off the main road there was no need to ask him to keep his eyes peeled and his mouth open; he knew the routine and automatically sat up, alert. Our eyes scanned the road surface and the bush as it flew by and I was glad when we eventually drove through the security gates of the homestead. Sarah and James rushed out excitedly, followed by Manka, with Caroline on her hip, and Peter emerged from the kitchen, his face split in a huge white-toothed grin, bearing special cornflake biscuits which he had secretly made to welcome the Nkosani home.

The next two weeks passed quickly, each day gloriously warm and relaxed. It was good being a complete family again. Humphrey and Molly came over a few times and we sat on the verandah watching the children make small bicycles out of fencing wire with the help of Ben, who'd been taught by Enoch, and then racing them across the top lawn. Without reference to me Peter produced the large jugs of lemonade I made from rough-skinned lemons in the orchard, and other little treats he'd cooked up himself which the children fell upon, despite my warnings about ruining their appetites. In the early mornings, with the dew still on the ground, we raided the citrus orchard and the avocado trees, holding up long poles tied to old tin cans, with sharp Vs cut in the side, to sever ripe fruit from their stems high up on the branches, and took them in for Peter to prepare for lunch. We swam in the pool after lunch and fished for Tilapia in the dam in the late afternoons and when the evenings arrived I read to them, or made up stories for them, before kneeling around the beds in the night-nursery, thanking God for a lovely day and praying for protection during the coming night.

On the last Saturday we woke to another beautiful morning. It was Peter's extra day off and the tractor and trailer had already left to take the sixty churns full of milk to Bulawayo. Roll-Call came and went with nothing untoward reported. Not having enough petrol coupons, due to sanctions and rationing, to go in to town as planned, we spent a peaceful morning around the pool and invited John and Sheena to join us for a barbeque lunch. David and Sarah wrapped bacon around bream from their fishing expedition. I produced our own lamb cutlets, salads from the kitchen garden, Peter's homemade bread and naartjies picked from David and Rowen's hiding place. John and Sheena stayed on for tea, and as they left we began clearing away plates and glasses. Suddenly the Agric-Alert siren burst into full volume, shock striking all of us out of the lethargy of the day.

Piercingly, on and on and on. Relentless. We knew that this was no false alarm.

Dear God, who this time?

We stood. Waiting. Paralysed. No one cut in.

Only Control could override the alarm. *Only* Control had the board with the lights flashing against the number. Only Control knew who it was.

Where the hell are you Control? Why doesn't someone speak?

On and on and on. Splitting through cohesive thought.

We ran to the bedroom and stood in front of the set, fingers in ears. Waiting.

Then a voice.

"Two Seven. Two Seven. Control. Come in. Over."

Silence.

Two Seven? Oh God. No. Secret Valley.

"Come in Two Seven. This is Control. Two Seven. *Come in* please."

Silence.

"Two Seven. Come in."

Silence.

"Roger, calling all stations. This is Control. All stations. Stand by."

We stood by, knowing the rest of the farming community would be too, waiting for instructions.

Tim was dragging on his camo-kit.

Agric-Alert spluttered and died.

No one spoke. Confused noises. Muffled. A shot. Screaming. More shots.

Silence.

"Four one, Four One. This is Control. Go to land-line."

Time to get a grip. No time to indulge in emotions. I swung around to gather up the medical bag, supplies, sensible shoes.

And froze.

David was standing in the doorway, facing me. White. Rigid.

We looked at each other. He slowly opened his mouth. His voice staccato.

"That's Tammy's grandfather. And she's there."

The land-line jangled.

I grabbed David and held him tightly to me. There were no words.

On the phone Control spoke calmly, it was time for business now.

"Martin Olds' reaction-stick has mobilized," he said. "They're in the area. Williams is scrambling his plane. Knight's already in the air. Green route into Secret Valley may be compromised. They may need to pick you up. Remain on stand-by."

We waited. The medical kit packed. Weapons, spare magazines, Rat-Packs, Molly's fruit cake and other supplies ready in the Friendly. A suspicion that Green route may have been booby trapped or mined meant air-wing had the best chance of getting there and I hoped Martin's stick may even go cross country on foot if necessary.

"Stand By," Control said.

But I had already decided I couldn't go. David had gone limp, motionless, his face pale and impassive. I hoped he wasn't remembering the battered bodies of old Mr and Mrs Beale. I could not leave him. All recce-sticks had received some training in basic war injuries, they'd manage, and Martin was well trained. They'd be alright. We would stay and wait for news. And hang on to hope no matter how unrealistic.

There was no further contact from Two Seven and, as time dragged on, only spasmodic snatches of information from security forces. Indications were, they said, that a gang of about fifteen terrorists had fled into the bush, making their escape before disappearing under cover of darkness. Tracking would be impossible before morning. Martin and his stick, having scouted for booby traps, had secured the area and gone in.

After that it was over very quickly. Eric and Christine Stratford, Tammy and Candy, were still tied to their kitchen chairs when Martin found them. They'd been tortured and shot through the head. Multiple shots. There was no need for medical attention.

"Calling all stations, this is Control. All stations Stand Down. Over and Out."

I debated about giving David a dose of Valium from the medical kit but didn't. It was healthier to deal with the pain if possible. Much later, when the children had gone to bed, I sat quietly by his bed until he too went to sleep. Then, on leadened limbs I made my way back to the verandah and stuck four more red pins in the map on the wall.

30

We took Monica to the Stratford family funeral. Apart from the awful brutality of the incident, it was also the first time children of white farmers had been deliberately murdered – and the shock waves rippled far beyond Nyamandhlovu and mourners came from all over Zimbabwe and South Africa. There was still a part of us that couldn't quite believe what had happened. And as we sat there listening to the eulogies spoken over muffled sobbing in the background, a part of me wondered who would be next and where it would end. The priest spoke words of comfort which brought no comfort to the unbelieving. We sang the Battle Hymn of the Republic. We'd sung it a lot in recent times and we knew it by heart.

Few children attended with their parents, but Whitestone's had arranged their own service of remembrance in the little thatched school chapel which they hoped would be less harrowing; a quiet affair and just for Tammy and Candy's school friends.

At first, being townies, our guards had been jumpier than we were, tapping on the bedroom window every time the Litany Bird called, or a jackal barked. It constantly amazed me that Tim never had sleepless nights. His sleeps were deep and dreamless while I struggled with light or sleepless nights, with a heightened awareness of noises, scents from the garden and the children in the adjacent night nursery; afraid that as I drifted into deeper sleep, the nightmares would surface. But having the guards did give a certain peace of mind, and particularly encouraged David who sometimes fretted about us on the farm, and who'd already seen too much in his short life to be reassured by mere words.

The export business Tim set up with Jacques Schwartz took up more of his time and involved frequent trips to Harare but eventually, because of the political climate, it failed to come to anything. At other times, while John ran the farm, Tim went down to the mine, usually leaving early in the mornings and returning in the late afternoons. Usually I didn't go with him as Sarah's lessons took priority.

I found that teaching came more easily this time and, having done it before, I knew, more or less, what to expect; but Sarah's and David's interests and personalities were very different and each day continued to produce new interests and challenges.

One morning we walked over to the verandah after lessons to find the mail bag had arrived early and John was sitting on a chair with the *Bulawayo Chronicle* spread out before him, laughing to himself.

"Listen to this," he said and began reading out aloud.

"An explosion, thought to be a 35kg charge, ripped apart a municipal office in Gwelo." He paused, wiping tears from his eyes. "A black policeman who was in bed at his home about 150 meters away said the explosion occurred at 12.50am. 'It was a tremendous bang,' he said. 'The whole house shook and every light bulb dropped out of its socket and smashed on the floor. I thought Jesus had come.'"

"Poor bloke," said John. "Or on the other hand, perhaps he thought that would have been good news."

He held his coffee cup out for me to refill and lit another cigarette.

"It makes a change from the blank columns since self-censorship came in."

"I hear on the grapevine the gooks are spreading east and southwest now."

I wondered how far and how long this would go on.

During all this time of lawlessness not one person had been arrested or prosecuted or held accountable in anyway for any of the murders or atrocities and I was beginning to feel the situation was slipping beyond control.

"By the way," John went on. "I took a couple of phone calls for you, someone called Brendan something, Seery I think. He wants to come out. He's a journalist. Sounds OK. A South African."

"And the other?"

"Oh, I think the other one said his name was Ross Benson — frightfully English. He wants to spend the night."

"I've heard of him. He's on one of the London papers."

"He said the Daily Express."

"John, if Tim's not here will you speak to them?"

"You're kidding."

"Luckily, by the time the press arrived Tim had returned from Ngede and he came out to join us on the verandah and agreed to be interviewed. John sat quietly listening, interjecting from time to time with snippets of up to date information he'd gleaned from some of the labour force. But it was the children and me they wanted to photograph.

"More emotive," John whispered. "Women and children tug more at the heart strings and produce more outrage against the bastards. People like being outraged, it sells papers!"

The phone rang and I got up to answer it. It was Kathy Olds reporting that rabies had broken out down near Compensation.

"It's a long way from you, but it could spread back your way again so this is just a warning to be aware. Dot Crosby's son-in-law's been undergoing the jabs," she chuckled. "His tummy's so swollen and sensitive he's going around wearing his wife's kaftans. Can you imagine the fun they're having with that down in Nyama?"

John got up. "Oh hell, I'd better go and warn the dairy boys."

Brendan Seery knew Africa well. One of his recent articles on Matabeleland carried the headline: 'Back In The Laager Again' and most of us felt he'd got it right. But this time he wanted broader information, he wasn't in a hurry and as the day became hotter sweat dripped onto his note pad and he wiped it away with the back of his hand. Birds chatted furiously around the fountain behind us and I glanced around just in time to see a harmless grass snake disappear into a shrub and I wondered what else was hidden just out of sight and if it might be something I could catch for the schoolroom. Brendan raised his voice slightly and asked how we viewed the politics in Harare, the latest security situation in Matabeleland, and the way we organized protection. "And why did I see your tractor driving out of town with branches of trees sticking up from each of the four corners?" he asked.

John turned back, "It's an agreed sign to the 'dissidents' that we are not hostile but going about our daily business driving the milk to town. For some reason that works wonders and they leave the tractors alone." He wanted details of our experiences and what systems were in place with our neighbours.

On the other hand, when Ross arrived later that afternoon, we discovered his main interest revolved around the human story – gun toting wives, children's reactions, the day to day lives of brave, beleaguered, suffering whites.

"God it's hot. How do you stand it?" Ross asked as Peter brought out a tray of pre-lunch drinks and he turned to look out over the two great spaces of sky and veldt. Clouds had been piling up on the far horizon since early morning and, as the humidity increased, so did the hope of a late rain. Below the escarpment John's Land Rover could be seen approaching along the farm track from the direction of the compound.

"You will want to talk to him as well," I said indicating towards the comets of dust churning up in his wake. "John has his ear to the ground."

Moisture dripped and beaded on Ross's forehead and he wiped it away. "Do you mind if I remove my jacket?" he asked.

Over lunch Tim told Ross he'd had a conversation with the Bulawayo station master earlier, who informed him that when the railway coach arrived from Victoria Falls this morning he'd had to clean it up. "Apparently," Tim said, "he'd removed a body from the loo and four others dead in the carriage. One survivor told him she saw a woman have her head blown off and split in half."

Ross looked as if he was going to be sick.

"Eat up," John said cheerfully, popping his head around the door.

With that, the Agric-Alert alarm screamed through house. We all jumped.

"Shhh, listen," Tim said as Ross began to say something.

"Control, Control, this is Two Four. My boys have been shot. Five dead. Please advise ETA".

192

"OK. Willco, Two Four. asap."

We glanced at each other. Marion Rankin again.

"That woman's a lightning rod for the gooks," John said.

Agric-Alert spluttered, fell silent and then spluttered again. Ross looked uneasy. A few minutes later her voice rang out again. It was lighter this time.

"Control, this is Two Four. I made a mistake, only two are dead." A small apologetic laugh. "The other boys haven't been shot after all. Only bayoneted. But the bodies are in the dairy. It's *full* of blood. It's everywhere, *everywhere* and the cows need milking. Right now."

"Roger that Two Four. "

And, again we knew the reaction group would not leave camp until they were certain the Red Berets had finished their business and departed. So far only her labour had been attacked, but surely it couldn't be long before she got it too and our complete impotence to do anything left us angry and frustrated.

Brendan Seery took it all in his stride and it didn't make a dent in his appetite, but I felt sorry for Ross. Fresh out from England, and despite spending part of his childhood in Africa, he gave the impression, with his perfect manners and exquisite grooming, of being more at home on the London social scene, and a memory came back of having read somewhere that when he went to conflict zones he appeared in his bespoke war reporters suits. Despite our assurances that we had all possible protective systems in place – Agric-Alert, fences, alarms, guards, good labour relations, and an efficient network of ground cover information, he didn't look particularly relaxed. He wasn't stupid. He knew even the best systems can fail. That labour, under threat themselves can betray, information may be flawed, that ambushes happen.

Thinking Ross may like to think there was even one more pair of ears and eyes in the house I persuaded Brendan to stay the night also.

Because of Big Bonisa's size and topography, we'd been designated the safe house for the immediate area, the place where women and children would be brought behind the fence in the event of a major incident, and for this reason I'd kept a supply of new toothbrushes and spare toiletries.

As the sun went down and the day cooled we took Ross on to the bottom lawn and showed him how to use the G3. He surprised us by taking to it quickly and saying that he understood it was the same automatic as used by the SAS and he'd rather have that than a pistol. He told us how, although he'd been in 'hotspots' before, this situation was somehow the more unnerving.

"It's not just a sudden emergency which is quickly over," he said. "It's constant. It's trying to live the small things of life, while poised, holding your breath, waiting for something to happen which, at any moment, could be life changing." And he was still looking thoughtful when Peter came through before dinner, to say goodnight to every one. I'd told him to go back to the compound early because of the activity around Marion Rankin. As he turned to leave, Sarah called after him:

"Good night Peter. Don't get killed on the way home."

"How old is she?" Ross asked.

"Five."

"God," he said, "what a way to bring up kids."

194

31

It was not long after we turned out the lights before thumping on our bedroom door had us up and out of bed again. Ross stood in the doorway to the courtyard, trying, unsuccessfully, to look unconcerned.

"There's a snake in my loo," he said. "I can't shoot in an enclosed space." Grabbing our dressing gowns we followed him across the courtyard to the guest quarters.

"I'll go first," Tim said pushing open the loo door. We peered in. There, coiled together in one corner, two shiny black intertwined chongololos writhed, sliding around on the cement floor, frantically trying to mate.

"They're millipedes," Tim said. "Large ones, admittedly, but harmless! You're lucky it wasn't a black mamba. They're all over the place at the moment; in fact there's one living in the golden shower on the front drive and, just last week, one of Bates' herd boys met one on the farm next door. He was fighting a fire; shame, poor chap. Ian took him to Nyamandhlovu Clinic where they promised to observe him. They did too – as good as their word. They didn't actually do anything else, but they did observe him – until he died."

The article Ross eventually wrote covered a double page centre spread in the London Daily Express and carried an emotive photograph of me, looking glum, with two of the children and a pistol on my hip. He wrote well, but in making full use of artistic license some of the things he wrote hurt me and hurt my friends in town. He made much of the contrast between rural and urban lifestyles, implying that 'townies' showed little interest in the farmers lives and had different values. Theirs were superficial, glamorous ones, they obsessed about their competitive dinner parties and Gucci T-shirts and, worse, he implied some of these views were mine.

I was appalled. Since the troubles began, Bulawayo friends, commercial businesses and even acquaintances had been constant and unwavering in their generous support of the farmers and, angry, I vowed not to give interviews to the media again – a decision I stuck with until much later when, just before we left, I was trapped by Philip Haydon and Jeremy Paxman, who unexpectedly swung round to me after interviewing Tim for a Panorama programme.

A few days after his visit Brendan Seery's article appeared in the Cape Argus. He also stressed the 'human interest' point of view but with factual, if somewhat sensationalised, reporting, which appeared under headlines shouting out from the Cape Argus: 'Don't get killed on the way home.'

Peter came out to the verandah, stopped, looked at the newspapers lying on the verandah table, shook his head, and deliberately put the coffee tray down on top of them.

"Miss Mary, she will see this? She's also is in London?" he asked.

"Yes, I expect she will Peter. Did I tell you she's coming to stay again very soon?"

Peter liked Mary Buxton. She appreciated his cooking, thanking him after every meal and, when everyone else was busy, she would slip in to the kitchen to enquire about his extended family and their difficulties in these troubled times. But it wasn't only for the fact that she always arrived laden with presents for everyone (and tipped generously when she left) that he looked forward to visits from her; it was because, although originally Malawian himself, he regarded Zimbabwe as his adopted country, he was proud of it and genuinely wanted guests to enjoy their time here.

Mary Buxton, as Tim's Godmother, had been a constant factor in his life and she'd taken an almost possessive interest in him. As she had grown older her yearnings to be married had never waned and now that she was over seventy, the loneliness pressed in on her more and more, so that by the end of winter the bleakness of her luxurious London flat held no pleasure and had become almost more than she could bear alone. Timing her visits to arrive after the intense heat of the Zimbabwe summer had died away and before autumn turned into winter, when everything shrivelled and the veldt turned brown, Mary developed a little routine. She always invited herself for two or three weeks, but over time we learned what that entailed and planned accordingly. It happened every year. As the time to leave grew closer Mary discovered she had swollen glands.

"I couldn't possibly travel like this Darling. Not feeling as ill as this. It's not only the glands I have a sore throat as well," she said, gently wrapping her hands around her neck. Paul Fehrsen smiled and agreed to support her self-diagnosis for the purposes of cancelling her tickets and in case of any airline dispute. And so three weeks invariably turned into six or sometimes eight. As the date of her arrival approached I began selecting a few Bulawayo friends to come and stay a night or two during the time she was with us. People with mutual interests in literature, art or music (she had been secretary to the Bach choir) who, when we were busy, would help fill her days with stimulating company.

This year I also invited Simon Rhodes, Margaret's son, who flew down regularly from Harare. He and Mary had met on previous visits and, although still in his early twenties, he sensed her situation, and paid her courtly attention while regaling her with unlikely and amusing stories. Needing little entertaining himself, when the mood took him he happily picked up a gun and went out to shoot for the pot.

"Have you heard about Herbert Ushewokunze?" he called out one evening as he handed three guinea fowl to Peter before walking over to join us on the verandah where we were waiting for drinks to arrive. "It's all over Harare that he's trying to set up a police/intelligence force answerable only to himself and no other body."

"You mean to him as Minister of Home Affairs?" I asked.

"Nope, to him personally as Dr Herbert Ushewokunze."

"Surely Mugabe won't allow that?"

"It's all rather sinister," Simon said. "He's thoroughly evil. Have you noticed his lack of expression? Just like a psychopath. Evil."

"But what about CIO?" I said.

"Nothing to do with them. This is to be a separate organization. Bloody terrifying isn't it?"

A powerful, eloquent speaker who had no discernible allegiances except to himself, I'd been mildly afraid of Ushewokunze ever since he became a public figure. During the early days of independence he'd been Minister of Health and on his frequent trips to Bulawayo had demanded to have several nurses from Mpilo Hospital waiting for him in his suite. He got away with it because it only involved black nurses who had no power to object. But as the rumours flew around whispered speculations grew: 'What if future demands were for white nurses?' and hatred and fear of him spread through both Mpilo and the Bulawayo General Hospitals.

I wondered if Colin Shortis knew about Ushewokunze's latest plans and concluded that he probably did. There wasn't much he didn't know, but I would have liked to have talked with him about it and to ask if he had told Mugabe, at one of their frequent meetings, that another secret force, particularly under Ushewokunze could be a threat to him. But as I thought it through I decided he probably wouldn't discuss it with me anyway, and it may even be too politically sensitive to discuss with Mugabe.

Simon's weekend on Bonisa had to be extended when a report came through that gunmen had set up a road block on the main Bulawayo/Harare Road near the airport, and had fired indiscriminately with automatic weapons on cars, buses and a goods train. They killed three and injured twenty and although Simon may have got through, clean-up operations took time and, to the children's delight, we persuaded him to stay on for a few more days.

Although the children had each other, one of the things I'd regretted was the infrequent opportunities for the children to play with other children and I decided to give a children's birthday party on the farm and include a cake for Mary, whose birthday fell in the same week as, and half way between, David's and Caroline's.

Mary revelled in the bitterly cold early mornings and then blossomed in the warmth of the sun at midday, and as the days went by it seemed she drew life and energy, as if by osmosis, from having company around her. But the noise and liveliness of only four children always left her wilting by the evenings, and I hoped she would be able to endure a whole party.

"I do love them Darling," she often said, "but I'm always surprised to wake each morning and find they are still only children. I half expect them to grow up or go away overnight. Or at least not to be so consistently energetic. It's most peculiar." But the security reports, the Agric-Alert and fence alarms didn't disturb her at all. I privately suspected she enjoyed it, that it added a frisson and some welcome colour to her life.

Simon busied himself outside. He and John got on well, they shared a love of the land and while Simon worked at extending the brick barbeque he'd built on the bottom lawn a few months before, adding a concrete tabletop over an alcove for storing firewood, John graded the farm track, which was in a bad state following the rainy season, with newly formed pot holes and corrugations. Mary and I busied ourselves with planning the party, and David and Sarah, using their newly acquired copybook writing skills, helped with invitations to all the friends they could think of in the district, in Bulawayo and from the Hebrew English Nursery School.

Some of the replies brought excuses but others sounded enthusiastic, offering to gang together and arrange a meeting point to form a convoy with three husbands volunteering to accompany them in armed escort vehicles.

32

Each day after the sun had burnt the chill off the early morning air, Mary took herself out to sit on the verandah and spent her days doing tapestry or writing letters and hoping someone would come and keep her company. Simon was already there when I made my way over after Sarah's lessons. Mary had reached what she called 'The Age of Anxiety' which, she explained, increased as one grew older. Little things mattered more these days, she said, especially things over which one had no control, adding as she pointed towards the fluffy white clouds building on the horizon "I hope it doesn't rain for the party," but I just said I thought rain unlikely.

"No chance," John said throwing himself into a Morris chair and lighting a cigarette. "Those ones are white and fluffy and anyway the season's almost over."

Simon stood up to examine the map on the wall.

"There are a few more pins in it since I was last here," he said.

"There's been a bit of activity, a few attacks, and an abduction. You heard about the Stratfords. No one else wiped out since then," John said. He paused for a moment. "I'm talking about whites of course – the blacks are being clobbered all the time. Actually I popped in to say I'm going over to meet the new manager on Willoughby's Winter Block section of Umgusa Block after lunch, a chap called Dave Walters. Would you like to come? It's a fair old distance, out on the Falls Road, so we'd be gone most of the afternoon."

Mary looked as if she was about to invite herself as well but I intervened saying that we were expecting Monica for tea and we also really needed to begin planning, to make shopping lists and prepare for the weekend. She looked disappointed but, too well mannered to push herself forward, she sat up straighter and the moment passed. Apart from anything else, there had also been an occasional ambush out on the Falls Road and whereas John and Simon would defend themselves if necessary, it would not be fair to make them responsible for her as well; although I suspected she would probably enjoy a lively drama, and she'd often said she wouldn't mind dying.

We spent the afternoon sitting around the verandah table, leafing through children's party recipe books and making notes, until Monica's car came into view ahead of a trail of dust, and we watched as it slowly made its way up towards the escarpment. Mary and Monica had little in common. "She's a strange one" had been Mary's verdict when they first met, and this meeting was, for both of them, an annual duty which they performed, playing their roles to perfection; Mary leaning slightly forward with studied concentration, and Monica with an air of carelessness and a tendency to interrupt. I kept on neutral ground relating anecdotes about Solomon and the gold mine, about his funny little ways and his devotion to James, and I told them we'd discovered another use for the crucible. Apart from smelting gold and silver we'd taken to smelting expended brass cartridges, collected after each battle or attack, and turning them into extraordinarily heavy, conical door stops, which were much admired by everyone except Peter who, padding around in bare feet, frequently stubbed his toes.

Eventually, as Monica got up to leave, I wondered why we go through these type of rituals, and decided it was probably something to do with preserving a civilized society.

Peter spent the next two days cleaning and polishing with extra vigour, while Mary and I took over his kitchen and made sweets, fudge, toffees, chocolately rice-bubble biscuits, and when fresh cream arrived from the morning's milking we turned it into mango and Grand-Marnier ice-creams.

We designed three birthday cakes – one for the boys made into a Puffing Billy, like the ones that went through the farm, complete with a liquorice cow-catcher on the front; and one for the girls shaped like Cinderella standing on grass made of green coconut and holding a tiny shoe from a Christmas cracker. We debated making something more relevant to Africa for Mary but, apart from Tarzan and Jane which didn't really seem appropriate, we couldn't think of anything.

Mary cut thin strips of liquorice and applied them to some meringue mice, hedgehogs and snails I'd made. She gave them whiskers, tails, quills and antennae and added tiny pieces of glacé cherries for pink eyes, before deciding she'd had enough and needed to go and rest.

"Would you like a tray of tea? I'll tell Manka to bring one to your room," I said.

Later, Manka took the children to the orchard and returned with baskets of fruit. Peter turned the lemons into large quantities of lemonade, and the oranges we halved, scraped out, filled with jelly and, when set, quartered them to make little boats with children's names written on paper sails stuck into the jelly with toothpicks.

I woke early on Saturday, before Roll-Call and while the air still held the night chill. There was still a lot to do, much of it, like the tables, sandwiches and small sausages, Peter or Manka could do, but I planned to do last minute baking for the adults and make Mary's cake before the guests arrived.

But for now there was no one else about and I went outside and walked to the far end of the top lawn. I sat under the jacaranda, alone and yet not alone, absorbing the achingly glorious beauty of Africa, becoming part of it in those brief moments before the Queen-of-the-Night folded her flowers back in, as if re-gathering her petticoats, withdrawing her scent, readying herself for the day. I remembered reading somewhere that it was possible to turn our 'desert of loneliness into a garden of solitude." This is it, I thought. This is why Mary comes. The aloneness here is not lonely. In the tall bottlebrush beside the courtyard fountain brightly coloured birds preened themselves, singing and chattering to each other and, beyond the front lands, the veldt, drenched in pale gold, stretched as far as the eye can see. How could we ever leave this? As the sun, a large white pearl, slowly rose in the eastern sky, I got up and returned to the bedroom to await Roll-Call and Manka's morning tea tray.

By the time the convoy drove up at twelve o'clock, Peter and Manka had changed into clean uniforms and were putting the finishing touches to the tables laid out in the garden and we attached the last of the balloons to the trees. I managed to persuade James that it was important to keep his clothes on, that there would be photographs, which he might regret in years to come if he didn't, but by the time the first cars drew up all the children had discarded their sandals and were no longer particularly clean.

Friends from the Nyamandhlovu area arrived individually but others, like MG and GG Fleming and Paddy and Paul Fehrsen, drove out from town strung between lead and rear vehicles kitted out with automatic weapons. As this was something of an occasion everyone came up the front drive, through the rarely opened eastern security gates, and entered in the hall, piling their gifts on the kist (carved in Cyrene mission station by Sam Songo), propped up their rifles in the corner, and placed their spare magazines, as we did, on top of the curtain pelmets. But no one removed their side-arms. We didn't expect them to.

Mary took a photo of the hall.

Unsurprisingly Monica decided not to join us, but Dot Crosby did, and she, Molly and Humphrey walked over through the kitchen garden when they heard the last vehicles coming in the back drive along the Little Bonisa fence.

There were momentary pauses when Agric-Alert spluttered a few times but no one commented and when nothing further was heard conversations quickly resumed.

Paddy and Penny Thomas came through from Redwood Park. Their dairy farm out on the Victoria Falls Road neighboured Biggar Estates, the Fleming ranch. It was there, sixteen years ago, that Duncan and I began our life together, and I knew the area well. Just beyond Redwood Park and Biggar Estates lay a group of Willoughby ranches including Spring Block and Winter Block, where John and Simon had gone a few days before to meet Dave Walters.

"I presume you've met Willoughby's new manager? What's he like?" I asked one of the others from that area.

"He's OK. Mid twenties. Must have married young because he's got two kids about six and four."

"I hope his wife can stick it," I said.

"He's sensible, he takes an armed guard everywhere and a mobile Agric-Alert. He'll be OK."

"Yes, John said much the same thing – I think they may become good friends."

As the food and drink disappeared some of the parents took their children swimming while others chatted or stretched out on rugs around the pool. Mary circulated, her eyes alive and cheeks flushed with, what I felt certain, had more to do with enjoyment than swollen glands, and it gave such pleasure to see others warmed to her.

After the last ones left, Manka took the children off to bath, John and Sheena stayed to help clear up and Mary said she was exhausted from all the activity and would like to go to bed early with a supper tray in her room.

"Just some soup Darling, and perhaps a boiled egg, and a small glass of sherry would be nice. Please don't fuss about me, I don't want to be any trouble, but it's my glands. They're up again and I've got a bad headache. I'm sure I'll be better in the morning."

I was sure too. But I was also sure that wouldn't mean she would be well enough to travel.

Having worked uncomplainingly without a break, I gave Peter an extra night off and Simon suddenly announced that I should also have a night off.

"I'll cook a luxury, slap-up dinner for you, Tim and me."

"I didn't know you could cook. Can you?" I asked suspiciously, "What will you make?"

"Wait and see. You will be amazed." And he went off to ferret around in the pantry.

He was right. I was amazed. Aghast in fact.

"What on earth have you done?" I asked, looking at the kitchen sideboard on which lay the open tins from three rat packs.

"Wait 'til you taste it – it's delicious – everything in together. Couldn't be easier."

I looked in disbelief at the debris of empty containers. Baked beans with frankfurters; pilchards; chopped ham; savoury mince;

corned beef; orange segments and squeezed out tubes of jam and condensed milk.

All in together?

I looked again at the mess which by now had been smothered in parsley.

"I'm not eating it," I said.

"Yes you are. Be grateful I didn't throw in the box of matches," Simon said, enjoying himself.

Tim put a fork full of food in his mouth and looked up, surprised.

"This is rather good," he said. "At least give it a try."

Tim would eat anything. Someone had once remarked that he'd probably been born under the sign of the goat, in which case that would be expected, but I didn't believe in such things. By now both men were eating with gusto, ignoring me. I tentatively lifted the loaded fork to my mouth and was astounded to find it wasn't as bad as imagined.

Unusual, unattractive, but not absolutely dreadful as anticipated.

33

As suspected, Monica turned down her invitation to Jack Ehlers' wedding and, as John and Sheena, not really knowing them, hadn't been invited, they offered to drive Mary and Simon, who were leaving the same day, out to the airport, in time for the late flight to Harare, calling in to say goodbye to Monica on the way. As they drove away down the front drive Mary opened her window and called "I'll see you next year." But I had an unexpected premonition that she would not be returning and that this was the last time we would be waving goodbye to Mary as she left Bonisa.

Although the wedding wasn't due to start until 2.30pm, we wrestled the children into clean party clothes and left Bonisa early, hoping to have time to freshen up at the other end before the garden ceremony began.

The day warmed up and after the first few miles the children kicked off their shoes and fell asleep. Manka dozed with Caroline sprawled across her chest, and I turned my attention to the passing scenery. Beneath the wide, empty sky the veldt stretched for miles. Sparse areas of dry sepia grasses sprouted from the red soil, and occasional patches of lilac blossoms fell, like waterfalls, from thin branches of wild wisteria trees. From time to time small herds of impala leapt high across the road kicking up dust, and just beyond the Khami river we spotted a lone sable bull, standing aloof and unconcerned, on the side of the road. So beautiful, we stopped to watch it for a minute. My thoughts went on to the afternoon ahead and I wondered, not for the first time, how well Joy really knew Jack, if she knew of the Mimosa Park curse, and what she thought of the absurd alterations to the interior of the homestead.

The rest of the journey passed uneventfully and we had made good time when we arrived at the turn-off onto the Mimosa farm road and drove through a stone gateway complete with colourful coat of arms newly emblazoned on either side.

"Delusions of grandeur," John had reported the month before when he'd gone over to deliver the wedding present for us. "In fact, I wouldn't be surprised if they didn't add a 'Von' or Joy's name and somehow change plain 'Ehlers' into a double barrelled name for an added illusion of refinement."

I smiled. Maybe Jack would like that, but I didn't think it sounded like Joy. From all accounts Joy, the widow of a wealthy tobacco farmer from Mashonaland, was a 'fine woman' with 'her feet on the ground', a successful woman in her own right, although in what field no one seemed to know. She had the indefinable look of a perfect Nyamandhlovu farmer's wife, capable and with a certain style, and I imagined she would bring respectability rather than pretentiousness to Mimosa Park.

Further along the track we drove through the security gates into a rush of colour. In place of the bleached monochromes of the bush, purple, red, orange and white bougainvillea climbed up high trees until they could go no further and then cascaded back down, dripping blossoms on the grass. Scattered around the garden, mature oleanders, covered in lusty warm pinks, and, as if in competition, stout bushes of Yesterday-Today-and-Tomorrow, displayed a profusion of varying blues. Sweet perfume from the yellow scented frangipani wafted around the garden and, across the lawn, tubs planted with Pride-of-India disciplined into standards marked a walkway leading to the latticed arch which had been especially erected for the wedding arbour and woven with greenery, wild wisteria, and bougainvillea. Looking around the garden I marvelled, as I so often had, at the variety of plants that, defying drought conditions, could be coaxed into such splendour.

On a table in the pink and mauve haze under the arbour, more flowers, pink and white this time, draped across a white cloth and flowed over the edge. Two velvet kneelers waited side by side on the grass in front, and facing these, rows of white chairs stood either side of a central aisle.

"Where do we take the children?" Kathy Olds asked one of the Ehlers' servants after we'd dropped off our weapons in the hall.

"Isihlahla," he said, indicating towards a large spreading jacaranda on one side of the lawn. Toys, books, biscuits, and cool drinks had been spread over several rugs and we settled the very young ones in the shade with Manka, and Kathy's nanny.

We suspected a few early guests had already been drinking, and a small group had gathered around a belligerent Bronco who was airing his opinions about the security situation.

"It would," he said, "all be over by now if it weren't for a few jumped up munts." His wife, sensing danger, moved away from him to find safer conversations, but discussions didn't vary much, constantly revolving around 'the situation' or the drought.

One of the young men had just driven down from Kezi – Chief Sitole's area – and told that six men had been shot at Shashane Store, and then buried in shallow graves, three to a grave. "Worse than that," he said "several other men were beaten, thrown alive into a well and then hand grenades lobbed in on top of them."

Several farmers had already bought themselves flats in Bulawayo 'just in case,' and Kathy Olds had decided to move into town with her baby daughter until things 'settled down.' Her husband, Martin, continued to run to farm and she joined him at weekends.

Some, perhaps the majority, wouldn't even consider the possibility that things wouldn't settle down. They had, in days gone by, mainly been supporters of Ian Smith and relied on him to restore normality to their lives, accusing those who left the country of taking 'the chicken run'. But now 'Good Old Smithy' was no longer in charge, he'd not restored normality to their lives and with the appearance of Mugabe's Fifth Brigade a new expression had sprung up – 'taking the wise owl run.'

"You're lucky; you're over the worst part," Tony Sharp our next door neighbour said to a young couple who had shyly confessed that they were emigrating. "The really difficult bit is making the decision in the first place; after that the dye is cast and there is nothing to do but get on with it." And in many ways he was right.

Mingling amongst the guests I noticed a quiet respect for Joy, for her courage in leaving her part of the country which was now enjoying relative peace, and coming to live in Matabeleland in the thick of the bush war.

From somewhere behind the arbour an unseen piano began playing a medley and, taking our cue, we made our way to the chairs to wait for the ceremony.

Jack walked stiffly down the aisle to the front, removed his Stetson placed it under his chair, and stood staring straight ahead. The trek priest followed, more relaxed, carrying his small, battered Bible, and turning to face us, he adjusted his stole, gave us a wide smile, and prepared to receive the bride.

She didn't keep us waiting. The medley faded away as the piano launched into *Here Comes The Bride* and Joy, a reassuringly comely figure, in floating pale blue gossamer came down the aisle. Her broad-brimmed hat, with delicately hand-stitched fresh frangipani and rose buds around the brim, drew murmurs of approval as she serenely made her way, unattended, between the standards of Pride-of-India, holding in front of her a huge bouquet of mixed pink and white flowers from the garden.

We were beginning to wilt in the afternoon heat, and were grateful when the short service came to an end and the chairs moved back to enable us to circulate again.

By now the children had found a hose pipe from somewhere and were bare foot, soaked to the skin, and covered in red mud. I'd begun teaching them from an early age that, as they go through life, they must leave behind good footprints; but what the pale verandah sofa now bore was not what I had in mind.

"We could always throw them in the swimming pool with a cake of soap," Kathy said jokingly. But, glad to have got them this far looking relatively tidy, we gave up, as did all the other mothers, and it was clear that the nannies who, still crisp in their uniforms, did too and stayed sitting on the rugs drinking tea and catching up on their gossip.

As the sun moved towards the horizon and the strong heat ebbed away, servants in bare feet, white uniforms and red sashes cleared away the tea tables and, because of curfew, brought out early drinks.

Whisky, Brandy, and Gin appeared, all produced in Zimbabwe, some almost drinkable. Made by adding different imported essences to cane spirit, they all had an unusually high alcoholic content. There was even a bottle of pure Cane Spirit for those who liked the effect and weren't fussy about flavour.

The atmosphere was relaxed and mellow when suddenly, from inside the homestead the Agric-Alert siren blasted out. Some of the guests, instantly sobered, decided to go home rather than run the risk of running into curfew. Recently activity in the immediate vicinity had increased and, although no one had been killed, the terrorists were getting bolder.

"If you need to go that's up to you," Jack said. "I think it's OK but, man, just this morning my cook was abducted for the second time. It was before dawn, they locked him in an out-building again and only released him as you lot began arriving. He was not harmed and I wasn't going to say anything, but they're obviously about. Of course the Police never did arrive and it's too late now. You're all welcome to spend the night here on Mimosa Park, grab beds or sleep where you can, and set off at daybreak after curfew lifts."

But nothing further happened and this time it turned out to be a false alarm.

In the days that followed, Joy became accepted as a member of the district in a way that Corrie had never been. She had a steadying influence on Jack and, by appearing to be happy herself, she enhanced his credibility, until he too became more accepted and the memories of Jack and Beryl, Jack and Corrie de Koek and all their excesses receded.

34

Following each successive drought we swore we could see the Kalahari desert encroaching further into our territory. Tjolotjo Tribal Lands, west of Nyamandhlovu, were already desolate. Overgrazed by cattle, chewed to the quick by goats, denuded of trees by tribesmen building their huts and cooking fires, it had, over the years, cleared the way for desert sand to advance over the baked earth, and famine had become a reality for the tribal people. Food Aid Agencies tried to help but little reached those in real need. Government road blocks confiscated donations coming in on the backs of lorries, selling them on to the highest bidder and Nyamandhlovu farmers reacted by opening up back tracks on their land and smuggling the grain through.

The lacerating heat, seemed to last forever, but one day, as we watched from the verandah, purple clouds began stacking up on the horizon, rapidly blowing closer and bringing the smell of rain on the wind. Thunder rumbled in the distance, lightning played around the sky as the afternoon grew dark. And then it broke. Glittering rods of rain, blocked the view, spattered mud on the walls and washed dust laden leaves. Overnight the veldt greened and the air filled with smells of wet earth and blossoms and Matabele ants, pungent and pervasive when stepped on. Just behind John's cottage the Mpopoma River came down in spate, sluicing over the spill way into the Khami and sending torrents rushing down into the dam.

The season continued as it began. Daily downpours soaked the parched soil. We were kept busy with the increase in honey flow and milk production, and, as the crops flourished, the work force began clearing out abandoned silage pits, for the first time in years, in anticipation of a bumper crop.

Peter and Manka took the children off to harvest flying-ants, breaking out in patches from their nests in the earth, rising triumphantly to begin a new life, only to be beaten down by flailing black hands into zinc baths of water, and then, as a sheen of detached wings appeared on the surface, to be scooped out and fried in oil. Some said they tasted like peanut butter but I could never bring myself even to try.

Symptoms of diarrhoea and vomiting began showing up at the morning clinics, which I hoped was more to do with feasts of fatty flying-ants than cholera, and I drilled everyone on the necessity of washing hands and soaking vegetables in a weak dilution of Pot Permang before cooking.

"With babies in the compound we can't take risks," I told Peter.

"No Madam."

I wasn't really concerned about Peter – his on-going love affair with carbolic soap almost guaranteed good health, but I remained deeply suspicious that the solution of Pot Permang I sent down for use in the compound had probably been discarded.

As the grain ripened, noisy, compact flocks of queleas swooped over the maize lands in their thousands – some claimed millions – moving as one, like dense, fast-moving clouds of dark smoke, in some areas overtaking locusts as the scourge of seed-growing farmers. There had even been reports of branches breaking when vast numbers of the tiny birds came to roost, and it would be a race against time to get the crops in before they were decimated by them.

John told me later that Monica had complained about crop spraying aircraft flying low over the farm. "It's only right that you should share your food with the wild life," she said. "And I don't see why the night-shift should have to go on all night, banging tins around the lands near my cottage. It keeps me awake."

"I'm sorry," John said. "But we have to keep the buck out somehow, it's only for a short time and not a total solution but we do want to reap something. There'd be nothing left if we didn't. Have you seen how many there are this year?" Monica had driven down to New Farm, at the other end of Bonisa, where John was dipping cattle and swarms of flies attracted to the nearby pens of sick calves added to her irritation.

"Let's go to your cottage," she said. "I want to see your new baby."

As the rains usually fell in the afternoons I'd planned to take the children and Koki to the Mpopoma for a picnic in the morning, calling at New Farm Cottage on the way. Koki, her energy undiminished by her pregnancy, annoyed Monica and so I put her outside with John's dog, Zonda. I was constantly surprised that Monica who, although loving bush animals almost as much as her bush children, appeared not to like either domestic varieties.

John's wife Sheena greeted us warmly and went off to make coffee. Monica glanced briefly at the baby in his crib and rummaged in her bag.

"I've brought you a card," she said when Sheena returned with the tray. "But no coffee for me thank you; I'm on my way to visit the Hendersons. She's having a terrible time with her arthritis and I'm taking her some flame lilies." I privately thought Monica might have done better than that.

Just before John and Sheena's baby had been born, the car containing the bag packed with baby clothes ready for a dash to the hospital had been shot up by one of the guards. He'd tried to take it for a drive, found he didn't know how, got out and, in a fit of pique fired shots into it. The baby clothes, riddled with bullet holes were useless and when word got around several friends rallied together and replaced them. "Michael ended up the best dressed kid on the block," John said. "He probably ended up looking like one of Monica's 'Better Offs.'" But Monica's heart was for the young picannins and it was good seeing the way she cared for the forgotten poor ones, very few others did.

"Well you've got a long way to go. Don't want to hold you up," John said, winking at David as he moved towards the door.

"Hamba Gashly, Mrs Barrington," David called after her. "And don't run over a Nightjar — Mummy says it's bad luck." I threw him a 'don't-speak-to-her-like-that-or-we'll-be-talking-about-this-later' look.

Michael slept soundly, but, seeing Sarah's rapt expression, Sheena picked him out of his crib.

"Would you like to hold the baby?" she asked her.

"We've got a baby too. But you can't see it, mummy's looking after it," Sarah said.

"Where? Where is it?" demanded James, looking around.

"In her tummy… can't you see?"

"No Darling, not this time," I said.

Steam was still rising off the muddy track, after a sharp, unexpected downpour, as we left the Zurnamers and drove, following the water course, to Mpopoma Dam. Chutes from recent cloud bursts gushed over the weir and we stopped beside it under a canopy of thorn trees to spread a rug and off-load the picnic basket before going off to explore.

The river flowed strongly, imprisoned between cliffs of red earth which narrowed into a cutting a few yards before the spill way, and I sat on the side listening to the children watching flocks of startlingly beautiful Carmine Bee-eaters darting in and out of the hole-studded banks.

"They move into the holes of the Little Bee Eaters," I explained to the children. "But they don't stay there more than three years because bugs build up in their nests and drive them out."

"Why don't they just eat the bugs?" Sarah asked.

"Because they are small ones, too small to see, called parasites and bacteria."

David, pointed to a Malachite Kingfisher arrowing into the water and called "Look," as it emerged, in a glinting spray of water, with his catch.

The red earth appeared redder in the wet and, with the dust settled, the air felt fresher, almost sparkly. In between showers the sun seemed to fill the sky like a big, hot, bronze shield but the heat was somehow less punishing. We decided it was time to open the picnic and began walking back to the thorn trees.

In the distance, a single shot rang out. Followed by… nothing. James went rigid, Koki raced back and tried to hide herself between my legs. David and Sarah didn't move. Monkeys scampered off the bank opposite, and behind us a small herd of kudu crashed away, unseen, through the bush. My mind raced. *Don't panic.*

"It's probably John killing a calf too sick to survive," I said, hoping but far from certain I was right, and I decided not to drive back that way for another hour or two in the hope the situation would have clarified by then.

"Come on, time for the picnic. Who's hungry?"

It was a relief when, a few minutes later, John slewed up the track in his pickup.

"Bet that woke you up," he said. "Sorry if it startled you kids – I had to put a heifer down. By the way you must watch out for the barbel – they congregate in their hundreds, flapping around in the water at the sluice gates on the dam here – we've no idea why but it's quite a sight."

We hadn't seen much of John lately. Dipping cattle, increased to twice weekly since the rains began, occupied most of his time and we missed him dropping in each morning and afternoon as he did during the drier seasons.

"Will you take me riding?" David asked him.

"Sure, when it's not so busy. You can also help me to shoot the bloody monkeys," he said. Sarah gasped. "They're vermin," he went on, helping himself to a boiled egg and giving one to Koki. "Tuck in kids, it's good."

The children dived in to the picnic box and John drew me to one side.

"There's spoor on the track. Gooks. I don't know, maybe ten or eleven and they're fresh since today's rain. You'd be better back at the homestead – behind the fence. Pack up slowly, don't frighten the kids. I'll go ahead of you – to take the first shots," he grinned. "But seriously, don't toot if you get bogged down, and if we happen to run into them make sure you keep Koki quiet. We don't want to stir things up."

We had a clear run with John leading the way and arrived back at the homestead in the middle of the afternoon. Peter had found another use for his carbolic soap and was on the lawn scrubbing seasonal mould off leather belts and shoes. Mkava sat with him, waiting for us.

"Madam must be careful," Mkava said. "There have been soldiers here. Not like the other ones. These ones are Tsotsies, bad ones. Very, very bad ones."

"What do you mean Mkava?"

"Aah. These ones are not ours. These ones are the Red Berets. They are no good."

"What did they do?" John asked.

"Nothing. They do nothing. They just talk bad."

"OK," I said. "Let me know if they come back." And suddenly thought "How do we warn Monica?"

John sighed. "OK, I'll go to the cottage and leave a note for her." He stayed for a quick cup of tea and left to check the dairy on the way to Red Bank Cottage."

An hour later Mkava was back. But this time he wasn't alone. He didn't want to come, he was brought up from the compound at gun point, by five Red Berets.

"We caught this man hiding in a kia. We are taking him with us," the strutting bantam of a soldier said.

Mkava stood gazing rigidly ahead, his face expressionless but grey and strained.

I began to feel light-headed and wished John was still there.

Who were these strange people? Why do they want Mkava? What the hell is going on?

I dimly heard Peter's voice somewhere in the background, calling Manka, and I realized he was alerting her to get the children out of the way. Breaking the spell, it brought me back to reality.

With as much anger as I could contrive I turned on Mkava, ripping vehemently into him.

"What the hell do you think you are doing hiding in the compound?" I snapped. "You're late. You were supposed to be here half an hour ago. How can I do the bees without you?"

Confusion spread over his face and I turned quickly, to the Red Berets, drawing their attention away from him.

"Thank you so much. It was very kind of you to bring him up here. He's not lazy, he forgets things, he's a bit penga." I tapped my head, pulling a face which I hoped conveyed the impression that this man was subnormal.

A momentarily flash of recognition flew into Mkava's eyes.

"Sorry, too sorry Madam. I forget. It will not happen again."

"You see? He's not bad, just a bit mad," I said to the soldiers. "Leave him to me, I know how to handle him. Would you like cook to make you tea before you go?"

Disconcerted, they looked at each other. They hadn't expected this. Then an older one thanked me. They were glad to be of assistance he said, but they must be going.

"Where? Where are you going?" I asked innocently.

"Somewhere," came the enigmatic reply and I wondered if from guile or if even they didn't know.

Peter, watching from the kitchen, once again immersed himself in frantic activity and when the Red Berets left he emerged with a large tin mug of hot tea and thick slabs of bread spread liberally with jam which he handed to Mkava. He'd heard of these ones, he said. These ones were big trouble. And now he thought Mkava was lucky, very lucky, and so was Madam.

I wondered where Fifth Brigade went that night. We didn't want them on the farm, but on the other hand nor did we want them causing trouble for the neighbours. But they did. And the next morning brought in a flurry of reports.

Tim had left to catch the early morning plane to Harare when Mrs Rankin came through on Agric-Alert at 6.30am. She could hear automatic fire she said, "And my houseboy has appeared saying he'd been threatened but had managed to run away." Control asked her to describe the attackers. "They were wearing ordinary military camouflage and red berets," she replied.

At 6.45am she came on again reporting she now had all the dairy boys in her kitchen and she was dishing out bandages for injuries, "none of them very serious, just a few bayonet wounds."

At 7.30am Barbara Henderson came through using the 'speak button', "Red Berets are all around the fence and my husband is outside talking to them. They said they were Fifth Brigade."

Various other reports came through in quick succession – some farmers were hearing sporadic automatic fire, one reported "Mortar explosions in my vicinity."

Nobody was getting much work done.

Peter Henderson managed to disengage himself from the conversation he was having with Fifth Brigade and announced on Agric-Alert, that one of his boys had been shot in the thigh the day before. He didn't report it at the time because "it didn't seem important", but later he'd taken the boy to Mpilo Hospital and returned early this morning to find the whole work span had been abducted as they were riding to work on the tractor and trailer and no one had seen any of them since. During his conversation at the fence, Fifth brigade denied all knowledge of them.

As the first flurry of reports came in Mike Wood drove through from his farm near Nyamandhlovu and took over the police camp because, he said: "In all cases Nyamandhlovu police are conspicuous by their absence." He sat there, refusing to budge, arguing with officials in Harare until mid afternoon, trying in vain to get Fifth Brigade withdrawn.

I called John to ask if Sheena wanted to bring her baby down to Big Bonisa and stay until the area was clear. He said Sheena was fine and that as far as he knew everything was quiet on Bonisa but not to take the children for a walk this afternoon in case the situation changed.

As I put the phone down Mrs Rankin called over Agric-Alert again. Most of her labour force had been uplifted in army vehicles by Fifth Brigade. "And," she said, "so far I have four dead, plus one pregnant woman with serious bayonet wounds to her stomach, and another who's had her belly jumped on. It doesn't look good for her. And more women and children have been abducted from my compound."

At first we didn't understand what was happening. Why, when Mashonaland was peaceful, was Matabeleland erupting like this? Why were these Red Berets rampaging around the area? Why were they killing the innocent local people? Then we found out. Entumbane had been the catalyst, the excuse for Mugabe to send his North Korean trained praetorian guard, his Fifth Brigade, in to Nkomo's territory, to 'root out the dissidents and protect the whites.' At least that's what they claimed. And that's how it initially seemed, but before long we began to suspect genocide, not against dissidents but against the Ndebele people, and we wondered if it would stop there or if the white farmers would be next.

A dusk to dawn curfew was re-imposed with immediate effect. We couldn't rely on support from the Nyamandhlovu police camp and we took it upon ourselves to increase Roll-Call to three times daily. We applied to have our automatic weapons re-issued but Government refused. The country is at peace we were informed. This is the New Zimbabwe. We even have a New Currency to prove it. We are one nation and the Fifth Brigade are in Matabeleland to protect the white farmers.

"Bull shit!" said John.

35

One afternoon a few weeks after the Ehlers' wedding Monica's Mpofu presented himself at the kitchen door. This time he came without a note. He had a message of his own, he said, and insisted on speaking to me himself. Although reluctant at first, Peter eventually agreed to call me, and when I followed him to the kitchen door he stood firmly between Mpofu and me. Mpofu averted his eyes, there was none of the old arrogance, and I sensed a fear, or possibly guilt, in him.

"Madam, the Nkosikasi, she is very, very sick. Maybe is better if you come," he said. I never trusted Mpofu and hoped it wasn't a trap, but if she really was ill I couldn't refuse to go. On the other hand why hadn't she phoned me herself?

"She too sick," Mpofu said. I told him to meet me at the Land Rover, gathered up my medial bag, asked Peter to inform Boss John where I was going, and left him in the kitchen shaking his head and clucking to himself.

As we drove to the cottage I checked for spoor, but the only recent and obvious tracks could be explained as belonging to Mpofu. There was no sign of Fifth Brigade and no other vehicles or markings. I walked towards the back door with Mpofu trailing behind and called out. There was no reply. I told Mpofu to go to his kia and wait until I came for him and I went inside alone.

Red dust covered the surfaces of tables and in the gloom I could just make out the picture of her friend, Douglas Bader, above the fireplace. All the windows were shut, the curtains closed and an odour of neglect hung in the air. I called again and listened. Monica's voice came indistinctly from the bedroom and I pushed open the door. The bedroom curtains were slightly drawn back letting in a little more light. She lay on top of the bed muttering incoherently, her movements restless and spasmodic, her nightie damply clinging to her. The sharp, acrid smell of stale urine and sweat permeated the room.

"For goodness sake. Monica! What's wrong? How long have you been like this?" I said.

She gripped my hand like a vice and opened her eyes, looking at me without recognition. Jumbled words streamed from her, something about Albert and the Mission Station and names I didn't know. My heart sank. I knew this was beyond anything in my medical bag and, prizing her hand off mine, and hoping the party line would be free, I went to ring her doctor. I knew him from the days I'd worked in the Bulawayo Central Hospital and I'd not had much confidence in him then.

"I think it looks like cerebral malaria," I said when I finally got through. "Perhaps you could send an ambulance?"

But he said he didn't think that would be necessary.

"I'll leave as soon as I can but it will take an hour or so to get to you. In the meantime do what you can," he said, "You're a nurse, you know how to get her temperature down. See what you can do."

The whole cottage seemed to breathe heat. I opened the windows, found some methylated spirits and, fighting off her physical resistance, began to tepid-sponge her. Her temperature dropped a little, but not enough. She refused to drink and seemed to be in pain but unable to tell me where and I sat down beside her, holding her hand. Eventually I rigged up a wet sheet across the open window which cooled the room a little.

Outside the western window I could see the sun lowering in the sky, casting shadows from Mpofu's kia over his scruffy mealie patches. Monica was calmer now, but her breathing was deteriorating, and I hoped help would arrive soon.

About five o'clock the doctor drove through the open security gates and I went out to meet him.

"I don't like this. She's very ill and should really be in hospital," I told him. But after examining her, he was convinced it was just a bad 'go' of ordinary malaria.

"It always looks like this in the acute stage," he said.

I felt impatience welling up in me. "I know what it looks like. I've had it a few times myself. But this? – this is excessive. We don't know how long she's been ill. Mpofu won't tell us the truth because it would make him look negligent, but it must have been for some time, and she's very dehydrated. Couldn't she do with a drip?"

He opened his bag and took out a syringe.

"This should do the trick," he said, gently inserting the needle into her buttock. "Keep in touch and I'll pop out again in a few days. In the meantime get her to drink as much as you can. The crisis will pass soon. She'll be fine in a day or two."

But the crisis didn't pass and she wasn't fine. Tepid-sponging, no longer effective, almost seemed to hurt physically and she fought me off. I wondered if I should try and ring her sister and then remembered Jane MacKenzie was too far gone in her own dementia to be able to comprehend. *Who else was there?* The Beales were dead and I realised how shamefully little we knew of Monica beyond Nyamandhlovu.

It was clearly going to be a long haul and I rang Tim and asked him to bring me some food for the night. When he left again Mpofu followed him out to lock the security gates and return to his kia.

As the night wore on Monica's ramblings came and went, becoming tormented at times. There was little I could do but sit with her, sponging her face and holding her hand.

And then suddenly the pain hit. She thrashed around, flinging herself away from the light, moaning and fighting when I tried to examine her pupils and a cold fear crept into my heart as I knew my fears of cerebral malaria were correct.

The doctor, when I rang him again, said no she could not be moved and neither, because of curfew, could he come out again until morning; but he would leave Bulawayo at first light. In the meantime we would just have to let it run its course.

The night dragged on. I sat there reflecting on how little I knew, not of her history this time but of her as a person. I wondered how old she was, had she ever allowed herself actually to enjoy life, or had it all been duty? Had she been lonely, or did she really prefer her own company? Had she reached her full potential? We all knew she had strong opinions, and stood by them, yet she was not opinionated.

She could be demanding and difficult, but not controlling. She could, and did, manipulate but not to feed her own ego and, although maddening at times, she was unfailingly kind to those she thought needy, and she did it with no expectation of reward. Long forgotten phrases popped into my mind:

"Make sure that what you do in life is enduring." And, "It is given to man to die but once and after that face judgement."

If our time here is supposed to be a preparation for the life to come, how did Monica do?'

"Judge not that ye be not judged," came the inner rebuke followed by an awful thought:

How am I doing for that matter?

I wandered back in to the sitting room and stood looking at Douglas Bader in his spitfire above the fireplace. Monica had claimed a special friendship with him but beyond that I knew nothing and now wished I'd tried a bit harder, asked a few more questions.

Through the open window a forest of stars lit up the clear night sky and, as I gazed at them, I thought how small and insignificant we are and how GG, when in reflective mood used to re-read Bronowski's *Ascent of Man,* which put everything in perspective for her. Somewhere behind Redbank siding a jackal called and I strained to hear if there were other noises, ones that were not bush noises, intensely aware that the cottage didn't have Agric-Alert.

She died easily, eventually, a 'good death', in the early hours – at that time of night when the human spirit is at its lowest ebb, and for the rest of the night I sat, looking into the night, thinking about the mystery of life, love and death and beyond.

When the doctor arrived next morning and brusquely informed me that "Cerebral malaria is vicious, nearly always fatal and very quick," I kept silent.

"Nothing more could have been done," he said. "You did your best."

I did my best? What about you?

"I'll just ring for an ambulance to collect the body, and then I must get back to the surgery."

The body? It's not 'the body' It's Monica's body!

When she had been taken away, I walked over to Mpofu's kia and told him to clean the cottage out properly and I would speak with him later.

36

Despite the problems, visitors kept arriving. Pam Scott, Xan Smiley's aunt from Kenya, came alone and, although a little reserved, she was made of strong, no-nonsense stuff and we loved having her. Her farm at Deloraine, Rongai marched with that of President Moi's and she told the story of being introduced by him at an official function where he praised her lavishly and then added "she may look white, but she has a black heart". Tim had known her some years back and we were sorry her time with us didn't coincide with Xan's.

Christopher Mitchell-Heggs, Jacques Shwartz, Tim and Jeni Webb, Sue Ramsbotham and several others, including friends and Fleming family from Bulawayo came to stay, bringing uplifting and stimulating conversations. Just before Christmas Antonia Gibbs, Tim's twenty-four-year-old cousin came out to visit from London, collecting, on her way through Bulawayo, her friend James Maberly. James had been at school in Plumtree and was very much at home in the bush. But it was all new to Antonia. Her father, the head of our branch of the Gibbs family, was the one who knew most about the large number of relations, and from him she'd heard stories about the farm, about Humphrey, Molly and 'the cousins'. Even so, nothing had prepared her for how quickly and deeply she would become captivated by Bonisa, the bush, the way of life and the view from the verandah stretching away towards the Congo, always the same and constantly changing according to the weather and the time of day. She arrived in 1982 at the end of a particularly prolonged dry season, in time to watch, amazed, as the bleached out colours of the veldt were transformed by violent electrical storms. The bush smells that followed, the red dust turning into rivers of mud running down the escarpment and all the raw wantonness of Africa laid siege to her and held her in its magic. But it was also a tense security time and for that reason I was glad when, after a few days, they both left, James to make his way back to Botswana and Antonia to return home to London.

Antonia didn't get very far. She rang from Harare before boarding the plane for Heathrow. She couldn't leave, she said, she simply wasn't ready to leave it all.

"It's too hard to go and I'd like to help." I hoped she wasn't going to say what I anticipated. "You see, I've never done anything for anyone in my life apart from giving financial donations and I'd really like to come back to Bonisa and help you for a few months. What do you think?"

I didn't think much of the idea at all.

For Antonia life on Bonisa had been new and exciting but for us it was constantly precarious. She had been a cadet at her school in Surrey but we didn't feel that would have adequately equipped her to live in a bush war, especially in a country with people and customs she didn't know. A visit for a few days, we felt, was quite different from learning to live in it over a longer period and it had taken time for us to learn the task of adapting to unpredictable situations and conditions on a daily basis. It was nothing personal but initially the thought of having responsibility for someone else as well for the children did not appeal to us.

She understood my reluctance, she said, but continued to press her case and I gradually began to see that, whereas it would not affect Tim very much, a little extra help for a while could be particularly beneficial for me. But I was still cautious.

"You would have to agree to accept our authority in matters of security – and that includes any instructions from John or anyone else who knows the ropes."

"Yes, of course," she agreed.

"Even when the reason is not immediately obvious to you?"

"Yes. And I could take over the schoolroom and teach Sarah."

"But you don't like getting up early."

"I'll do it," she said.

A few days later I collected her from the airport and brought her back to the farm. Although initially a 6am start didn't come naturally to Antonia, and her natural inclination to be monosyllabic at that hour needed working on, after a little prodding, she adapted quickly, rose early each morning, was a good teacher and Sarah became devoted to her. It was rewarding, she said, watching Sarah learn and grow under her tutorship.

"Great job satisfaction," she said and, apart from the help she gave, I simply loved having her with us.

I found having the burden of the schoolroom lifted from my shoulders liberating and, although the days remained busy, now there was also time to catch up with domesticity, telephone calls and correspondence.

From early on Peter became Antonia's slave. She sympathised every time he stubbed his toe on the brass door stop – something we'd long given up doing – she admired his highly polished floors, and his cooking, insisting that her all time favourite food was 'Peter's Green Soup'.

But John was not Antonia's slave. He grew fond of her and, finding her intelligence and feistiness challenging, he set himself the enjoyable task of taming her. In the late afternoons, for an hour or so before curfew, and sometimes in the early morning before lessons, he took her out in the Land Rover game viewing or hunting for the pot which she loved and whenever possible Egalandi saddled up the rather unkempt ponies for them to ride out together. One day they returned to the homestead without the usual banter or exuberance of a new discovery. This time John appeared frustrated and Antonia was quiet and thoughtful.

"We decided to skirt the lands and see if we could pick up the herd of kudu just this side of the Mpopoma," John said, "but then we ran into a bedraggled group of refugees – about thirty-five of them walking towards Bulawayo from the direction of Tjolotjo. They said they were going to the townships to escape from 'Ma Soldiers', who were 'killing, killing.' I asked who they were killing and they said 'Everyone at Mbamba School'"

"Awful," Antonia said. "They were hungry and thirsty and John offered food from the store but they said there was no time, they had to hurry, they wanted to look for their relatives in town before curfew, although they did accept water."

"That's another thirty miles."

John shrugged. Although dangers left Antonia largely unflinching, even taking the regular appearance of snakes and creepy crawlies in the house in her stride, seeing the refugees so ragged and poor, so defenceless and afraid, with no possible recourse to any sort of justice, was sobering.

With Tim still going away a lot – to Bulawayo, Harare or the gold mine – having Antonia's company filled some of the gaps. She had become very much part of the family and, while the children rested in the day nursery during the heat of the afternoons, Antonia and I swam, or sewed, chatting, in the Billiards Room. Between us we made all the children's clothes including pyjamas and towelling tracksuits on an unreliable old sewing machine, and when that went wrong she stoically carried on stitching by hand.

We were used to some established routines and stuck to them, but it was easy to become lax about closing the security gates during the day, or having the wireless turned up just too loudly and thereby masking any tell-tale noises, or failing to investigate immediately when the fence alarm went off because it was probably just a bird or an animal.

But then Colin Shortis came down again and, without saying anything in particular, he managed to convey the impression that, although there had not been any recent incidents, we should be particularly vigilant at the moment.

Colin and Antonia had met before, on Antonia's previous brief visit when it was obvious that they were total opposites. Antonia, tall, outspoken and in some ways undisciplined (or 'relaxed' depending on your point of view) met her match in Colin who, shorter in stature, older, guarded, very disciplined, sensitive, and accustomed to man-management quickly got her measure. At times he teased her and other times he ignored her, especially her small indulgences, such as bringing her book to read at the breakfast table.

The year was drawing to a close and we sat on the verandah, sipping our sundowners with Antonia, talking about the early days of Nyamandhlovu and Bulawayo. She'd already met a couple of the 'old timers' and had become intrigued as she listened to them reflecting on 'the good old days.' The days when everyone, including the majority of the blacks, felt safe and sure of their future even during the moments it didn't show much promise. The days when boundaries set out in the 'Master/Servant' Act were largely observed and when people such as Farewell Roberts, Civil Commissioner in Bulawayo, and men like him, fulfilled their duties to the best of their ability, holding the welfare of all Rhodesians at heart.

Tim brought the small battery radio out to the verandah and we paused to listen to the news bulletin. Then the report came: "Security forces announces the abduction today of Mr Benjamin Williams, along with his twenty-one-year-old grandson, Mr David Bilang from Mr Williams' farm near Turk Mine. Nothing has been heard of them since and security forces are following up."

I went cold and felt as if some sort of vital energy drained out of me. We knew Benjie and feared that he would not be diplomatic with his captors. He would be furious, possibly reckless, he might even blame them for the death of his son, Huntsman. Painful memories came flooding back of the day Hunty died and the way, being out of range of medical help, he'd bled to death when his arm was ripped off by a rocket fired into the cab of his vehicle. No, I was sure Benjie could not be expected to be circumspect.

Despite the slightly cooler evening air, mosquitoes whined between silent attacks and we went inside, which wasn't much better as the gap between the top of the walls and the thatched roof simply made them fly a little higher, and we each lit one cigarette after another, blowing the smoke around us to little avail.

Antonia offered to bath the children and I walked down to the dam and sat, alone, on the bank's hard baked earth watching a small flock of pelicans.

Please God let them be alright. Give Benjie patience and wisdom.

I reflected on the times we'd had together – the occasional shooting parties at Battlefields Ranch, and Bonisa, the lunches and dinners we'd enjoyed, and visiting Ineke and Hunty's baby, Sasha, for the first time, and I could hardly imagine what the rest of the family must be going through. How were David's parents, Cyril and Sharon, coping?

After a while, old, familiar questions began tumbling around in my mind.

And us? What if it were us? Or our children?

Although young children had not been abducted so far, what guarantees were there that they would always be spared? After all, we'd thought that before and then the Stratford grandchildren were murdered. What would happen if that began?

What are we doing?

As usual, no reassuring answers came to mind and I sat for a long time trying to concentrate on being realistic rather than emotional. The air cooled and chilled as the sun sank rapidly towards the far dam wall. I got to my feet, waited a minute to watch the fish eagle swoop low over the water and fly off again empty handed, and then walked slowly back to the homestead, the questions still unanswered.

A few weeks before, Benjie's daughter, Sippy, had invited us to a New Year's Day lunch party in their magnificently landscaped garden high on the hill overlooking Bulawayo, and we wondered if she would cancel it; after all it would be only twenty-four hours after her father and nephew had been taken. But she rang to confirm that the lunch would be going ahead, saying that Benjie always said 'life must carry on,' everything had been prepared and the most comforting thing is having family and friends around.

Those of us who lived in the bush understood – these were times for uniting, for standing together in the deeper, darker moments while preserving as normal a life as possible, at least on the surface. Over the years, living on two levels at the same time had become a way of life. And so we made plans to leave the children in Bulawayo with MG and GG and continuing on to Hillside to be with Sippy, her husband Boo and other friends.

37

Just before New Year Tim had flown up to Harare for a meeting with Mugabe, and to meet with Jacques Schwartz and Senator Showina again. Although Mugabe seemed to be encouraging new businesses, and the security situation in Mashonaland had settled, the plans for setting up an export business were not going well. Perhaps the timing wasn't right but, whatever it was, they needed to find the reason before taking it much further. He expected to be home before evening, he said; after all no business would be done on New Year's Day.

I was sitting on the verandah, wondering what it would take for Mugabe to accept Joshua Nkomo and make way for Matabeleland to become as stable as Mashonaland, when Peter brought out a tray of coffee and placed it on the big table under the map. There were two more white pins off to the side of the map representing Benjie and David and I hoped and prayed I would soon be removing them and they wouldn't turn red.

A few minutes later John came in from the New Farm to join me. I could see at once that something was wrong. He stood, facing out over the lands, his eyes focussed on the horizon, his jaw muscles working.

"Coffee John?"

He didn't reply immediately and then said: "Just heard, the new ones, the Walters, on Lonrhos – they've been hit."

"What? Are they alright?" I said.

Before he could answer Agric-Alert burst into life, we turned the volume up to listen to security forces at the scene calling Control in Nyamandhlovu.

As the whole horror of the situation began to unfold we knew that others would also be listening in shocked disbelief as Control asked the questions and monosyllabic reports came back, in unemotional almost matter-of-fact tones.

"Negative Control, he's dead. Negative, he's also dead. Negative, two children ..... also dead."

John lowered himself heavily into the chair and the questions raced around in my mind competing to be asked.

"Where were they? They've got Agric-Alert haven't they? Why didn't they use it? What about his wife? You didn't mention her."

"No time," John said. "They were off-loading maize meal from the railway siding out in the sticks. Another bloody ambush. Dave had the mobile Agric in the Land Rover but they were taken out before he could use it."

We sat for a moment not speaking.

"I make that six dead. Can't be right can it?" I said.

"Y..y..yes," John took a deep breath to his stutter and went on. "It was Dave, his two sons, Sean and Michael I think their names were. Oh God, I think they were both under five. D.. D.. Dave's brother-in-law, John Hearn, a good sort, also got it and two security guards – a Frog, Phillipe Boiron, and a local, called Themba Ndebele. I'd heard Dave had employed them but I'd not met either of them."

"And his wife?" I repeated.

"Michelle's in shock but I don't know where she is now. She was in the house when it happened, with a Japanese girl – The Frog, Boiron's, fiancée. Apparently the telephone was out of order, or so they said. Sod's law."

When lessons were over, Antonia came through from the schoolroom to join us, and John repeated the story. Talking it over seemed to help and I asked John if he and Sheena would like come up from New Farm and spend the night on Big Bonisa. Unusually, I suddenly felt it would be good for us all to be together that night. There was plenty of room. Tim was still in Harare and, although Humphrey usually came over from Little Bonisa when activity erupted in the district, Molly often went to stay with friends in town for the night. When John returned from ringing Sheena, I went off to tell Manka to make up three extra beds and ask Peter to take another guinea fowl out of the freezer.

In the coolness of the evening we sat on the Morris chairs again, watching the red and gold streaks of sunset. Tim had returned on the late afternoon plane. John and Sheena had come up just before curfew and, when all the young had taken their cool drinks out to play on to the top lawn, John turned to us and said: "I spoke to Sunray earlier. Dissidents have set up road blocks on all the main roads out of Bulawayo again. They're firing indiscriminately. So far this week three have been killed by them and twenty injured – all blacks so you won't hear that on the news."

"These ones not Fifth Brigade?" I asked.

"Sunray said Dissidents, but I don't know. He also dropped in that Dave and the others had been robbed of their shirts and wrist watches. I'm told one of the neighbour's kids, the one about eight, said to his father that if that had been him he wouldn't have had a very long life would he?"

"Did he have any further news about Michelle?" I said. "Do hope someone in town is looking after her."

"No. Sunray told me she's been admitted into Bulawayo Central with slashed wrists."

Tim turned on the radio and Comrade Mugabe's voice crackled over the airwaves halfway through a sentence "….when apprehended and proved guilty they must receive the sternest of all punishments – death. Those who kill in cold blood must suffer nothing less than death in cold blood." Maybe some believed him, but I didn't. Even then.

Over the next few days more than 2,000 troops arrived with tracker dogs, helicopter gun-ships, spotter planes, armoured cars and other vehicles to sweep the East Falls Road area. There were no arrests and the by now familiar feeling of restlessness filled each of us. Again we found ourselves becoming hyper-alert.

To add to the difficulties a severe drought hung over the land, and with it the stench of death. There were reports of starving cattle overrunning gardens, and eating flowers and vegetables. Around kraals baboons began eating goats and chickens, prompting one old kraal chief to say: "Baboons have become leopards because of the drought." The Christian Aid charity used ingeniously devious methods to bring food to tribesmen beyond Nyamandhlovu, deep in the Tribal Trust Lands of Tjolotjo. Disguised as travelling fertilizer salesmen they brought coarse salt, sugar beans, powered milk, dried Kapenta from Kariba, peanuts and maize. They used interconnecting farm tracks. And they got away with it. As dams dried up the death toll soared. To the north of us ninety-eight elephants were found dead in Wankie game reserve, and further south elephants and cows fought for muddy pools – the cows usually being the losers. Tribesmen lost count and stopped skinning the dead cattle.

But, perhaps due to its size and specific catchment area, Bonisa Dam still had reasonable water. Large numbers of birds began arriving and we continued to hear the soul cry of the fish eagle outside the bedroom window every morning.

A few days later Tim, as Vice-chairman of the Matabeleland Commercial Farmer's Union (CFU), met with the Security Minister, Comrade Emmerson Mananagwa, and the Defence Minister, Comrade Sydney Sekeramayi, in addition to Rex Nhongo, who led Mugabe's fighters in the bush war and who was now the head of the Zimbabwe Army. Nothing came out of the meeting beyond vague promises to 'look into the situation'.

38

The next day was New Year's Day and after dropping the children off at Mzinzini with the Flemings, we arrived at Sippy's a few minutes late. Patches of coloured shrubs stood out in front of the ranch-style house, and we walked around the side to the front garden. Here, sweeping down to the edge of the hill overlooking Bulawayo, a lawn, lush, green and springy under foot, hinting at a copious bore-hole, was dotted with several tables laid out with highly-polished silver and glass, on white cloths. To one side of the grass the swimming pool dazzlingly reflected the white-hot sun. Surrounding the lawns flower beds, scented shrubs and blossoming trees splashed colour against the pale blue sky.

We drifted down towards the pool and the large shade trees at the side where several other friends were gathered. Sippy, one of the most beautiful women in Bulawayo and a vision of slim elegance in a dress of soft blue silk, came down the lawn to join us. Despite her cheerful conversation her face was pale, and behind her eyes lay an unexpressed anxiety.

The day before, as soon as the news had come through that Benjie had been abducted, Boo had gone out to Turk Mine, taking only his hunting rifle for protection because we had recently been disarmed of our automatic weapons. He returned later saying the place was "swarming with security forces and fairly chaotic. They described the exact area being searched by the follow-up team and the bleak revelation, volunteered by Benjie's cook, that Benjie had verbally lashed out at his abductors and called them names." It was understandable but, no matter how justified, it did not bode well, especially in the New Zimbabwe and a sobering silence fell. Our hope now was that the abductors might hold their hostages for a reward. It was a slim hope but we clung onto it.

"Boo isn't here. He sends his apologies," Sippy said. "He has gone up to Harare to see if the High Commissioner can do anything to help – Pat Wesson flew him up in his plane and so, with luck, they will be back a bit later."

Several servants in white-starched uniforms, bearing trays of drinks and silver boxes containing cigarettes, moved amongst the guests. Conversations revolved around the usual topics and we were not surprised to find that, apart from a smattering of personal gossip, politics and 'the situation' dominated. The first question on each new arrival's lips was a quietly voiced: "Any news?" But otherwise no one mentioned Benjie or David by name – it was too raw.

Antonia said afterwards that if she hadn't already known, she would never have guessed that there was anything wrong, that the day was anything other than a happy gathering in an extraordinarily beautiful garden. In the few days since Antonia had arrived with us she'd assimilated a lot regarding 'the situation' and, although younger and the only outsider in a group who knew each other well, she was well-informed and held her own.

Sippy's father and her young nephew, David, had been close during the past few years – since Benjie's son, Huntsman, had died and David had matured. It had been a tough time for the family but they were a strong family and now we hoped that father and nephew would be restored to them soon.

I talked with Paddy and Paul Fehrsen and, as everyone's doctor, I thought of how many of us Paul had seen through difficult times and It was good that he was there too.

"I believe that Ant and Ginnie Johnson are coming in from Botswana," Paul said. "I hope he's brought lots of contraband!"

Ant had been one of Duncan's closest friends and he'd done the same thing for us when, three days before Duncan died, I'd arranged a large Christening party for Sarah, who was only a few weeks old. It was a good excuse to gather his friends, to give them an opportunity to say goodbye and to give Duncan a lot of pleasure without an awareness of how ill he was, for that was something he always said he didn't want to know.

236

As the day grew hotter, ice melted, drinks warmed, the edge of cheerfulness blunted and two or three of the older ones were beginning to droop. I was sitting next to Ant.

"You're not thinking of joining the rush to leave are you?" he said.

"No! I'd like to make contingency plans, just in case, but Tim doesn't want to go that far just yet. He'd really like to believe there's hope. I would too, but I'm not so sure."

"You know what? It won't be one of the big incidents that makes you pack your bags. It will be some officious little creep at the border post or the cocky waiter or petrol attendant that will be the last straw."

Towards the end of lunch one of Sippy's servants lent over and whispered something to her. She excused herself, rose from the table and slipped up to the house. A few moments later I also went up to the house. As I entered the hall, Sippy was holding the telephone. She was very still but not speaking. It was her cousin, Phil Williams, on the telephone from his farm at Turk Mine. They'd found Benjie's body. He'd been beheaded. David had not been found yet.

"The others need to be told." Sippy looked dazed, her voice flat. I nodded and stepped out onto the lawn again. I began walking down towards the tables. But this time I couldn't do it, I needed just a moment to myself. Turning aside I walked off to beyond the shrubbery and stood on the edge of the hill looking out over Bulawayo. My throat felt paralysed with a deep sadness mixed with inner rage. There was a sound of foot fall and someone came and stood next to me. I didn't turn around. It was Ant.

"Benjie?" he said. I nodded.

"Dead?" I nodded again. After a short silence he said matter of factly, "Too hard? It's alright. I'll do it." He turned and walked slowly back across the lawn and after a moment I followed.

By the 20th January 1983 large advertisements appeared in the national newspapers offering a reward 'For correct information leading to the release and safe return of Hostage: David Bilang. A substantial reward payable in cash or in cattle.' A few weeks later David's body was found near a rocky out crop not far from where they were abducted.

39

What appeared to be specifically targeted farmers and their families began receiving threatening letters containing promises that they would be 'dealt with' in the same way as they had dealt with Benjie. But as the letters didn't come with any demands or caveats none of us knew what was expected of us.

Another two weeks passed before Robert Mugabe came down from Harare and met with farmers in Marula, a village south west of Bulawayo, where, once more, he promised to 'look into your problems'. John was there when Dave Joubert, a local farmer, in his own idiosyncratic way giving scores out of a hundred, told him to his face that the problems were 80% security, 55% drought and 15% economic (especially petrol and diesel shortages). Mugabe responded "Don't worry about what you read in the press. Watch what I do, not what I say!"

Nothing changed.

An underlying weariness pervaded us all. My hope was slipping away and in its place a deep sense of foreboding began rising until once again I said to Tim that we ought to be making contingency plans, or at least have some sort of strategy, in case we were thrown into our own emergency and had to leave in a hurry. But Tim remained optimistic.

"It's a bad patch,." he said. "It'll blow over and will come right in the end." But it didn't and when, on one of the outlying properties, an elderly farmer was brutally stabbed to death, Henry de Lange, for one, had had enough. He closed his stores in Nyamandhlovu and Inyathi saying: "Roads in the remote areas are just too bloody dangerous now." And he and Petronella moved into town leaving only Martin Old's Butcher shop still open for business in Nyamandhlovu. The district itself seemed to be dying, and Nyamandhlovu took on the atmosphere of a ghost town.

Joshua Nkomo fled into exile, illegally crossing the Botswana border dressed as a woman, or so it was reported; a charge he later denied.

He was going "to look for 'solutions' to the Zimbabwean problems abroad," he said. To the consternation of his people in Matabeleland 'The Father of The Nation' claimed political asylum in Britain, and while there he was interviewed by Jeremy Paxman. "I had to leave, I was under threat to my life. The Fifth Brigade raided my house. The Fifth Brigade is a political army, and they killed three people in my house when they raided it. I had to go." He repeatedly denied any connection with dissidents calling them 'vermin' and saying that there were hundreds of bodies rotting in the bush, being eaten by wild animals and vultures, and blaming it all on the Fifth Brigade.

However, back in Zimbabwe, two of Nkomo's senior military men, Dumisa Dabengwa, ZIPRA's Intelligence Chief, and Lookout Masuku, Commander of ZIPRA forces, were put in detention and, along with four others, were charged with treason. They were acquitted, but nevertheless the government ordered their indefinite detention and, although Dabengwa was eventually released, Masuku was detained until a few weeks before his death.

On April 5th the curfew was lifted and two days later the BBC rang and asked if I would be interviewed on The World Today. With all my antipathy to being interviewed I formed the word "No" in my mouth but it was "Yes" that came out. The interviewer was professional, respectful and kind, and I remember saying something about the "law of the jungle" and that "the threat of death gives added significance to life. Priorities get sorted out and tolerance for other lesser values evaporated." *Where did those words come from?* I put the phone down, thinking it was soothing to have managed to express something of the gradual changes that had taken place in all our lives, changes that had been largely hidden or ignored by International powers and the British Government in particular.

Colin Shortis understood our apprehensions and the risks involved in speaking with the media. My main concern was of us being misquoted, and when he produced a special recorder for attaching to our telephone, one that would record all conversations, it gave us more confidence.

"It feels odd tapping our own phone," I said.

240

"Should anyone try and make a false statement you will now have proof of the conversation," he replied.

The next time Colin came to visit us he brought with him Brigadier Edward Jones, a particular pleasure for us as he was a cousin of Tim's we'd not met before; a Green Jacket, who was due to take over as Commander of BMATT from Colin now that his term of office was coming to an end. We would miss Colin enormously but also liked Edward immediately, and hoped he would be as good and a regular visitor. He said he intended to continue using the web of ground-cover Colin had built up and that this was his induction trip to Matabeleland. The nights were becoming chilly and that evening, after dinner, I lit a huge fire in the drawing room and we sat talking until the small hours.

"You do realise that no matter what crimes they commit, soldiers of the Fifth Brigade are protected by an indemnity act – a remnant of white minority rule – that shields government troops from prosecution for atrocities carried out 'in the interests of national security'," Edward said.

"Even when two little girls at a village school had their hands chopped off," Colin said, and went on giving Edward more of 'the story' of Matabeleland and asking us questions to fill any gaps.

The flamingos were temporarily back on the dam on their way north in the migration, and next morning we took Edward and Colin to see them. John told them that some expert ornithologist had come out to the farm and said the variety of bird life was exceptional – over 200 different types. There were only a few flamingos this morning and as they took off we also noticed Spurwing Geese, Egyptian Geese, Hamerkops and Saddle Billed Storks along with a few Whistling Ducks. "A bird watcher's paradise," Edward said. "You could almost believe this was heaven and will continue for ever."

Colin asked after Antonia and I told him that her mother had sent tickets for the six of us to have a holiday in the UK. "We think Antonia must have told her the stark facts about 'the situation' here," I said.

"Go and enjoy it," he urged. "Go and join Nkomo!"

We thought hard about the difficulties of leaving the farm to fly to the UK but, like Colin, both Humphrey and John urged us to use the tickets and go, and "go now, before second thoughts take hold," and we did.

As we landed at Heathrow and then took a taxi along the motorway to stay with Margaret in Windsor Great Park, I was struck by the awful smells – smells of exhaust fumes, diesel, and the heavy, dank air, and I felt as if the sky and the traffic were crowding in on us. But the greenness of the park with its tall sturdy trees and the warmth of Margaret's welcome gave us respite in a more familiar environment of space and fresher air. At the instigation of Antonia's mother, Mary Aldenham, we began to plan dates for a tour from the south of England to the north of Scotland, visiting some of the large Gibbs family who were known to Tim but not to the children and me. One of the cousins lent us a car. It was a marathon with four children but, unbeknown to us, there was a purpose to it all. Mary had not only provided the tickets, she'd also asked that our last two nights before returning to Bonisa would be spent with her and Anthony.

"What do you think of England?" she asked on our last morning.

"A breath of fresh air," Tim said which, remembering my first impression, was not quite the expression I'd have used, but it did feel like a safe haven and we told her how grateful we were to her for providing us with the most wonderful holiday. The children had changed during the three weeks we were there and we'd not realised how much we'd needed it.

"Anthony and I would like to make that permanent," she said. "If you would consider coming over here to live, the first thing you would need is a roof over your heads. I've asked another cousin, Sam Goodenough, who I know is coming to stay with you and who you may not know is chairman of Knight Frank and Rutley, how much money would be needed to buy a suitable house for you and your family. Anthony and I would like to lend you that money, in cash, for you to choose your own home. It would be interest free and you need only begin paying it back when you are able to afford it."

We were stunned.

"Don't give us an answer at the moment. But now you have options. When the right moment arrives, you will know this offer is available."

It is hard to thank adequately someone who has made such an offer. Perhaps the speechless filling of my eyes told her. In any case, from their point of view the matter was closed and she changed the subject to how many trout they'd caught that season in the river running down the side of their manor house. But, grateful as I was, and recognising that this could be part of the answer for a contingency plan, I still yearned to get back to Bonisa.

We flew back to Zimbabwe revitalised and feeling greatly supported, but I was also in turmoil. Even as we circled Bulawayo, looking down on the parched veldt where military vehicles stood around the perimeter protecting the runway, I just knew I couldn't leave – not yet, I just couldn't leave yet.

40

After Nkomo had turned up in the UK in self-imposed exile, there were no further incidents, and for several months life on Bonisa settled back into the usual routine. Tim felt encouraged; perhaps that was the end of dissident and Fifth Brigade activity, he said and Ian Brebner, another Nyamandhlovu farmer, said he now had a 'tentative hope' when they met a few days before at the Farmers' Club. Martin Olds and Broncho Greaves had chipped in and vowed that, whatever happened, they were staying until things returned to normal or they would be the ones to put out the lights. Even so, what was regarded as 'normal' included the unspoken questions: Where? When? and Who next?

It was 14th June 1983, David's 9th birthday, and a beautiful crisp morning, heralding one of the last days of autumn. After a run of visitors we were having a quiet family time for a week or so before Sam Goodenough was due to arrive. Roll-Call had not begun and it was too early for the children to be up, so I strolled out on to the top lawn and sat on the edge of the escarpment in a moment of pure contentment, watching the meercats playing around the big old tree stump. A brief golden glow spread across the expanse of pale blue, its warmth penetrating the chill.

Although Tim only had a drive of fifty miles or so to the gold mine, he'd left early because the road was rough, hazardous and slow as it wound through the Tribal Trust Lands, and he wanted to be there to start Solomon and the team on what promised to be a demanding day.

I was preoccupied, daydreaming, in the beauty of the early morning when spluttering erupted from Agric-Alert, sending meercats scattering across the garden to disappear down holes. A deep African voice poured out of the set.

"Good Morning everyone, this is Control. Standby for Roll-Call."

Reluctantly I got up and returned to the bedroom.

When everyone in the district had been accounted for, I took Sarah off to the schoolroom and left David, James and Caroline in Manka's care. Tim had planned to bring sludge back from the cyanide tanks that afternoon and smelt it in the crucible over a gas cylinder he'd set up behind the kitchen. I'd promised the children they could stay up late that night to watch and in return they had promised to be 'good'. Manka nodded – she never had a problem with them, to her mind they were always good.

After school Sarah and I joined the others around the courtyard fountain for their mid morning cool drinks. Peter, oblivious to the sound of his bare feet slapping gently on the cement floor, clicked his tongue to announce his arrival and put his coffee tray on the verandah table just as the telephone rang. I went inside and picked it up.

"Hello, Sue?" his voice urgent, Tony Sharp from his farm over the Khami went on, "Sue, Ian Brebner's been shot."

I went cold.

"Jenny's hiding behind the cattle troughs and can't get to him – he's probably dead anyway. Hello, you there Sue?"

"Yes."

"The problem is," he continued, "that three separate workers ran all the way to the Nyama Police Camp, completely of their own accord apparently, but all of them were turned away. The district police simply didn't want to know."

"We'd hoped it wouldn't come to this."

"They must have disabled their Agric-Alert. Anyway, for the first time it didn't work. So I rang Sgt. Moyo – he refused even to accept the report. You know why of course."

"Yes," was all I could say.

"Because," he went on, his anger increasing with every word, "once they accept a report they are required to respond and the incompetent bastards probably know it was Fifth Brigade... shit scared they are! Only interested in saving their own black skins."

What can I do? Struggling to think practically I said, "OK... I'll see if I can contact Colin Shortis. He'll know what to do. I'll get back to you on landline in case Agric is compromised. "

"I was going to suggest that. The British chap would be better than that idiot Nhongo, and he outranks him."

My own belated rage began surging up through me, but I sent up a silent prayer of thanks as I was put straight through to Colin the first time of trying. He sounded businesslike and impatient as he picked up the telephone with a curt "Yes?" but then listened in attentive silence as I poured out my story.

"Jenny needs to be rescued if they haven't already gone for her too... And now," I reminded him, "none of us can go and help as you will remember the Zimbabwe Army disarmed us some time ago. At least four reports have been sent to the Police Camp, three on foot and one by 'phone, and still they won't react."

"Won't they indeed!" was his terse reply and he hung up.

I suspected Colin might have to battle with Brigadier Rex Nhongo. Although Colin never said, our impression of Nhongo was of a secretive, puffed up little man, who was deeply resentful that the British had sent out a man of higher rank than himself and there was nothing he could do about it. But Colin was the only man in the country who would be capable and willing to resolve the situation and of doing it quickly.

Hope was tempered by an overwhelming sense of personal helplessness and despair as I wandered through to the courtyard and sat on the wall of the fountain pool, staring at the goldfish swimming peacefully between the water lilies. It didn't feel as if time existed any more, but it could not have been more than an hour or so later when a deafening cacophony of clattering rotor blades shattered the quiet over the thatched roof surrounding the courtyard. James ran into the courtyard, screaming, into the downdraft, as the bottle brush bent over, scattering its blossoms around the fishpond. I looked up. Three helicopter gun-ships tilted slightly, one after the other, and thundered off towards the west and Brebners' farm.

Bush telegraph worked quickly and within a few hours every farmer knew that Ian had been killed almost instantly and that his body had been recovered and taken to Bulawayo. But for Jenny, forced to watch, hiding behind the cattle trough, it had been merciless. To everyone's relief she had been rescued, uninjured, and taken to relatives where she was still being looked after.

Tim returned home from the Ngede in the late afternoon. He'd had a good day.

"Best day for weeks," he said. "All the labour force turned up, not one of them drunk. They'd hit payload a couple of days ago and revealed what looks like a rich seam. Solomon did all the right things, the three-stamp mill worked all day without breaking down, and quite a lot of crushed ore went into the cyanide tank. I've brought back copious amounts of sludge to smelt — it looks good. I knew Solomon was a good one when I hired him." I'd never heard Tim talk so much. "And," he went on, "they've also graded part of the road in the Tribal Trust Lands. I suppose it's still too early to have a drink to celebrate. How was your day?"

"It's not too early to have a drink. But it won't be a celebration one," I said.

And I told him about my day.

He was silent for a while, his jaw working, and his grim face said it all.

"Right. That's it. We're leaving Zimbabwe," he almost whispered, "Let's have that drink now."

41

A few days later an article by Stephen Taylor appeared in *The Times* of London under the heading *Fear and Fatalism down on the Farm*. In it he described the service at the Church of Ascension 'jammed with mourners, mainly deeply-tanned men' but he neglected to mention the women. More often than not it was the women who were left behind, who swelled the congregations at funerals. Stephen wrote that Ian had been killed by a band of eight men who stepped out from behind a reservoir and shot him and that he'd been the twenty-eighth white to be killed in the past sixteen months. He went on to say that the numbers of white farmers in the Nyamandhlovu district had dropped from sixty to twenty-five in three years. But Matabeleland farmers made up only about fifteen per cent of the 4,500 of the country's farmers, the great majority of whom were in little danger.

Bob Sayers farm marched with the Brebners' and he was a veteran of the bush war. But now he said he'd had enough. His children were at Whitestone's prep School with the Tavenor girls and when Tammy and Candy, with hands tied behind their backs were murdered with their grand parents, Bob's children, just like ours — especially David — had been affected. "I'm packing up," Bob was reported as saying, "I can see no future for us on the farm."

We didn't hear from Colin again for two weeks, but when he next came to stay I told him how much we'd all appreciated such a rapid response to my call and I asked how he'd managed it.

"How did Rex Ngnongo react? Did you ask him politely or did you have to stamp your feet and pull rank? " I said. But, he told me it would be better if I didn't ask, and refused to discuss it. We'd heard stories about Rex Ngnongo but although, as head of the Zimbabwe Army, he would have been a difficult person to deal with, Perence Shiri, head of the Fifth Brigade would have been worse. Shiri, a cousin of Mugabe, liked to be known as Black Jesus because it was said that he could "determine your life like Jesus Christ. He could heal, raise the dead and he could say if you lived or not."

Colin said he'd seen movement around Monica's cottage as he arrived and it was only then that I remembered Mpofu.

Was he still there? Did he have food? Had he been paid? What would happen to him now? I drove down to the cottage. A cooking fire was burning outside his kia but there was no sign of life. His belongings lay untidily strewn around on the ground. Pushing open the kia door I peered into the small, dingy room and felt a surge of anger. There, propped against the filthy wall on the far side was Monica's picture of the spitfire with a smiling Douglas Bader waving out of his cockpit into the gloom. I hadn't noticed it had gone from the cottage. I decided Mpofu was probably in the beer hall and would be back as time for curfew drew near. Picking up the painting, I returned to the homestead.

It was now the end of June, and two weeks since Tim had announced that we were to leave Zimbabwe. Two weeks of living with inner doubt and turmoil, which was strange because, since the spate of violence and murders around the New Year, I had been urging Tim even more fervently to discuss a possible range of contingency plans for leaving which, if necessary, could be brought into action quickly. We'd seen others making decisions on the spur of the moment, in the middle of a personal tragedy, ones that had not been right for them and had only added to their misery. I'd wanted to avoid that. But during that time Tim had not believed 'the situation' would last for ever. He'd been confident that peace and prosperity would eventually return to Matabeleland and that what we were going through was just a hiccup.

I didn't regard the on-going incidents, the murder of white farmers and the genocide against the blacks in the same way, and I persistently tried to persuade him to change his mind. But now the situation was reversed. It was bewildering that, in the instant Tim had said "we are leaving" something in me rebelled, and inside I was silently screaming '*NO, I love it here,*' and I knew that, despite all my efforts, I wasn't ready to go.

Tim's parents, our family, John Zurnamer and his family, put together added up to eleven whites on the farm – not a good number statistically when set against the fact that ten per cent of the whites in the Nyamandhlovu District had been murdered in the previous six months. Logically, it was the right decision, but desperate, illogical 'may-be's' played over and over in my mind. Maybe Fifth Brigade would be withdrawn, maybe Ian's death would be the last one, maybe the Ndebele would rise up, maybe the rains would come...

Following Ian Brebner's murder the government had, under pressure, re-armed us with G3 assault rifles, but we knew when these were eventually withdrawn once more we would be left vulnerable again. In the meantime, we continued to drive around in armoured vehicles – the Leopard or the Friendly – to sweep the sandy soil leading up to the security fence each evening and examine it for foot prints each morning; to employ armed guards to patrol around the house inside the security fence day and night; to answer Agric-Alert Roll Call three times a day; to check on neighbours; and after changing for dinner each evening to sit, pistols strapped to our belts with the radio turned down low while we half listened for any untoward noises. It was business as usual. At some level we knew this was not the way to live but we had become slowly conditioned to it over the years and for us this was normality.

A few visitors still came to see us and when Sam Goodenough, an unmarried, middle-aged cousin, arrived from England we didn't mention Tim's decision to leave, because I had unexpectedly found myself inwardly still unable to completely accept it. I was looking for some sort of sign, something more specific, before coming fully to the same decision. And for this reason we'd not told Humphrey and Molly nor anyone else. If Sam was a joy to us Peter found him perplexing. He appeared each morning in Peter's kitchen, sometimes in his pyjamas, and insisted on cooking his own bacon – unheard of behaviour in a guest. When done to his satisfaction he then poured 'Madam's honey' all over the bacon in a way that did not meet with Peter's approval. After joining the family to eat the rest of his breakfast, which Peter had set out in the dining room, Sam picked up his paints, brushes, easel and folding chair and disappeared into the bush until it was time to eat again.

From time to time friends from Bulawayo and other places within Zimbabwe joined us for a night or two and the international press continued to arrive, usually staying only a few hours, but occasionally overnight, before moving on with their stories. With the local press heavily censored, we co-operated with the ones from outside as much as we dared. We regarded getting the truth of what Fifth Brigade were doing out to the rest of the world as a form of secret weapon. Most reported factually, respecting our sensitive position, but a few glossed over the terrible suffering of the blacks and came close to romanticizing the dramatic plight of the whites.

Amongst the honourable ones were Jeremy Paxman and Philip Hayton from the BBC who would only take first hand information and, as far as we later heard, they reported accurately.

The agony of my indecision continued to bubble away beneath the surface of every day life. There had been no further attacks recently and, apart from a few reported 'sightings', security had generally settled down into a quiet patch. Although we welcomed this, it was also true that this was often the most dangerous time, when vigilance did not seem so critical and farmers began to relax a little. The lack of activity encouraged Tim's cousins, Rupert and Luke Ponsonby to visit us from London, bringing with them Henry Bowring, a young bachelor friend of theirs. They came with all the vitality and optimism of youth, lifted our spirits, and injected energy into us. Tim and I didn't discuss the future any more and my decision-making was temporarily forgotten in the fullness of each day and now the good company.

On their last night with us, as we took our coffee out onto the verandah to look at the stars, we told them of Ross Benson's visit, revelling again in his encounter with the chongololos. Henry had a shotgun in his hand and looking up said, "Would you like a real snake?" Swinging the butt to his shoulder in one swift movement he took aim at overhead gum poles supporting the thatch and fired. We all leapt out of our chairs except Henry as, at our feet landed a fat, five foot long python. Henry broke the astonished silence. "This place is *such* good fun," he said.

When Peter came out to collect the coffee tray and say goodnight Tim suggested a game of billiards and lead the way through the courtyard to the big room at the back. It had been raining and the room, although not cold, felt damp. Tim put a match to the logs already laid in the cavernous fireplace and threw open all the windows. At one end of the room David and Sarah played snakes and ladders while James and Caroline sat drawing and colouring in their books on the sofa covered in denim by Elias; I didn't mind if it got paint all over it. Looking at the happy family scene I decided that to leave this might mean giving up too much altogether. Maybe more than I could bear. I leaned against the mantelpiece watching Tim, Rupert, Luke and Henry engrossed in their billiard game and felt a deep contentment, something I'd not known for a long time.

Stretching out my arms I put my hands behind my head. Everyone heard the tearing sound as the shirt sleeve split open over my left elbow – my favourite shirt! dark blue with little white motifs, in Egyptian cotton. A few years before I had admired it on Peter Foote and he had gallantly taken it off, there and then, and given it to me. I treasured it and when the collar and cuffs became threadbare I had even taken the trouble to turn them. But it was obvious that it was now beyond repair. Before allowing the temptation to patch it again to take over, I took it off and threw it in the fire behind me.

There was a momentary silence. Everyone was watching. Sarah, aghast, ran over and hugged me around the knees, crying.

"That was your funeral shirt," she said. "Now what are you going to wear to all your friends funerals?"

Something in me snapped, shocked she had assumed that friends would continue to be murdered as the natural way of life.

I looked at Tim who was still watching,

"Right. Yes, now I am also ready," I said.

42

Although we'd made the decision to leave we decided to plan it properly and in the meantime to maintain an appearance of normality, and not tell anyone until we ourselves had a clearer idea of when, and where we would go. Making investigations without revealing the purpose proved challenging, but then the BBC *Panorama* team from London arranged to visit. When Jeremy Paxman and Phillip Haydon arrived with their cameraman early in the morning Peter brought coffee out to the verandah and we spent a while talking generally about Zimbabwe and events in the wider world which, thanks to the airmail edition of *The Times*, we felt reasonably informed enough to discuss. But when Jeremy asked if I would also agree to be interviewed, I refused "Because," I said, "I don't think I could add to anything Tim might say," which they appeared to accept. They took the big Morris chairs on to the top lawn and sat there putting questions to Tim while filming him from various angles. I stood behind their chairs, watching and trying to keep the children quiet. Tim answered each question carefully, aware of a possible backlash if his words were transmitted within the country, and managing to avoid any mention of our future plans. At last, when it was over, they got up to leave. Phillip turned towards me, smiled and said how difficult it must be bringing up children in these circumstances.

"Yes," I said, recoiling from the fluffy microphone which was suddenly thrust in front of my face. "Yes, and we do wonder how much longer we can stick it out."

He had half turned and begun walking away, but then abruptly swung back again. The microphone shoved closer.

"Does that mean you're thinking of leaving?"

Seized with panic I stammered something which I hoped afterwards had sounded noncommittal, or even like nonsense, anything other than disclosing our plans. But in the event it turned out to be all too revealing. The cameraman glanced triumphantly at

Phillip before dismantling his equipment and packing it carefully in a zip bag.

As we walked with them back through the courtyard to their cars, Philip assured us that anything I was concerned about could be edited out before going to air and I, naively, assumed this meant that it would be. I thanked him and relaxed. As we passed the kitchen the faintly earthy smell of freshly dug potatoes cooking wafted through the door and I asked if they would like to stay for lunch. They declined, saying they had another interview to do with John Barry on M'pandeni but asked to speak to cook. As we stepped in to the kitchen Peter continued energetically forcing raw venison through a mincing machine without pause, but he answered freely when asked about his experiences and what difference the situation had made to his life, as a Malawian who had spent most of his life in Mashonaland.

Later, when the children were in bed, Humphrey and Molly made their way through the kitchen garden from Little Bonisa for our weekly dinner and game of bridge. Unusually, conversation stalled early on in the evening and as Tim poured Molly's gin and Humphrey's whisky ("Don't be too careful with the tot measure Tim") an awkwardness crept in. In the developing atmosphere we became acutely aware of the crackling of Molly's yellow plastic fertilizer bag. Humphrey, Molly and Tim said little and, rushing in to fill the gap, I could hear my voice, trying to ease the uncomfortable feeling, too bright, and too much.

Eventually Humphrey took a breath and casually said that they'd received a telephone call just before coming over for dinner. It was from a cousin in England who had been watching the BBC TV news at six o'clock. One report carried an excerpt of the interview that had taken place with Tim that morning which they thought was alright, although it had clearly been edited and they'd have liked to have heard more. Following Tim a picture of me flashed onto the screen. I was standing to one side with James on one hip and a pistol on the other. An emotive picture, Molly said. It seemed nothing had been edited. Apparently, with a slightly startled look on my face I had admitted in a round about way that yes, we'd had enough, we were thinking of taking the children and leaving.

News spread around the family up and down the country and, by the time the same news item was repeated on the 9 o'clock news, various relations had their video recorders ready.

Hot with embarrassment I apologised.

Although at some level both Humphrey and Molly must have known the likelihood of this day arriving, and had probably sometimes wondered at what stage the decision would be made, hearing the news in this way must have come as a shock to them both and I was full of regret. It was more than fifty years since Humphrey first bought the Bonisa land and begun establishing the farm. His were the memories of the virgin bush from which he'd developed the dairy and dam, made roads, built the homestead and sunk bore holes, which enabled Molly to create a beautiful and extensive garden surrounding the house which over the years had matured into the trees and shrubs we were now enjoying from where we were sitting with our drinks on the verandah. It was more than their house, it was a way of life, the base from which they'd raised their five sons, and, despite the ten years when they were restricted to Governor's Lodge and then Government House, it was still 'home'.

Although, in one sense, I was lured into saying what I did, the thought that they had found out in such an impersonal way, filled me with distress. But there were no recriminations. They knew this was not the way we'd have wanted it. Tired now and aware that this day, which had hung over us for years, had arrived sooner than we wanted, left little to say.

Mosquitoes buzzed around close by and in the distance, audible through the splashing of the fountain in the courtyard behind us, the throb of the Lister engine on the bore hole and the rhythmical beating of African drums floated up from the compound below the escarpment. They too would suffer when we left and we hoped most, if not all, would find employment elsewhere. But in a way they would lose not only jobs but community and family connections which had seen three or four generations on Bonisa. So many lives would be changed. Somewhere out in the bush a jackal barked reminding me that even the dogs would have to go.

None of us felt inclined to play bridge and, to fill the void, we tried to discuss a few practical issues – who to tell immediately and in what order – the children of course, other Gibbs family, the brothers – Tim's and mine – Duncan's family, MG and GG, John Zurnamer who would also have to look for another job, and then the wider circle of family and friends.

There were details to be worked out. Some things would be given away, some sold. Government permitted us to sell the dairy cows which, over many generations and with the benefit of Artificial Insemination, Tim had developed into a fine herd. The beef cattle, other livestock and farm implements could also be sold without restriction but, according to law, the properties of Bonisa, Little Bonisa and Deeside would have to be offered to the government first. If government didn't want any of the land and then issued a 'Certificate of no Interest' we would be free to auction the farms on the open market.

Humphrey said he and Molly had long thought about this eventuality and had decided that when the day came they would not leave Zimbabwe and would, instead, move to Harare and buy a cottage where they still had many friends..

"And the staff? Lavu has been with you fifty years," I said.

"I'd always told Lavu that when he retired I intended to buy him a little house in Bulawayo, probably in Luveve Townships, with a garden – he said he wants to grow paw paws and mealies in his old age."

"And a pension," Tim said.

"Of course, I'll give him a pension for life which, if he keeps drinking as much as he does now, may not be for long! Manka could live there too and look after him. After all you won't be able to take her with you and she is his daughter."

"Where will you go?" Molly asked Tim. "South Africa?" Molly came from South Africa and would have liked that, but Tim said "Probably not. No, we don't want to take sons out of one situation to put them in another where they may end up fighting someone else's war in a country not their own."

"Australia?"

"Don't think so," Tim said. "Sue has property there but it's too far from anywhere. We're thinking of the UK. Antonia's mother has offered to lend us the money to buy a house. It's the best option for getting a roof over our heads and settling in quickly."

Friends understood. John was sad but stoical and young enough to find somewhere else to spend his energy, but we would miss him and Sheena. The children were apprehensive and not completely comprehending. Peter said he would go back to Malawi, but when I told Manka, she turned aside and wept.

Colin Shortis expressed his relief. "I'm glad you're going. This situation will run and run. Reminds me of Northern Ireland. It's the right decision, but I couldn't have said that before you had made it for yourselves."

There was a great deal to do and, with David weekly boarding at Whitestone School, GG suggested Sarah live with them where she could take the short walk through the bush each morning and attend Whitestone's with him which would make her happy and release a few more hours in my days to prepare for the leaving. Both David and Sarah were thrilled with the idea and although James and Caroline missed them we were all together for the weekends.

Despite the big decision having been made, and now out in the open, what followed was an avalanche of smaller decisions. There were restrictions on what we were allowed to take out of the country. The limit, we were told, would be £620 in cash and one bag each. However, depending on the mood of the authority vetting our application, one bed each may be allowed because, they claimed, the international definition of a refugee was one who had been forced to leave their country without their bed and the authorities did not wish to have Zimbabwe's reputation besmirched. I didn't know how true this was but we did know that the rules applying to the country stipulated that each family may be permitted to also take 'one of everything' – one stove, fridge, deep freeze, dining room suite and lounge suite, and, as we were also housing large quantities of furniture for the parents and the brothers, we planned to have everything packed, other than the few sale items, and hope for the best. And so, five dining room tables, extra sofas and chairs, ten beds and the full sized billiards table were designated for the containers which we were by no means certain would be given clearance for shipping.

Preparations gathered pace. We had large packing cases made from planks of a warm, deep-brown African wood, and filled them with tins of food from GibCan, (the canning factory in Mashonaland started by a Gibbs some years ago) hoping that, if the containers did make it to England, the contents would help feed the family until Tim found employment and began earning. The fine wood could be turned into bookshelves and small cabinets, and so I had more wooden cases made and filled them with clothes, mainly rather unsuitable khaki shorts and shirts for the boys, and three sizes of equally unsuitable BATA shoes for each child. They balked at the idea of having to wear shoes and socks, but then they didn't know how very different the future would be.

While Tim made arrangements, setting a date with the auction house, hiring extra security guards, and inserting advertisements for the auctions of the dairy herd and machinery, I planned the catering and made as many arrangements as I could for what was beginning to feel like 'life on the other side.'

I had repairs done to everything in need. Morden came over from the farm school and repaired furniture, the Indians in Bulawayo made up belts, several pairs of sandals, and advised me on the twelve dining room chairs with worn out leather seats which had been given to me by the Flemings when they sold their big house on the hill. Mr. Patel insisted that hide off-cuts from elephant belly would be the hardest wearing, most attractive and most economical leather for re-covering the seats. It would last forever he said. I took him at this word.

43

Tim arranged for the sale of farm assets, implements, machinery and livestock to take place a few weeks later in the Lucerne lands behind the Bonisa homestead.

John and Sheena spent most of their time in or near Big Bonisa helping to prepare, while the children played behind the fence with their nannies. John brought up the tractors which, because of sanctions, were now old and made up to a large extent of repairs carried out using spare parts made from scratch in the workshops or bits cannibalised from other vehicles. We were not expecting high prices but we did expect everything to sell, especially the Massey Fergusons, if only for their scrap value which was prized by all farmers as they struggled with the same shortages.

In accordance with the law we'd offered the farm itself to the government and, to our relief, they responded by issuing a 'Certificate of No Interest', leaving us free to sell on the open market. Jack Ehlers belonged to the 'Open Market'. He declared his interest. Despite owning Mimosa Park, he also wanted to buy Bonisa and he had the money. There were no other offers.

Jack gave a statement to the press: "No one can deny we have some problems but, problems or not, my place is in Zimbabwe. My latest investment is a demonstration of my unwavering faith in the country's future."

I thought back to the day Jack had called in to invite us to his wedding and his casual, almost throw-away, comment about wanting to buy Bonisa. I'd been angry then. *Anyone but Jack* my instinctive response; but times had changed. Jack was a good farmer. A rancher, he ran a herd of over 2,000 Brahmans including 200 pedigree bulls, and I could imagine Joy would take good care of the homestead and garden. I steeled every part of my being to wish them both well in the future, little knowing the disaster that lay ahead.

The sale was well supported by both local farmers and others from outlying areas who came, with their families, for a day out. They ignored the heat, dust and flies, standing around in their khaki shorts, drinking their drinks and talking with old friends as the dairy herd was brought out to be paraded before them. Smells of hot cow pats mingled with that of hot, freshly varnished metal as the auctioneer, with a fur of red dust on his hairy arms, bellowed out the bids.

I knew the majority of people there, if not well, then at least by sight. The widow of a recently murdered farmer from Kezi came up and introduced herself.

"I'm so sorry," I said. There must have been other things to say but at that moment I couldn't think of anything.

As I offered around the vast quantity of sandwiches Peter had made, along with a selection of virulently coloured jam tarts, I felt as if I were treading water; as if this were all real but not relevant to me. I'd been brought up to believe that pain was a private matter, that lacerated feelings were not to be inflicted on others and I remembered with clarity the only words my mother spoke to me after I left for school when my father died: "You will be going back to school soon, Susan, be careful not to wear your heart on you sleeve" and after that I never did and my father was never discussed again.

Mike Milne cornered Tim and repeated what Tony Sharp had said earlier: "You are the lucky ones. You've made the decision. That still lies ahead for some of us."

Snatches of conversations rose above the general hubbub:

"The skellem was probably high on M'banje."

"This had better be a good rainy season or I'm finished."

"One of Labuschagne's boys reckoned twenty-two of his family were herded into a thatched kia and set on fire."

"I hear the Grand Hotel's up for sale."

"Where's the Trek Church being held this month?"

Broncho Greaves shouted to someone on the other side of a tractor that the Cape Argos had written another article on the white farmers of Matabeleland. "You know what they wrote?" he demanded. "I'll tell you what they said, they said that our 'stubborn streak of

260

optimism makes us an endangered species'. What do they know?"
But Bronco also had a big heart. I remembered him being particularly
kind to Duncan and offering wise advice just before we were married
and now I suspected he was finding the diminishing district difficult
to accept.

Marian Rankin pushed past him. "I've come all the way from
Hilda's Kraal but don't think I can buy. Your Holsteins and Friesians
are excellent but my cows are Jerseys and it's better if ne'er the twain
shall meet. Pity," she said. In the event Humi Steyn's wife Joan, a
near neighbour, bought all the milkers and the Kays all the non-
milkers, with various others biding on the remainder of the livestock.
Steyn's and Kay's herd boys immediately drove the cows back to
their respective farms and, as I watched the last of them disappear
down the escarpment in eddies of dust, I thought of all the work
Tim had, often with the benefit of Artificial Insemination, put into
breeding them from prize bulls from several other countries around
the world.

All animals and implements in the auction sold and, after everyone
left and the day began to cool, I told Manka to take the children in
and bath them while Tim and I walked down to the dam to sit quietly
and watch the game come down to drink. Neither of us spoke about
our feelings that day, there was no need and a life time of keeping
emotions tucked away inside, if at times lonely, was also in a strange
way comforting – perhaps the one part of life it was possible to
control.

The next day it was announced that Foot and Mouth disease had
broken out in Nyamandhlovu and the Government, at the instigation
of the European Union, threw a Cordon Sanitaire around the area.

"What?" Tim said when we heard. "If we'd not got the cattle off
the farm yesterday there wouldn't be another opportunity for weeks
or even months."

We decided to rent a furnished house in Bulawayo for two or
three months which we could move into while Tim flew over to the
UK and began looking for a job and a house in which we could settle.
We found a pleasant modern house with a fenced off swimming pool

and garden in Burnside, quite near MG and GG, which belonged to a family who were going on an extended holiday abroad – an arrangement that suited us all.

In the meantime, as the old familiarity of the farm noises, smells and landscape changed, I decided it would be too painful to hold a farewell party on Bonisa and looked for a suitable place in Bulawayo. After investigating various venues, we eventually settled on a large reception room in the older, more traditional, Southern Sun Hotel and sent out invitations to friends and faithful business acquaintances.

The night before the move into town a team of packers came out to Bonisa with the Trek removal van for the enormous job of packing up the entire contents of the homestead. Humphrey and Molly sent some belongings over from Little Bonisa to be included in the shipment which we all hoped, but were by no means certain, would one day arrive in the UK. As evening approached and the large pantechnicons drove in through the security gates a violent storm hit. Forked lightning fractured the skies briefly lighting up the darkness, high winds banged windows, rain lashed in through the ill-fitting stable doors, and brought down power lines. I scrambled around in the black-out and found enough candles to burn deep into the night in each section of the house. Men, as black as the night and difficult to see, moved through every room talking loudly, wrapping, padding, filling boxes and in the confusion someone packed the casserole I'd made to take for our first meal in town into one of the many tea chests, but no one knew which one. I made my way through dark chaos into the candlelit hall just in time to see one of the packers, unable to fit the pendulum of the grandfather clock into the packing case, carefully bend it over his knee and with obvious satisfaction, stuff it into a tea chest. Too late to rescue it, I was almost beyond caring.

The next morning the pantechnicons drove slowly out of the drive and down the escarpment.

John and Sheena made their own way off the farm.

There was nothing left for us to do.

We left Peter with gifts for himself and his new family, loaded up the children and Manka and drove out for the last time.

Nobody said anything.

We drove past the dairy, now fallen silent and lifeless.

From the compound below the escarpment the smell of cold wood smoke from last night's cooking fires wafted over the dry, dusty veldt.

Further along the track the rusty old ploughshare nailed on a post still stood at the farm entrance proclaiming H.V. GIBBS. BONISA.

We drove on beyond the turn off.

Monica's cottage stood desolate, the garden long dead, the fence mangled and partly stripped for the wire, Mpofu's kia abandoned in the corner.

As we turned onto the Nyamandhlovu Road I finally said to Tim: "There will be moments of homesickness and in those moments we must always remember the reasons we left".

44

Although being in town meant I saw more of my friends, perhaps because of the season of loss and transition we were in, I didn't enjoy town life and when, after two weeks away in the UK, Tim rang asking me to fly over and join him in house hunting, and various friends offered to look after the children, I went. The short time we were in England was too short, too social and therefore not very productive and we returned to Bulawayo not having found a suitable home.

David and Sarah enjoyed the freedom of being in town. Attending Whitestone School as day students, being able to visit their friends living in the area and being able to invite them around for a swim or tea after school were all new experiences and they revelled in it all – even Caroline said it was good because she'd been 'tired of living on tooth picks'. GG found a friend who offered to give all the dogs a good home together and gradually final plans began falling into place and loose ends were tidied up.

We had made the decision before leaving Bonisa to give ourselves a final treat, to make our last days happy ones, ones to leave us with good memories. We would take the four children and Manka to spend the celebrations of Christmas at Victoria Falls.

The A'Zambezi River Lodge, about three miles upstream from Victoria Falls, was the perfect place. Right on the river bank, smaller, and less formal than the Victoria Falls Hotel (which was my favourite) it was an ideal base for a family holiday. The area, wild and free, had been a favourite haunt in my early years in Rhodesia and, full of nostalgia, was a good place to say a final farewell to the country we loved so much and in which all our children had been born.

It would be terribly hot in the Zambezi Valley at that time of the year, but we didn't mind, we were used to heat and the proprietor's wife had assured us of a great time, "a really memorable Christmas" she had promised on the telephone.

"Father Christmas will be coming down the Zambezi in a motor boat with a sack full of presents for the children. And then, for our guests, there is a full Christmas dinner with all the trimmings," she said over the 'phone and repeated it as she cast an appraising eye over us on our arrival at the reception desk. "The decorations are original too – all locally made stuff." Then, taking the cigarette out of her mouth, she indicated the way to our rooms. "You have lovely views over the river. Nanny's room is over there," she said, indicating somewhere behind a shrubbery, one of the waiters will show her where to go."

Sweeping lawns led from the semi-circular lodge down to a path running alongside the river, which was marked off by a flimsy fence and small gate which looked totally inadequate from a security point of view, but security concerns here had different causes – not terrorists, but wandering elephant or hippos coming out of the river to graze at night.

"That's where Father Christmas will pull in tomorrow morning, so bring the children there before 10am and they can watch him speeding down the river towards them. They'll love it!"

Tim and I made our way down to sit by the pool and ordered drinks while Manka took the children off to change into swimming costumes. Bright pink bougainvillea draped a tall tree by the thatched bar off to our left but otherwise the vegetation was all indigenous, and birds chatted noisily as they darted in and out of the surrounding foliage. Following the relentless activity of recent weeks we began to relax and now, in the heat of the day, lying on sun beds under trees, I gave up the struggle to stay awake.

The following morning, after an early breakfast, we decided to fill the time before Father Christmas' arrival by going for a walk along the river. The children had fun examining spoor on the path, guessing at the identity of which animals had left them, and how long ago. There were occasional glimpses of monkeys and at one point a startled warthog shot out of the bush, took one furious look at us and raced on ahead, its tail held high. Manka, superstitious about warthogs, felt uneasy and turned back.

Small islands stood out in the middle of the river, now it was no longer in spate, and on the nearest one we could see a few elephant. I hoped we'd see them swim across in single file, as they do, hanging on to the tail of the one in front, but either the river was flowing too fast or they weren't yet ready to return to the mainland, and they stayed languidly moving around the island. Indifferent to elephant, crocs lay basking on the warm sand banks.

The day was becoming warmer when we returned, as instructed, just before 10 o'clock, to the landing in front of the lodge where a small crowd, including a few children, had already gathered. The minutes dragged on. Murmurs of impatience arose, some strained to peer up river, hoping to catch a first glimpse of the speed boat roaring through the water, but the great Zambezi flowed implacably towards the precipice of the Devil's Cataract without a sign of man or boat. An irritated father went off in search of someone accountable. People moved away. Anyone with any authority seemed to have disappeared, no one offered any explanations.

Eventually, when the time came, we took the children into lunch and found our tables. We sat and waited. And waited. The woman who had greeted us on arrival breezed into the dining room.

"Sorry, but I'm afraid there's been a delay with the turkeys. I'm sure we'll have them for you by this evening but for now we are changing the menu to macaroni cheese. Sorry. Can't be helped. Sorry. Despite almost running out of the dining room she paused in the doorway to light another cigarette and could not have helped but hear the murmurs of consternation rippling around the room.

"It's all very odd," Tim said. But no one moved and no more information was forthcoming. We would just have to wait.

The temperatures rose even higher and some of the other guests went to their rooms to have an afternoon nap. But I gave Manka the afternoon off and, following a short rest for the children, it meant another afternoon around the pool for us.

Because Christmas dinner had been abandoned at lunch time, the parents got together and agreed on insisting we have an early

Christmas dinner in the evening when even the very young children were able to join in.

"It will give it a festive air for them," we said, making the most of it, but by the time the dinner gong rang out the turkeys still hadn't arrived. This time a man, with apparent authority, appeared in the dining room.

"Ladies and gentlemen," he said. "The train bringing our Christmas turkeys up from Bulawayo has been attacked, you know – shot up, down by Thomson's Junction. You will be glad to hear it was the goods train and there were no casualties... Apart from the turkeys of course. There are now more than a hundred of the damned things roasting in the veldt, scattered through the bush, beyond retrieving, probably being eaten by hyenas and vultures." And as he rapidly left the room, the woman came in again.

"Sorry. It's been a bad day. We had not anticipated being without turkeys and so all we now have for tonight's dinner is vegetables."

One of the irate fathers stood up and shouted.

"It sure has. And what happened to Father Christmas? We'd been told he'd be here this morning."

"Aaah. Father Christmas. Well, Father Christmas – he got pissed, didn' 'e?" she said. Then, registering the expressions of horror on parents' faces, went on, "actually, children, he got ill... poor Father Christmas. We found him face down in the bush this afternoon. It was too late to make him well again today. There was another Father Christmas who could have come but he didn't have any clothes and we didn't think that would be quite right."

As we left the next morning she looked up with a bright smile.

"Thank you for coming. I hope you enjoyed your stay and do come again."

On our return to Bulawayo we went to say goodbye to MG and GG. It was our final day and we sat drinking tea on their verandah until the last moment. They were clearly struggling, but controlled, as was I, but when we reached the car I looked back. They looked so frail standing on the verandah and I broke away and ran back to give a hug. As I approached them GG, crumpled and weeping

267

uncontrollably held up her hand, "GO Darling. Just GO!" was all she could say. I glanced at MG, turned and walked back to the car.

Paddy drove us out to the airport. I insisted she didn't wait so see us off. It was better that way.

The children were subdued and as we took off and I felt heavy with a burden of some vague unwanted knowledge gained through experience, and an apprehension about the future.

And through it all I was aware that tucked deep in my heart, the warm heart of Africa would always live on.

It is possible to leave Africa but you can't escape it.

— Unknown

Epilogue

On our arrival in England with £620 and one bag each, we were dependent on the generosity of the extended Gibbs family and Sir Charles and Lady Villiers set us up in a cottage in their garden in Berkshire while we looked for a home of our own.

We soon discovered that speaking English and coming from English parentage didn't automatically make us 'one of the tribe' and it was a time of a great many adjustments.

The first time we drove through Windsor Great Park, to visit Margaret, James dived down behind the front seat in terror of the Park Wardens in their green uniforms. "Do they kill you here?" he asked. I could not sit with my back to a window, nor at night in a room with the curtains open which, after all this time, still leaves me feeling vaguely uncomfortable.

Mary Aldenham gave us a generous cheque – the promised loan – saying 'go and buy a house' which we did in rural Gloucestershire and then, sometime later, we received a letter from her solicitor saying 'Lady Aldenham has withdrawn the loan and converted it into a gift.'

About the time we were settling in to our home, news arrived that Jack and Joy Ehlers, having been to Bulawayo to complete the paperwork for their purchase of Bonisa, were ambushed and murdered on their way back.

Further news said that Peter had died of malaria, Mkava had gone missing, to rumours of abduction and possible murder, and Manka was living happily in Bulawayo townships with her father Lavu.

After several months, having camped in an unfurnished house, we were both amazed and delighted when our furniture arrived and one of the first things we discovered was the prepared casserole which had been packed during the thunderstorm on the last night on Bonisa.

Humphrey and Molly lived peacefully in Harare until Humphrey died in March 1990, after which Molly moved to England and died in Kent in 1997.

GG Fleming died in Bulawayo in 1989, after which MG lived out the rest of his days in Australia.

Paul Fehrsen died in1993 and Paddy stayed on in Bulawayo.

John and Sheena Zurnamer emigrated to Australia with their children in 2006.

Martin Olds was murdered on Compensation in 2000 and his wife, Kathy, and her children, came to live with us in the UK until they were eventually granted political asylum.

Martin's mother, Gloria, was murdered on her farm in 2001.

David went to university in Birmingham, following which he trained as a journalist, worked in London and is now living in Australia and travels a great deal.

After university Sarah worked in education and now lives in Australia studying at Le Cordon Bleu.

James graduated from St Andrew's university and went on to care for problem teenagers in a safe house before obtaining his yacht masters, and has lived and worked at sea for five years.

Caroline obtained a degree in Criminal Justice and Sociology, trained in submarine operations/rescue and became a private dive guide/instructor and underwater videographer in the super-yacht industry. She is now based in Australia.

Robert Mugabe changed the constitution in 1987 and became executive President of Zimbabwe. The following year he wrote a glowing Introduction to *Beleaguered Governor*, Alan Megahey's biography of Humphrey. Two years later he began his next wave of hostility towards white farmers.

Big Bonisa and Little Bonisa homesteads burnt to the ground in 2003. New Farm, derelict, escaped the fire.

We are not victims of the past. We are heirs of the future.
— David Prior

Acknowledgements

My grateful thanks go to the *Catchword* team for their unimaginable persistence (pushiness) and bullying: Dr. Rona Laycock, Geoffrey Adams, Liz Carew, Martin Wilkinson, Nick John and Sarah King without whose collective carrots and sticks this record would probably not have been completed.

I am deeply indebted to Colin Shortis for reading through the manuscript and making helpful suggestions and to John and Sheena Zurnamer who shared the memories, read the manuscript, confirmed my recollections and added a few of their own.

Dick Cumming provided information, both historical and his own experiences on Mimosa Park, and Tim Longden gave permission to refer to Syd Longden's journal regarding the early days. I thank them both very much.

I also thank John Gaye and Paddy Fehrsen for their help in tracking down key people.

Arthur Cunynghame has been a patient help and a great encouragement which I have very much appreciated and for which I thank him.

Finally I give thanks to Tim for his encouragement and enthusiastic help in ferreting out people, photographs, information and for jogging the memories.

Also from Loose Chippings Books

The Cheesemonger's Tales
A good read for all food and wine lovers

Not Dark Yet
A very funny book about cricket

Cool Is The Reaping
Poems of rural England

Diary of a Shropshire Lass
A delightful autobiography

The Harts of Chipping Campden
Essential reading for all who admire the town or fine silver

Keeping Afloat
A light hearted tale of exploits on the canals of France

Roy The Eagle
*Children's Picture Story Book about how what makes us different
brings us together*

Walk With The Wise
*Reflections on thought-provoking quotations to stimulate and
guide those who are interested by life's challenges*

Spirit On The Water
A sometimes irreverent look at eleven extraordinary cricket tours

Full details from our website
www.loosechippings.org